The

Illustrated

Home

Recording

Handbook

PRICING OF EQUIPMENT

Throughout the text, mention is made of the cost of software and hardware. Rather than giving the actual price, a lettering system A–F is used instead. This gives the approximate cost of the equipment in sterling and dollars.

Pricing range:

A	Cheap Shareware/Freeware
B	£1–100/$1–150
C	£100–200/$150–325
D	£200–400/$325–550
E	£400–600/$550–800
F	Over £600/Over $800

Publisher and Creative Director: Nick Wells
Project Editor: Polly Willis
General Editor (this edition): Rusty Cutchin
General Editor (original edition): Ronan MacDonald
Picture Research: Melinda Révész
Art Director: Mike Spender
Digital Design and Production: Chris Herbert
Layout Design: Lucy Robins

Special thanks to: Julie Pallot and Claire Walker

07 09 11 10 08

1 3 5 7 9 10 8 6 4 2

First published 2004

This edition published 2007 by
FLAME TREE PUBLISHING
Crabtree Hall, Crabtree Lane
Fulham, London SW6 6TY
United Kingdom

www.flametreepublishing.com

Flame Tree Publishing is part of the Foundry Creative Media Co. Ltd.

© 2007 this edition The Foundry Creative Media Co. Ltd.

ISBN 978-1-84451-922-4

A CIP record for this book is available from the British Library upon request.

Printed in China

The

Illustrated
Home
Recording
Handbook

General Editor (this edition): Rusty Cutchin

Roger Cawkwell, Rusty Cutchin, Adam Crute, Stephen Evans,
Douglas Kraul, Orren Merton, Tim Oliver, Michael Ross,
Dave Simons, Scot Solida

Foreword: Sonic Boom

**FLAME TREE
PUBLISHING**

FOREWORD by Sonic Boom

Sound – the simple vibration of air – is omnipresent. Sound is perhaps one of the most pervasive and interesting of the sensual stimuli – something that we never "shut-off" or "turn-off". The possibilities available to us through the simple manipulations on any simple sound are themselves infinite. With today's digital home studio, we have access to a palette of tools and effects, the like of which has not been seen before. Hardly a day goes by without a new effect or processing algorithm becoming available, not to mention the regular arrival of more and more capable digital instruments, controller modules and recording pre-amps that can interact with your recording system in ever more useful ways.

Home recording has gone through many changes in the last decade – changes that were hard to envision in the tangle of equipment and knowledge previously needed to record at home with analogue equipment. One hardware unit or computer set-up can now provide all that is required – from the recording process itself to mixing and mastering – with the luxury of onboard effects, tone equalization and automated capabilities all thrown in . All the capabilities of the analogue studio and much more.

We should never forget, of course, that ultimately it is **what** we are recording, not **how**, that is most important. It will soon become evident that your ears and the way in which you use them are one of your most important assets, one that you must use and learn to trust in order to achieve good results. After all, if it sounds great to you, it probably will to everyone else ....

In truth, the essentials of a good recording actually remain the same, whatever the equipment. It is now easy to use high-quality, low-cost home recording equipment tools to perfect the process without the previous expense engendered by commercial studios, and all with the knowledge that good results are easily achievable by anyone. In this hi-tech age, the remaining advantage of a commercial studio is the engineer's experience – a world this book seeks to open up, demystify and guide you into in simply understood stages.

For me , there is only one real rule in recording: **anything you can do to achieve the sound you want is valid**. As long as basic precautions are taken, a little experimentation will go a long way. There are no right sounds or wrong sounds, no better or worse techniques, merely those sounds that are well-recorded and those which are not. Ease of achievement is not always the measure of the best result.

Experimenting is a vital and valid way to learn, and to get to know your ears and how best to analyze the sounds you are exploring or recording. Something learned during experimentation, though perhaps not always immediately right for the matter in hand, will often be found to be useful later on. It is well worth remembering, though, that trying to fix things "later on" is very different to actually getting something to sound great right from the start. If you think you can "fix in the mix", you are opening yourself up to a host of potential problems.

There is no reason why , with the information contained within this book, and some idea of your own as to what you want to record, you cannot quickly get results that will surprise and delight you. In combination with your enthusiasm, the possibilities are endless. While we must absorb a certain amount of technical knowledge to achieve good results, success is easily within the grasp of anyone prepared to experiment. The world of recorded sound is open equally to the musician and non-musician alike. No great technical proficiency or musical knowledge is necessary to be able to record great material – far more important is the ability to be able to make decisions based on the feedback the speakers give your ears and making the necessary adjustments so you achieve the required result. A little musical knowledge is always useful, however, whichever side of the microphone you are on – and the basics are worth gleaning as you go.

With this book, your imagination and your ears, the world of recorded sound will quickly become a familiar and fascinating place, a limitless zone of creativity and beauty. Turn on, tune up and sit down. A world of wonder awaits....

CONTENTS

INTRODUCTION

There's a revolution going on in music production – a revolution that's seeing the line between the home studio and the professional recording facility blurred to the point of meaninglessness. For some time now, the price and performance of hardware workstations, instruments and effects units have moved firmly in favour of the musician on a budget, with mass-produced units equalling and often exceeding the quality of the specialist classics of yesteryear. Even that, however, is nothing compared to what's been going on in the world of computers.

Over the last three years, the home computer has been steadily and dramatically increasing in speed and functionality, to the point where anything is possible in terms of digital media. The simple fact is that anyone with a Mac or high street PC and a few well chosen pieces of software and peripheral hardware has at their fingertips considerably more technological muscle than the world's greatest studios could boast only a decade ago, and at an infinitesimal fraction of the price. Software sequencers like Cubase, Sonar, Digital Performer and Logic make high track-count, multitrack recording and editing easy and intuitive, while plug-in synths, samplers and effects allow you to create incredible sounds to place on those tracks, all within the confines of your computer. And don't think for a second that the virtual studio is just a second-rate, low-budget substitute for the traditional tape-based recording environment – tape has become just as outmoded for music makers as it has music listeners. Even the most famous and respected professional record producers, engineers and musicians have enthusiastically signed up for the software revolution, seduced by the convenience, mobility and stunning sound quality that it's brought to their working lives.

The *Illustrated Home Recording Handbook* is your comprehensive guide to the brave new world of home recording in the digital age. No previous musical experience is required to read it – one of the best things about the democratization of music technology is that instrumental skills are a bonus rather than a requirement. Of course, if you can play an instrument, you'll be wondering what's in all this for you.

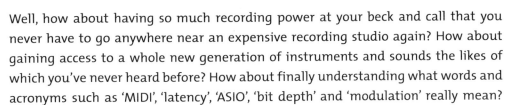

Well, how about having so much recording power at your beck and call that you never have to go anywhere near an expensive recording studio again? How about gaining access to a whole new generation of instruments and sounds the likes of which you've never heard before? How about finally understanding what words and acronyms such as 'MIDI', 'latency', 'ASIO', 'bit depth' and 'modulation' really mean? Make no mistake, once you've digested this book and implemented the concepts and buying advice it presents, your band will thank you for it and your musical output will improve. Dramatically.

The *Handbook* is divided into two main sections, the first designed to ease the aspiring music maker into the gear and techniques that form the basis of modern music production, and the second delving deeper into the details and practicalities. The writers behind the words are all renowned experts in their field – a crack team of professional producers, engineers and music technology journalists who many will recognize from their work on such respected newsstand titles as *Computer Music*, *Future Music* and *Electronic Musician*. We've aimed to keep everything as jargon-free and easy to follow as possible for the beginner, but utterly comprehensive in terms of coverage and depth. It's worth pointing out, though, that the music technology industry moves fast, and while all the information in this book is accurate at the time of printing, some things may have changed within months of publication, particularly in the area of product listings and prices. That aside, we've constructed a pricing table to simplify the market and make your buying decisions a bit easier. You'll find it on page 2.

If this is your first foray into making music, *The Illustrated Home Recording Handbook* will quite possibly change your life. Making music with technology is a hugely rewarding and creative way to spend your free time – the satisfaction of burning that first completed mix to CD and playing it to your friends and family just can't be beaten. And if you're a musician looking to expand your horizons and make professional quality recordings in the comfort of your own home, then you've come to the right place – once you see and hear this stuff in action, there's simply no turning back. So without further ado, let's get to work...

Ronan MacDonald, *General Editor* (original edition)

START HERE

This book provides a very wide range of information which can be sourced for your needs. Start here to find out where to go first.

I WANT TO EXPLORE THE POSSIBILITIES

🖥 *For the cost of a personal computer, it is possible to bring your music to life in a way that sounds great and then sell it over the Internet.*

↬ **Go to page 10** to find out what recording at home is all about.

🖥 *Do you want to know how your home environment can be adapted for recording and mixing, whether you can use some of the gear you already have and what else you might need?*

↬ **Go to page 110** to find out more.

I WANT TO PUT MY MUSIC ON THE INTERNET

🖥 *Although it is not difficult to upload your track, you do need to understand some fundamentals before you can begin.*

↬ **Go to page 170** to learn more about MP3 compression and the practicalities of putting music on the web.

I WANT TO BE A PRODUCER

🖥 *There's nothing like learning how to mix and master like a pro to give your track that extra edge.*

↬ **Go to page 144** to discover how to achieve professional-sounding mixes.

🖥 *Want to know how some famous producers got started?*

↬ **Go to page 210** for profiles of some top people in the business.

I WANT TO WRITE AND SELL MY SONGS

🖥 *The "Projects" section of the book will give you valuable tips on how to go about writing and recording your songs, including:*

↬ **Go to page 164** to discover how to master basic song structure.

↬ **Go to page 182** for advice on how best to record yourself sing.

🖥 *Once you have your song, now what do you do with it?*

↬ **Go to page 168** to see how to put your song on the Internet.

↬ **Go to page 172** for guidelines on how to make a podcast for the Internet.

- *If you do not want to go down the record company route, but still want to get your music into the public domain, there are many ways of doing so.*
- **Go to page 200** for advice on MP3 and computer-based DJ mixing.

I WANT TO RECORD AND PROMOTE MY BAND

- *Whatever type of band you are in, or whatever your ultimate ambition, you want to make sure that you are the best you can possibly be.*
- **Go to page 184** to see that it's actually possible to make good recordings of live performances at gigs or at home.

- *Different instruments have different needs when it comes to recording.*
- **Go to page 136** for top tips on recording a guitar, whether it be electric or acoustic.
- **Go to page 188** for advice on recording a piano.
- **Go to page 192** if you are recording wind instruments or brass.
- **Go to page 194** for the best way to record a group of singers.

- *There are countless ways to promote your band, ranging from the sensible and practical to the outrageous and absurd.*
- **Go to page 369** to learn all about press packs, self-promotion, radio stations, music magazines....

I WANT SOME BACKING TRACKS

- *How about a sample, drum loop or groove?*
- **Go to page 88** to discover how to get hold of them.
- **Go to page 92** and see how easy it is to make your own samples.

I LOVE MY MAC

- *Whether you love them or hate them, Apple Macintosh computers are deeply established in the world of music and recording.*
- **Go to page 332** for information on the advantages of a Mac, and the OS X platform.

- *Apple's position will be strengthened with their recent purchase of Emagic and the entire Logic Audio platform.*
- **Go to page 224** to discover more about Logic Pro, the Mac-only software sequencer.

I LOVE MY PC

- *For music, PCs do the job just as well as Macs, although they can require more setting up and optimizing to really get the most out of them.*
- **Go to page 26** to discover what the likely cost will be for buying your new PC.

THE BASICS

WHAT IS RECORDING AT HOME?

Are you an aspiring songwriter looking to make affordable high-quality demos? Does your garage band need a demo to pass out to prospective promoters? Would you like to expand your freelance video work to include music and soundtrack recording services?

Do you dream that your self-styled dance music and "beats" will be played by club DJs? Or are you just someone with a deep love of music and a desire to share your creations with friends and family? These are just a few of the many ways in which a home recording studio can be used.

Musicians of all means have long sought a personal studio capable of professional results. There have always been impediments though, such as cost, the need for a large room, and complexity. Professional results required special training and experience. However, today's affordable computer music tools rival what was possible a few years ago only in the best commercial studios. You can even squeeze an entire studio into something as portable as a laptop computer! Better yet, these new tools can be learned by any willing musician. Computer technologies such as recordable CDs, MP3 files and high-speed internet connections have made it possible for your recordings to be heard by almost anyone.

If you have the talent and motivation you can produce music in your own home and make it available for a worldwide audience, or for one as intimate as your immediate family. The computer home recording studio promises to liberate the musician in all of us. So why not join the revolution today?

WHAT DOES A HOME RECORDING STUDIO LOOK LIKE?

The diagram below shows the functions found in a traditional home recording studio. One way to assemble a personal studio is by acquiring hardware equipment for all the individual pieces and connecting them together. An easier way is to use a fully equipped personal computer.

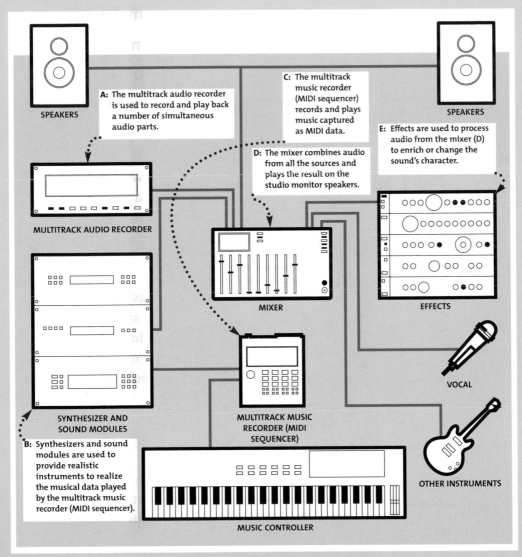

A: The multitrack audio recorder is used to record and play back a number of simultaneous audio parts.

C: The multitrack music recorder (MIDI sequencer) records and plays music captured as MIDI data.

D: The mixer combines audio from all the sources and plays the result on the studio monitor speakers.

E: Effects are used to process audio from the mixer (D) to enrich or change the sound's character.

B: Synthesizers and sound modules are used to provide realistic instruments to realize the musical data played by the multitrack music recorder (MIDI sequencer).

SPEAKERS

SPEAKERS

MULTITRACK AUDIO RECORDER

MIXER

EFFECTS

SYNTHESIZER AND SOUND MODULES

MULTITRACK MUSIC RECORDER (MIDI SEQUENCER)

VOCAL

OTHER INSTRUMENTS

MUSIC CONTROLLER

▲ *A conceptual model of a home recording studio.*

AUDIO RECORDERS

A **multitrack audio recorder** is used to record separate instruments and vocals, each to its own **track**. Multitrack recording can be used to record two or more instruments at the same time, or it can be used to build up a complete song, by recording them one at a time. One problem with recording at home is that you probably need more instruments than you know how to play yourself. Having a band or orchestra always on call is hardly practical. What you need is a type of music shorthand and special studio equipment that takes the music you write or record in that shorthand and creates audio with the desired instrument sounds. **MIDI** (musical instrument digital interface) can be used for this purpose.

Jargon Buster

TRACK refers to a separate part of an audio recording.

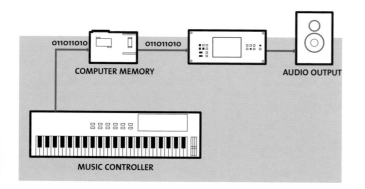

011011010   COMPUTER MEMORY   011011010   AUDIO OUTPUT

MUSIC CONTROLLER

▲ *A keyboard or controller converts musical notes and other performance gestures into MIDI digital data, which is stored first in the computer's memory and ultimately on the computer's hard drive. The performance is replayed by sending the data to a MIDI synthesizer or sound module.*

Musical performances such as notes and other gestures are recorded as special MIDI data instead of audio. The MIDI data is recorded and edited with the multitrack music recorder or MIDI sequencer, similar to the one shown in the diagram. During playback, the MIDI data is sent to a collection of MIDI sound modules and transformed into audio. The MIDI instruments serve as your personal orchestra or band, ready to perform musical parts 24/7/365! Audio effects processors are important to modern music production. Each audio processor provides one or more different treatments called effects. A typical studio will have a number of these processors for variety, so that different parts can use different effects at the same time.

The audio mixer allows you to control the audio levels to and from the various parts of the studio. You listen to the audio using studio monitor speakers.

WHAT IS A DIGITAL MULTITRACK AUDIO RECORDER?

The basics of digital multitrack recording are shown below. Each audio part, also called a track, is recorded as a separate file stored on a computer hard drive. Sophisticated editing is possible because the file data is easily manipulated by a computer. The number of files that can be recorded or played at the same time determines the track count. A 24-track recorder uses up to 24 simultaneous files, one per recorded part. The technological magic behind digital recording is known as **sampling** (see the diagram below right). Recording quality depends on the sampling rate, which is how many times a second the data values are captured. Faster is better, but remember that a sampling rate of 44.1 KHz (44,100 times per second) is used on commercial CDs and is considered sufficient for professional results. However, you can use the highest rate provided by your equipment and convert the rate in order to make a CD at the end of the process.

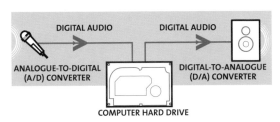

▲ A simplistic digital audio recorder transforms sound with the analogue-to-digital (A/D) converter into numbers stored on the hard disk drive. The sound is played by sending the data from the hard drive to a digital-to-analogue (D/A) converter.

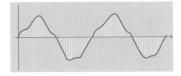

▲ An audio signal is converted to digital by periodically measuring its value. The rate at which the measurements occur is called the sampling rate. The number of digits used in a value is called the sampling resolution.

Sample resolution – the number of digits used to store each data value – also affects quality. Sample resolution is stated as the number of **bits** used for each data value. More bits are better. Commercial CDs use 16 bits, which is considered the minimum for good-quality playback. However, 24-bit resolution has become the standard in home and professional studios and is available on even budget equipment. As with the sample rate, you can covert the resolution at the end of the process to make a lower resolution copy on a medium such as an audio CD.

Jargon Buster

BIT (short for "binary digit") describes one digit of the binary numbering system used by computers.

➡ What Is MIDI? pp. 28–31; What Is a Synthesizer? pp. 32–35; What Is an Effect? pp. 68–79

REAL MUSIC OR COMPUTER MUSIC?

The words computer and music in the same sentence often conjure images of something that is, well, not quite "real music". The popular press would have you believe that computer music suggests cold, sterile and possibly strange-sounding music that was somehow created by the computer as if it were both composer and musician.

But why does recording and editing musical performances with a computer have to mean you are making computer music? After all, no one speaks of "multitrack audio music" just because a multitrack audio recorder is used!

THE FIRST COMPUTERS IN MUSIC

Musicians and computers took their first awkward steps together in the middle of the last century with some seminal experiments, in which the computer was used both as a composition tool and as a means of playing the resulting score. These extraordinary accomplishments gained notoriety. The music, though, was often mechanical, rigid, and lacking in depth or emotion. This reflected the aesthetics of the musicians as much as anything, but still the publicity forged a lasting bond between computer and not quite natural-sounding music.

◄ *Computer music to your ears: although traditional instruments such as keyboards were used, the majority of material on Deepsky's In Silico was produced by using virtual instruments, and was mostly mixed on a PC-based virtual studio. The title of the album reveals its digital roots.*

THE MIDI REVOLUTION

Thirty years later, this scenario replayed itself when the first MIDI sequencers and synthesizers were used in studios. The limitations of the equipment and the lack of sophisticated techniques often led to mechanical-sounding drum rhythms and other programmed music (a telling description!). Again the computer was somehow seen as the progenitor and the myth of computer music grew.

The reality is far different. Computers and synthesizers are pervasive tools used in nearly every type of musical production. Popular music today depends upon, and indeed thrives on, using computer recording and synthesizers. Even some of the live music heard at West End and Broadway plays and musicals is now partially performed by personal computers and synthesizers.

The computer can either be neutral to the creative process or colour the results, depending on how you choose to wield it. The computer does not define the span of musical possibilities. It is your imagination, your musicianship, and your command of the tools that determine the music produced. As it turns out, the computer is one of the most flexible pieces of music technology thus far conceived.

▲ Computers and synthesizers are at the centre of music by groups like Orbital; they are a far cry from the unwieldy apparatus of days gone by.

CAN COMPUTERS BE USED FOR REAL MUSIC?

A related criticism of using computers and synthesizers is that the result is somehow not real music because it seems to allow individuals without any formal training or any instrumental competency to make music. Some people incorrectly confuse musicianship with music education and mastery of a conventional instrument, such as the guitar. When someone who possesses neither skill creates music – no matter how good it is – there is an attempt to minimize the achievement and attribute it to the computer, as if it were some type of alchemist capable of transforming amateurishly played leaden notes into musical gold.

A USEFUL TOOL

The computer can amplify the musician's abilities and overcome deficiencies such as limited playing technique, but it is still just a tool. Harnessing this power requires skill, which is often as hard won as learning to play any musical instrument. There are no one-button compositions or performances. Mastery still requires dedication, study and practice!

◀ *A scenario that perhaps was unthinkable 30 years ago: the computer is now the mainstay of all recording studios, and because of advances in technology it is possible for more people to experiment with making music using their computers than ever before.*

Real music also suggests acoustic instruments; orchestral instruments; band instruments such as guitar, bass and drums; and, of course, the human voice. You are probably thinking, "How could a computer possibly help with this type of music?"

Computers can be used as multitrack audio recorders. In that sense, therefore, computers are applicable to all types of recorded music. The benefits of working with digital audio using a computer are immense, which is why nearly every professional recording studio today counts computers as part of its necessary equipment.

A ROLE TO PLAY

Even synthesizers and samplers have won their place in most musical styles, and computers are often used to record and play the MIDI performances that control these instruments. Many of today's film composers use computers to develop their scores. This allows them to hear the composition before a single note is played by an actual orchestra.

If you write songs that use instruments such as drums, keyboards, guitars, bass and even orchestral instruments, you can use the computer in a similar manner. Each of the instruments' parts can be played by tools within the computer, while the vocal parts can be recorded later. Many songwriters now work in this fashion on their songs or arrangements. This way of working has democratized songwriting.

In the final analysis, there is really no computer music, at least not in the same sense that there is orchestral music, guitar music or piano music. The computer is simply a tool to assist composers or musicians in transferring the sonic imagery within their minds' creative ears into something we can all hear. It is a powerful and highly flexible tool, but in the end it is just a tool. What music you create with it, and its qualities, are totally up to you!

➡ *Profiles pp. 210–215*

▲ *Today's film composers can work out their ideas using new music technology before the score is actually written, as Philip Glass did in the film* Koyaanisqatsi.

THE BASICS

WHY USE A COMPUTER?

There are numerous ways to assemble a home recording studio, but the personal computer represents the most economical, and arguably the most powerful, approach. Technological innovations have produced inexpensive personal computers with enormous capabilities, which, when harnessed with music software, can replace and surpass the facilities of traditional studios.

The traditional home recording studio shown on p. 13 has been absorbed into the music computer. The diagram opposite shows the computer version of a home recording studio. The once complex (and expensive) traditional studio has been reduced to a personal computer, special music software and a few inexpensive components.

The computer runs special programs to replace the audio and MIDI multitrack recorders, the rack of synthesizers and sound modules, the rack of effects processors, and the mixer. The sound that results from all this software activity is sent to the monitor speakers through the computer's **audio interface**. Different models provide varying numbers of inputs and outputs.

Jargon Buster

An **AUDIO INTERFACE** is a computer device that contains the necessary components to convert audio to and from a digital format.

The computer recording studio can extend beyond the capabilities of a typical home studio. Special composition tools can assist you while you write your songs. Your music can be displayed and printed as traditional sheet music. You can burn CDs or DVDs of your music to share with others. MP3 versions of your songs can be made and placed on the Internet for others to hear. Your studio can adapt as your needs and interests change. Tools can be replaced or improved by installing new software. A new, faster computer will enhance your studio's capabilities as if you had bought more synthesizers or effects, or had replaced your multitrack recorder with a more capable version.

➡ *Put Your Song on the Internet pp. 168–171*

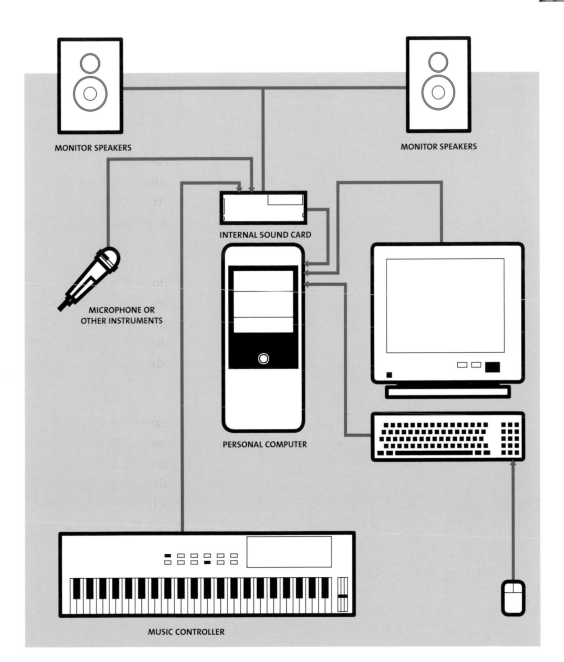

▲ *A typical computer-based home recording studio.*

WHAT HAPPENED TO ALL THE STUDIO EQUIPMENT?

The home recording studio shown in the diagram on the previous page consists of a personal computer, an audio interface, monitoring speakers and special software. So what happened to the rest of the studio?

▼ *When it was first built, the Moog synthesizer was one of the most advanced in the world. It can now be replaced by a computer running a software instrument.*

R.A.MOOG

DESIGNERS AND MANUFACTURERS OF ELECTRONIC MUSIC INSTRUMENTATION

come visit and use our back room

studio at R. A. Moog, Inc. –a working showroom for "State-of-the-art" instruments

The electronic music studio at R. A. Moog Inc. is among the most complete and up-to-date anywhere. The company extends an open invitation to experienced professionals and qualified students alike to use this facility for whatever purpose they may choose. This studio has the distinct advantage of being located at our factory in Trumansburg, New York where Moog instruments are designed and built.

The Moog studio provides an atmosphere of maximum creativity, free from the many pressures normally encountered in a facility of this nature. Here the musician may carry on a creative exchange with engineering and marketing personnel, and the manufacturer can keep abreast of the changing demands of a growing medium.

70-001 page 1

The multitrack MIDI and audio recorders have been replaced by software running on the computer. These are usually combined into one software application called a **sequencer**. A sequencer lets you record, edit and play back audio and MIDI parts. You can even incorporate audio and MIDI parts from other songs or sources into your current song. You can, for example, take a drum part from a previous project and reuse it in a new song. This makes it easy to build up a personal library of reusable musical elements.

The synthesizers and sound modules that would normally play the MIDI parts have been replaced by software **virtual instruments**. These special software programs are true synthesizers in every respect and offer audio quality and versatility equal to or surpassing the actual hardware synthesizers they replace.

Effects processors have been replaced with **software plug-ins**. These programs process the digital audio recorded on the computer hard drive, or the digital audio created by software virtual instruments.

The mixer is part of the sequencer program. Like a real mixer, it allows you to adjust levels and send audio for effects processing. You can use **automation** to record changes to the mixer settings while the song is playing, and have those changes exactly repeated every time you play the song. Unlike a real mixer, this one has an adjustable number of inputs that can change according to each project's needs.

The audio interface uses digital audio technologies to transform audio back and forth from digital data. The audio interface is your computer's ears and mouth. audio interfaces can have as few as two inputs and outputs, or as many as eight or more. You can use the extra inputs for recording more instrumental or vocal parts at the same time, and the additional outputs for extra monitoring flexibility or even listening in 5.1 surround sound.

HOW ELSE CAN THE COMPUTER HELP?

Software tools offer incredible power to create and manipulate your music. For example, you might import a musical passage or an entire series of passages from a library of pre-recorded musical snippets called loops. These loops can even be broken down into individual sounds and controlled by MIDI. You might record a few **bars** of a musical idea yourself and use cut-and-paste editing features (similar to a word processor's) to use those bars repeatedly throughout an entire song. Creating the initial material is fast and efficient. Editing can be used to reorder, alter and even create new musical sections or passages. You can try out alternative ideas and preserve each result, all the while retaining the option to go back and try a different approach. This flexibility comes from sophisticated audio editing facilities and from using MIDI data as a more abstract way of representing the music.

> ## Jargon Buster
>
> A **BAR** (measure) is a way of locating your place in a song. It lasts for a fixed number of beats (usually four in popular music) set by the music's time signature.

The computer's display and user interface offer tremendous advantages. Your musical ideas can take shape literally before your eyes. You can display the song in easy-to-comprehend graphics, as microscopically detailed MIDI data or digital audio, or even as traditional music notation. It is easy to zoom in and out of the details as needed, or to change from one type of representation to the next.

➡ *What Is a Sequencer? pp. 44–47; What Are Virtual Instruments? pp. 48–51; Other Methods of Recording pp. 342–353; How to Read Music pp. 364–368*

WHAT DO I NEED?

The very thought of purchasing a home recording studio probably brings one of two images into your mind. Either that any studio that can yield professional results will cost a princely sum, or that an affordable studio will only produce a pleasing but hardly masterful sound.

You will be pleasantly surprised, therefore, at how little you will need to invest to create not only a useful home recording setup, but one that can readily grow into an amazingly powerful tool for crafting music.

Jargon Buster

VIRTUAL STUDIO
is a way of describing a computer-based recording studio, in which all elements of the production, such as audio recording, effects processing and MIDI instruments, are realized by special software.

HOME STUDIOS

Let us examine three studios: a budget starter studio; an intermediate, more accomplished studio; and a studio that will enable you to produce professional results. The proposed studios are **virtual studios**, replacing mixers, synthesizers and effects with computer software. Even if you think you would favour a combination hardware and computer studio, you owe it to yourself to sample the compelling benefits a virtual studio has to offer. You can always pursue a more traditional studio using the virtual studio as a solid foundation.

The computer-based virtual studio is the most economical and easiest approach to creating a working studio. It is simpler to use and takes up less space. It is also easy and affordable to upgrade or enhance.

THE KIT

A Mac or a PC can be used for a home recording studio, so choose whichever you are excited about and comfortable using. This is your art, so your tools should inspire you! The price ranges in the examples given in this book reflect typical PC prices, so figure to pay a little more if you opt for a Mac. A desktop computer is assumed but laptops work well, too, albeit for extra money.

Even for a powerful studio, you do not need the latest top-of-the-line computer. The final 10–20 per cent improvement usually costs dearly. Even if you have the budget you should resist the top model and invest the savings in other studio equipment such as better monitor speakers or microphone preamps, or save for your next computer upgrade.

There is more to computer performance than just the processor, so do not become enchanted by the lure of clock speeds. The difference between a 3.2 GHz processor and a 2.8 GHz model may seem a lot, but it is less than 15 per cent, something you would hardly notice. More memory, or a DVD writer instead of a CD-R/W drive, will usually be more beneficial.

Technology moves too quickly to make specific model recommendations. Music computers are also different from office or home computers, so you will need to make your selection carefully. Although Macs initially were more popular for music recording, the gaps in ease of use (which favoured Macs) and in price (which favoured PCs) have narrowed in recent years. Whichever model you choose, the computer will perform its musical tasks well from the first moment you turn it on.

➡ *What Will the Cost Be? pp. 26–27; How Do I Set Up My Home Studio? pp 110–135;*

Hardware pp. 332–341;

Studio Layouts pp. 354–363

◀ *If you already have a collection of MIDI synthesizers, effects processors and a mixer, they can still be put to good use in your computer studio.*

Part One: The Essentials

WHAT IS THE PLAN?

As in any great building, you need a solid foundation that lets you begin making music straight away and prepares your studio for future enhancements as your interests and expertise develop. You need the following to get started:

- A place for the studio – preferably a separate room – that does not unduly colour the sound
- Monitoring speakers, with built-in or separate amplifiers
- A computer
- An audio interface
- Sequencer software, virtual instruments and plug-in effects
- An optional music controller

Essentials such as microphones, preamps and other external devices have been omitted because not every studio requires them. Be sure to reserve some funds if you need these items. The recommended pro setup provides some clues about how you should focus your upgrade efforts. Hint: the computer itself is not where you should be investing more money!

SAVE AND INVEST

Try to obtain the highest audio quality as soon as you can afford it. This means focusing on two aspects: the quality of your monitoring system, especially your speakers and room acoustics; and the quality of your audio-interface, provided you intend to record external audio sources. If not, then even a modest audio interface will have sufficient output quality to satisfy your monitoring needs.

Software is a great place to save money by starting modestly. Free or inexpensive software tools are capable of some amazing results when used well. Many of today's budget recording applications are full featured, and, so one of these may satisfy you for a long time. Another option is a **software studio** – a complete "studio in a box" with sequencer, virtual instruments and plug-in effects. They are powerful, easy to use and just plain fun!

Some type of **music controller** is helpful, especially if you play keyboards. Even if you only have rudimentary (or no) keyboard skills, a music keyboard is a wonderful way to enter music into the sequencer. Controllers that feature **sliders** and **rotaries** (more commonly known as **knobs** or **pots**, after "potentiometers", in the US – see p. 56) are great for giving your virtual studio more of a hands-on" way of working by providing alternatives to the mouse and computer keyboard.

The gulf that separates a starter studio from a professional studio is not so wide as you might think. When wielded by a deft hand, a starter studio can produce some extraordinary results. As your needs develop, the professional home recording studio of your dreams is only a few, well-chosen upgrades away.

WHAT WILL THE COST BE?

The following lists have been put together to show you how much you might expect to spend on equipping three types of studio. For explanation on how the pricing works, see pp. 2.

BUDGET STUDIO

• Low-priced computer with 17-inch flat-panel	E
• Inexpensive audio interface (sometimes built in)	B
• Budget USB music controller	B
• Good computer or home stereo speakers	C
• Budget sequencer or budget software studio	B
• Other computer software	B
• Sample CDs and extra instrument sounds	B
Total	**~ £1,025/$1,675**

INTERMEDIATE STUDIO

• Medium-priced computer, 19-inch flat-panel monitor, extra RAM and larger hard drive	F
• Stereo pro audio interface	C
• Budget USB music controller	B
• Budget powered studio monitors	D
• Intermediate sequencer or top software studio	D
• Other computer software	B
• Sample CDs and extra instrument sounds	C
Total	**~ £1,620/$2,600**

PRO-QUALITY STUDIO

• Fully expanded computer, 19-inch or larger LCD display	E
• Pro audio interface	D
• USB music controller	C
• Powered studio monitors	F
• Pro sequencer	E
• Extra virtual instruments	D
• Mastering software	D
• Other computer software	B
• Sample CDs and extra instrument sounds	D
Total	~ **£3,100/$5,000**

Desirable upgrades (especially after achieving a pro-quality studio) include:

• Widescreen LCD computer display	E
• Sequencer control surface	F
• Extra virtual instruments	C and up
• High-end plug-in package(s)	E
• Top software studio	D
• Additional sample CDs and extra instrument sounds	B and up

CAN I USE MY CURRENT COMPUTER, OR MY SYNTHESIZERS, EFFECTS AND MIXER?

If you already have a recent-model personal computer there is a good chance that it can be used in the studio, provided it is properly set up for trouble-free music operation. You can find information about setting up a music computer in numerous music magazines and on Internet web sites. If you have a friend that already knows about it, get them to help.

The recommended computer studio does not require external equipment but there is no reason not to use equipment if you already have some. Keep in mind, though, that your overall studio will be more expensive and complicated. It will also take up more room.

WHAT IS MIDI?

MIDI, short for Musical Instrument Digital Interface, was created in 1983 when a group of like-minded musical-instrument companies banded together to solve the problem of getting two musical instruments to talk to each other.

It turned out to be one of the most important music technology developments in the second half of the twentieth century. MIDI provides a way for different musical instruments and computers to work together so that the full capabilities and features of each can be combined into a formidable music tool. MIDI is also a standard way of recording music – including capturing performance gestures – that can be edited, modified, preserved and later played.

MIDI COMMANDS

MIDI uses a type of digital communication to pass musical events in a special digital form from one music device to another. When a key is struck on a music keyboard, for example, a MIDI **note-on** command is sent. The information in this command specifies the pitch of the note and how hard or softly it was struck.

▲ *The synthesizer started it all. The MIDI revolution began as a result of electronic musical-instrument companies wanting their instruments to communicate with each other.*

Illustrated Home Recording Handbook

The arrival of the MIDI note-on command instructs the instrument to play it now. When the key is released, a companion MIDI **note-off** command is sent to signify that the note is no longer playing, whereupon the instrument stops making the sound. MIDI commands can specify an instrument's loudness, alter its sound character and even change pitch during a note – similar to how a guitar player or horn player bends a note. Some MIDI commands are used for administrative purposes and to establish a consistent tempo between instruments.

▲ *Most people imagine something like these MIDI cables when they hear the word MIDI because they think of it as a way of connecting instruments. MIDI is actually a language used to convey musical performances.*

The MIDI commands are very much like a type of musical language that can be used to specify a musical performance. This very powerful aspect of MIDI is perhaps its most compelling attribute. Normally you will not be required to read or write in this language, since the computer and other tools will hide these details, though it is useful and easy to learn.

MIDI is now regularly used as part of many musical tools, particularly software, even when there is no physical MIDI interface or cable being used. MIDI has far transcended its humble beginnings as a way of connecting two synthesizers.

➡ *MIDI pp. 252–267*

Part One: The Essentials

WHAT CAN MIDI DO?

A single MIDI connection can address up to 16 independent channels. For example, the connection could control 16 devices, each assigned to its own MIDI channel, or one device that can receive many channels simultaneously. So, for example, with a single MIDI connection you could control a 16-piece orchestra that consists of a mix of violins, cellos, trumpets, flutes and so on. A large MIDI setup can employ many MIDI connections to overcome the 16-channel limitation. Software sequencers usually support many MIDI connections to both physical MIDI devices and other software programs such as virtual instruments.

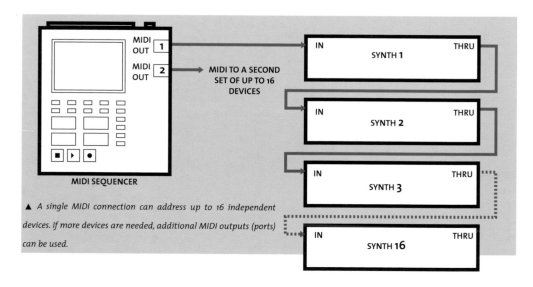

▲ A single MIDI connection can address up to 16 independent devices. If more devices are needed, additional MIDI outputs (ports) can be used.

Jargon Buster

A **SEMITONE** is one twelfth of an octave, the pitch difference between two consecutive musical pitches of the common 12-note scale.

MIDI divides a range of pitches that span far more than the pitch range of a symphony orchestra into 128 **semitone** notes. The 88-key concert grand piano keyboard's middle C corresponds to a MIDI note value of 60. MIDI offers enough pitch range for nearly any kind of music.

Other values, such as how hard a key is struck or how loud a passage is, are specified by numbers from 0 to 127. The specific meaning of these numbers is dependent, however, upon the actual MIDI device.

DO VIRTUAL STUDIOS STILL USE MIDI?

Sequencers can control external MIDI synthesizers as well as virtual instruments that also utilize MIDI for control information. External music controllers use MIDI as a means of relaying their information, sometimes using a USB connection. Even without any external MIDI devices, your virtual studio still uses MIDI as an internal representation of the music you create.

When you record a music performance using your sequencer, it stores the performance using a variation of MIDI. When you edit the performance you modify the underlying MIDI information. You may be moving a note around on the screen but underneath the software is actually altering MIDI note-on and note-off commands. Software virtual instruments and other music tools besides the sequencer use MIDI as a control language. If two or more musical

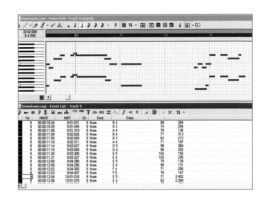

▲ *The top sequencer window shows a typical musical performance being edited graphically. What may not be clear is that the underlying musical information shown in the lower window is indeed the same MIDI date.*

tools are working together on the computer, they often exchange the musical information using MIDI. Some sequencers actually save MIDI information in their project files, while others offer a way of saving a project in a **MIDI file**. This is a special computer file containing MIDI information that describes a complete song or a portion of a song. They can be easily found on the Internet.

MIDI has become a type of scoring language for specifying musical performances. It allows music to be specified in a way that is more abstract than an audio recording but detailed enough that a particular performance can be recreated later. Computer software can easily manipulate the MIDI language to create powerful tools and, as we have seen, even hide the MIDI language details from the musician.

➡ *What Are Virtual Instruments? pp. 48–51; Sequencing pp. 288–305*

WHAT IS A SYNTHESIZER?

A painter has his or her palette of coloured paints. The composer or musician has a band or orchestra. Instrument tone colour is usually called timbre – which distinguishes, for example, a trumpet from a flute, or an electric guitar from an acoustic guitar.

Shaping **timbre** during the course of a composition once meant learning to control an entire orchestra using only written notation, a skill that requires many years of study and practice. This method of composition is very cumbersome because it is hard to hear what your music will sound like without having the orchestra play it. Yet who has an orchestra always at hand in a home studio? Today, from the confines of your home recording studio, you can command an electronic orchestra of traditional and new sounds created by synthesizers.

HOW DO THEY CREATE SOUND?

A **synthesizer** creates (synthesizes) sound, sometimes imitations of traditional instruments, and at other times unique, new sounds. The first synthesizers were little more than a collection of electronic devices, called

◄ *This is how synthesizers used to look when they consumed much more studio space and cost more than a small house! Not shown are the patch cords used to create different sounds.*

Illustrated Home Recording Handbook
Illustrated Home Recording Handbook

modules which you connected with wires called **patch cords**. This was called a **modular synthesizer**, and the sounds it yielded depended on the specific connections as well as each module's settings. The collection of modules, connections and settings used became known as a **patch** – a term still widely used today to refer to any recallable synthesizer sound. Early synthesizers were large, expensive, finicky and difficult to use.

▶ *Many synthesizers, such as this software model, offer an abundant library of easily located and used sounds. This can speed up production and let you focus on composition.*

▶ *A software version of a classic analogue modular synthesizer, complete with virtual patch cords.*

Modern synthesizers store sounds for later use and usually come with a collection of pre-installed sounds called **presets**. The range of available timbres is impressive: from familiar orchestral and band instruments to sounds unique to the synthesizer. You can adjust these presets more to your liking via the synthesizer's controls, make your own sounds from scratch, or add sounds that others have created.

Synthesizers come in the form of keyboard instruments, **sound modules**, or software virtual instruments. Although a synthesizer can take many forms, they are all the same in principle.

Jargon Buster

A SOUND MODULE is a sample-based hardware synthesizer that can sit on a table-top or be placed in an equipment rack. Usually connects it to the computer using MIDI.

Part One: The Essentials

WHAT IS SYNTHESIZER PROGRAMMING?

It is possible to simply use a synthesizer without learning to do anything more than select and play a sound. Learning to adjust sounds will broaden your sonic palette and allow you to make the presets more suitable to your needs. You will only unleash the true power of your synthesizers once you learn to create your own sounds.

◀ You can program a new synthesizer sound by adjusting its front panel controls, such as the ones shown for this software virtual instrument.

Sounds are made or modified by adjusting settings on the front panel of a hardware synthesizer or via the on-screen representation of a virtual instrument. This activity is known as **synthesizer programming**, or simply **"programming"**, which is not the same as computer programming. So never fear, you do not need to be a computer technologist to make your own sounds! Start your programming adventures by adjusting and studying presets, and before long you will be programming your own synthesizer sounds.

WHAT IS A PRESET OR PATCH?

Today, patches or presets are used interchangeably to describe a stored synthesizer sound. Some synthesizers offer an expansive library of presets that can be browsed and auditioned. This is very convenient when you are in the heat of songwriting and need a specific sound.

There are, however, negatives to using presets. Some synthesizer presets become popular and overused in commercial recordings. Even small alterations can help keep your music sounding original and fresh.

WHAT IS POLYPHONY?

When you play a six-string guitar, you know that you can strike up to six notes at once. A piano can sound as many notes as struck keys. These are examples of instrument **polyphony**, the number of simultaneous notes it can play. Do not confuse this with the range of pitches than an instrument can create. A flute can play many different pitches but only one at a time. An instrument that plays a single note at a time is usually called **monophonic**.

Synthesizer polyphony depends on the model. Many offer a polyphonic capacity of 32 or more voices, but some are limited to eight, four or even as few as one – although that would actually make the synthesizer monophonic rather than polyphonic. If the complexity of your music requires more simultaneous notes than you have polyphony, then you will either have to acquire more synthesizers or record some parts as audio, freeing up the synthesizer to begin its polyphony count-down again. One of the many beauties of virtual software synthesizers, however, is that you can call up several instances of the same model simultaneously, which usually renders polyphony limitations irrelevant.

PLAYING MORE THAN ONE SOUND AT A TIME
FROM A SINGLE SYNTHESIZER

When a synthesizer can play more than one preset at a time it is called **multitimbral**. Multitimbral synthesizers are very useful because they can play more than one musical part. A single multitimbral synthesizer, for example, might play the bass, melody and chords, each with a different instrument sound. Each multitimbral part is assigned to its own MIDI channel. Since MIDI has up to 16 channels per connection, 16-part multitimbral synthesizers are available. However, some offer less, and single-part (**monotimbral**) synthesizers are not uncommon.

Do not confuse multitimbral with polyphonic. Multitimbrality is the number of different sounds played at a time; polyphony is the number of notes played simultaneously. A synthesized piano might offer 32 notes of polyphony, but since it can only play one sound at a time it is not multitimbral.

➡ *What Are Samplers? pp. 40–43; What Are Virtual Instruments? pp. 48–51; Synthesis pp. 268–287*

WHAT IS A SAMPLE?

What if you could take any part of an audio recording and reuse it in a new song, but at a different tempo and/or pitch? Or perhaps you would like a library of professionally played and recorded drum phrases that you could incorporate into your songs, freeing up your time and creative energies to focus on more pressing aspects of a composition? Would you like to create a new song or an audio montage by combining parts of recordings that you have processed and modified?

Pro Tip

Technically, a SAMPLE is the individual number measured and recorded for each instance of audio, a sort of atomic unit of digital audio. Most musicians, however, now use the word sample to mean a short digital recording.

The **sample** is the key element in all of these examples. The term sample today has come to mean a part of a digital audio recording, usually short in duration. It is a kind of audio snippet. This can be any short digital audio recording, but the common usage implies that the source was an existing song, or a special collection of short audio recordings called a **sample CD**.

Samples have become a staple ingredient in today's music productions, including the music you find in record shops, advertisements and video or film production. The use of pre-recorded musical phrases can speed up music production while yielding a great-sounding result. This might seem like a type of dubious instant music, much like a paint-by-numbers oil painting, but it is really just another step in the evolution of modern music production. Use your own sense of aesthetics to decide if it is right for you, keeping in mind that it is just another technique in your musical bag of tricks.

WHAT CAN A SAMPLE DO?

We examined sampling on p. 13. The same methods are used to make a sample. Often samples are created by editing (sometimes called "lifting") a short portion of a longer recording (a couple of famous examples are the "Funky Drummer" drum loop, used exhaustively in hip-hop and pop in the early 1990s, and the Rolling Stones' orchestral strings used on the Verve's "Bittersweet Symphony"). Since samples are merely digital audio, and, therefore, a string of numbers in computer memory, they are easily manipulated using computer software. One of the most common manipulations is to alter the playback speed so that a drum rhythm played at one tempo can be reused for music at another tempo.

▲ *There are sample CDs available of virtually every kind of music or instrument you care to use.*

The easy way to alter playback speed is to play the sample either faster or slower. There is a problem, though. If you play a drum rhythm sample faster to make it have a quicker tempo, you will also inadvertently cause the pitch of all the drum instruments to rise. If you have ever recorded yourself on to tape and played it back faster, or listened while rewinding or fast-forwarding, then you are familiar with how this sounds. This is probably not what you had in mind, though it can be used to good effect.

A clever computer technique called **time stretching** avoids this inadvertent change in pitch. A complementary processing technique called **pitch shifting** does just the opposite: it alters pitch while retaining the original timing (duration and tempo). Both methods are widely used with samples.

LOOPING

You can create the illusion of a longer sample by repeating all or part of a sample over and over again. Imagine that you have a two-bar drum rhythm sample. You can create a 16-bar section by repeating this same sample eight times. This is called **looping**, and samples used in this fashion are often referred to as **loops**. Some musicians use the terms sample, loop and **sample loop** interchangeably.

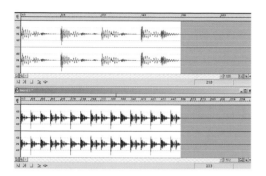

▲ *The top picture shows one bar of a four-beat drum sample. The picture below shows the same sample repeated four times to create the illusion of a four-bar drum rhythm.*

Any type of recording, including drums, vocals, guitar, and bass, can be looped. More complex loops can be made by combining different samples – either one after the other, or in layers – and looping the result.

Samples, loops and sampling grew out of using **samplers** (electronic musical instruments, see p. 44) and are closely related to digital audio recording. You can take all or part of a recording and make a sample; the difference is in how the result is used. Each and every one of your audio recordings, even those you have assembled previously from samples, is a possible candidate for sampling and further sonic exploration.

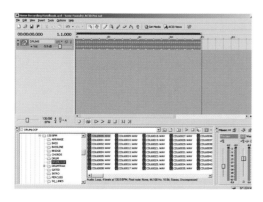

1. Let us use samples and a specialprogram to create 16 bars of music quickly. We start with a one-bar drum sample and repeat it 16 times.

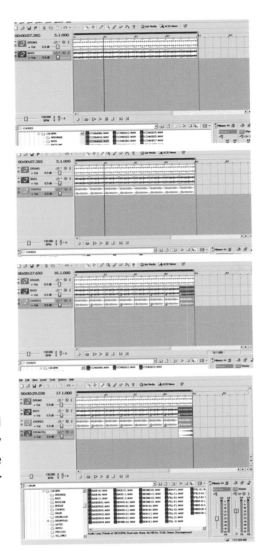

2. Next we select a two-bar bassline and repeat it eight times.

3. A sample of a synthesizer playing a chord for two bars is added and repeated eight times.

4. In order to create a more interesting chord progression, we use Acid's pitch-shifting abilities to change the pitch of both the bass and chord parts every two bars.

5. Finally, our 16-bar musical master-piece is completed by adding a drum fill on the last measure using another drum sample.

IS THIS LEGAL?

It is important that you respect others' work and only use parts of a recording if you have permission. Samples that you purchase on sample CDs (commercially available CDs containing samples specifically designed for music composition) will usually include terms of use that describe what you can and cannot do with them.

➜ *What Are Samplers? pp. 40–45; Samples pp. 88–103; Samples And The Law pp. 373–374*

WHAT ARE SAMPLERS?

How would you like to take any sound and turn it into a musical instrument? Or have a nearly endless library of instruments, including orchestral, band and some never heard of before? Maybe you make beats and want to transform a drum break into a driving dance track? A sampler can be used for these and many other applications.

Samplers are the most widely used electronic musical instruments, and nearly every recording today features a sampler at some point. It is a special-purpose recording device, which captures a sound and then replays that sound whenever you wish. Samplers use digital audio recording technology, just like a multitrack recording application or machine. The difference between a multitrack recorder and a sampler is the way in which the recording (the sample) is then used.

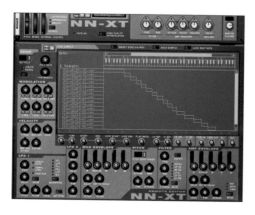

▲ These days software samplers are the norm since they are easier to use, more capable and cheaper than the hardware versions. Pictured is NN-XT (Reason's sampler component).

A sampler plays a recording, usually called a sample, as if it were a musical note. A MIDI note event from a sequencer track or a MIDI controller triggers the sampler to play the sample. Usually the sample plays for the duration that the note is held. A different MIDI note might play the same sample at another pitch, a technique commonly used to imitate actual instruments. Or the MIDI note may select an alternate sample, perhaps a different drum sound or sound effect.

PITCH ALTERATION

How can one sample produce so many different pitches that seem to go on forever? Well, once a sound is recorded, the sample is nothing more than some numbers stored in the computer's memory. To play a sample at its original pitch the sample's data is sent to the **D/A converter** at the same rate it was recorded. Higher pitches are possible by skipping some of the data. A pitch one octave higher can be played by sending every other data value. Lower pitches are possible by repeating sample data. A pitch one octave lower results if each data item is repeated twice before moving to the next one.

The problem with this type of pitch alteration is that the sound also changes: higher-pitched playback has shortened duration; lower-pitched playback is lengthened. Also, if the pitch change is an octave or more, then the character of the sound changes so that a guitar sample no longer sounds like a guitar or a piano sample like a piano. In spite of these limitations, most samplers use this type of pitch alteration.

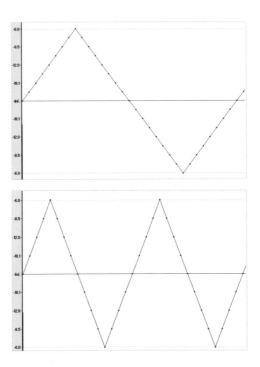

1. A sampled sound can be replayed at its original pitch and duration by sending each data point (shown as dots) to the D/A converter at the same rate as the original sampling frequency.

2. The same sample shown in the previous illustration can be replayed at twice the original pitch by simply omitting every other data point when sending the values to the D/A converter.

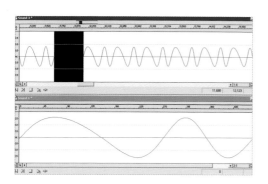

▲ *If a portion of a sample, shown highlighted and magnified, is repeatedly sent to the D/A converter, the illusion of a longer sample is created. Repeating a sample section is called looping.*

LOOPING

If you zoom in and look at the detail of an instrument note sample as edited by someone who knows what they are doing, you will find that once the start of the note finishes, the note tends to repeat a short segment of sound. This is true for many types of instrument sounds and is exploited by samplers to play a sample indefinitely by simply repeating a section. This is called looping.

Looping can be used to repeat very brief sections, such as within a single note, or longer sections, such as a whole bar of music. This last use is the original basis for sample loops.

MULTISAMPLING

Changing the pitch of a sample by more than a few pitches either way causes the sound to be different and often artificial. A way to avoid this is to make a collection of related samples, recorded at different pitches, and spread them across a large pitch range. This is called **multisampling** and the collection is called a **multisample**. It is an essential technique when attempting realistic instrument imitations.

Sometimes multisampling is used to spread many different sounds across a range of pitches. An example of this is a drum kit, in which each pitch triggers a different drum sound.

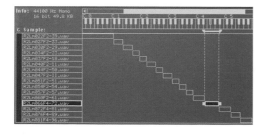

◀ *An example of using multisampling to assign a number of different samples across a range of pitches. Multisampling can either create more realistic instrument sounds or let you play a variety of sounds at the same time.*

Jargon Buster

A **SAMPLE EDITOR** is a computer program that lets you view a sample (or a digital audio track) and edit or manipulate it.

SLICED LOOP

A drum rhythm has different drum sounds at different rhythmic intervals, such as every 16th or eighth note. Sample slicing locates each of these rhythmic divisions and breaks the sample into smaller samples, one per time interval. This can be done manually with a **sample editor**, or with a special slicer software tool.

You can do some amazing things with a sliced loop (sometimes called "recycled" loops, after the popular Propellerhead program ReCycle!). If you assign slices to successive keys and then play each key in order, at the original tempo, you can recreate the original rhythm. Play slower to lower the tempo, or faster to raise it, all without undesired changes in pitch. Mix up the order in which you play the keys and you get a new rhythm. Since each slice is a separate

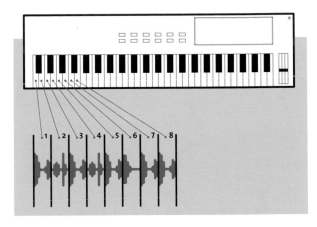

▲ *A one-bar drum loop sliced into eight samples, each assigned to a key. You can recreate the original rhythm by playing ascending eighth notes, or create new rhythms by changing the order.*

sample, you can manipulate it to change the tonal character of the sound without affecting the rhythm. Learning to use sliced samples opens up many new creative possibilities.

Pre-sliced recycled loops are available on CD-ROM or by Internet download, or you can get hold of the necessary software to make your own.

➡ *Samples pp. 88–103; Samples: Advanced pp. 248–251*

▲ *Dr.Rex is Reason's special sample player, which can load recycled samples and give you synthesizer-like processing of individual sample slices.*

WHAT IS A SEQUENCER?

The function of a sequencer is to capture a musical performance that can later be manipulated, edited and even totally redone. The captured performance is called a sequence, because it contains a series of either audio or MIDI musical events that detail the performance.

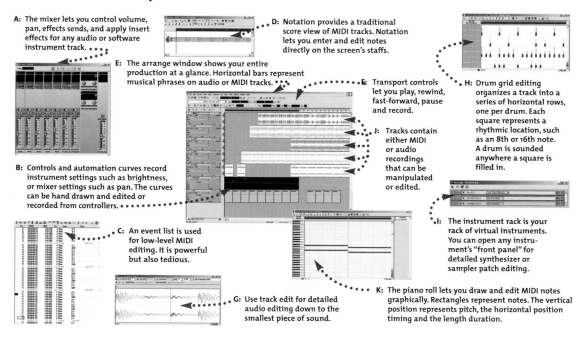

A: The mixer lets you control volume, pan, effects sends, and apply insert effects for any audio or software instrument track.

B: Controls and automation curves record instrument settings such as brightness, or mixer settings such as pan. The curves can be hand drawn and edited or recorded from controllers.

C: An event list is used for low-level MIDI editing. It is powerful but also tedious.

D: Notation provides a traditional score view of MIDI tracks. Notation lets you enter and edit notes directly on the screen's staffs.

E: The arrange window shows your entire production at a glance. Horizontal bars represent musical phrases on audio or MIDI tracks.

F: Transport controls let you play, rewind, fast-forward, pause and record.

G: Use track edit for detailed audio editing down to the smallest piece of sound.

H: Drum grid editing organizes a track into a series of horizontal rows, one per drum. Each square represents a rhythmic location, such as an 8th or 16th note. A drum is sounded anywhere a square is filled in.

I: The instrument rack is your rack of virtual instruments. You can open any instrument's "front panel" for detailed synthesizer or sampler patch editing.

J: Tracks contain either MIDI or audio recordings that can be manipulated or edited.

K: The piano roll lets you draw and edit MIDI notes graphically. Rectangles represent notes. The vertical position represents pitch, the horizontal position timing and the length duration.

▲ *Anatomy of a sequencer.*

A typical sequencer offers most of the features depicted in the diagram here. It provides multitrack audio recording, multitrack MIDI recording and a means of mixing audio tracks and MIDI tracks. The synthesizers are played and controlled by MIDI tracks. Many sequencers include provisions to involve **plug-in effects** or virtual instruments as part of the project.

MIDI SEQUENCING

MIDI sequencing helps abate many real-world constraints. For example, you can create compositions note by note and later select an appropriate tempo, or change keys and other performance parameters. Dense musical passages that challenge physical dexterity can be recorded over and over until you either get the perfect "take" or you have enough material to create a perfect take from bits and pieces of each separate attempt. You can amend mistakes using easy editing commands. MIDI sequencing helps musicians with modest or non-existent instrument-playing skills to record professional music.

AUDIO SEQUENCING

Audio sequencing is the offspring of conventional multitrack audio recording. It is used alongside MIDI sequencing to add actual instrument recordings, such as guitar and vocals. It offers great editing flexibility, plus many creative options for transforming recorded audio or incorporating the audio in interesting new ways. One example of this is using prerecorded instrument parts, such as drum-rhythm sample loops, to help form a complete song.

EDITING

A sequencer lets you edit audio in ways that either change the original (destructive editing) or merely apply the changes during playback (non-destructive editing). Non-destructive editing gives you a chance to "undo" a change that did not quite hit the mark. It also lets you apply different edits to the same section and use the results in various places throughout the song. Audio editing can be done in microscopic detail if necessary, right down to the individual data value of a tiny portion of the sound. This is called **sample accurate editing**.

You can work with the sequencer from the first germ of an idea until you have a CD-ready song. It replaces a multitrack audio recorder and, with MIDI or virtual instruments, gives you a more flexible way of recording than just using audio. It is your studio's personal assistant and collaborator that helps you sketch out song ideas using MIDI and audio, including pre-recorded sample loops. Rough ideas are polished with editing and visual arranging. Professionally polished final mixes are made with the help of plug-in virtual effects and total mix automation.

WHAT ARE SEQUENCER TRACKS AND PATTERNS?

A **sequencer track** is the recording of a single musical part. Tracks contain either audio or MIDI, although sometimes audio tracks use MIDI for automation. Sequencers offer a number of MIDI tracks, usually over 100. Audio tracks are normally more limited, either to something like 32 or 48, or by the capabilities of your studio computer, based on hard drive and processor speed. Music has many repeated elements, so it makes sense for a sequencer to offer different ways of working with those repeating parts. Repeated sections of a song or of just a single part of a song are called **patterns**.

Sequencers that treat each part of a song separately as a track from beginning to end are called **linear sequencers**. You repeat a musical part with this by making another copy in a different place. In contrast, **pattern sequencing** lets you reuse one or more parts from a section simply by referring to them. Most sequencers work in a linear fashion but include some pattern-oriented features.

WHAT ARE QUANTIZING AND AUTOMATION?

Quantizing lets you correct the timing of a recorded performance so that it better adheres to the rhythm. It is useful if you are playing difficult or complex rhythms, or if you simply lack the necessary skill. Quantizing allows you to correct the timing of where each note should be placed without resorting to time-consuming hand editing. Quantizing can be applied in degrees to help correct a performance without making it sound too mechanical. A special type of quantizing called groove quantizing lets you alter rhythmic feel so that it adheres to different styles of grooves and rhythms.

Jargon Buster

PAN, short for panorama, relates to how a sound is positioned between stereo speakers.

Over the course of a song, automation controls your track levels, **pan**, effects and even software instrument settings. You can record automation in real-time from a hardware controller, or you can enter automation data by drawing curves in a sequencer editing window. Automation lets you work on the details of your final mix a bit at a time and, when perfected, have it control all the mix settings for the duration of the song.

1. We start our 16-bar song by loading a drum loop, which will be used to make the entire drum part.

2. Next, we make the drum loop last all 16 bars by using the sequencer's loop repeat feature. Select the right edge of the loop and drag it to the start of bar 17.

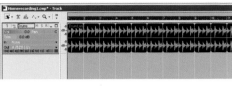

3. We use the Piano Roll Editor to paint four bars of simple chords and repeat them over all 16 bars using Copy and Paste.

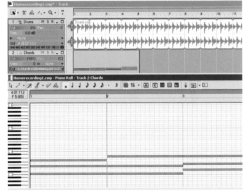

4. A four-bar bassline is recorded by playing a MIDI keyboard. Our sloppy timing is fixed by the Quantize command. A quick Copy and Paste extends the four bars to 16.

5. Inspired, we improvise an electric-guitar part, setting the sequencer for "loop play" and recording multiple passes without stopping. Afterwards, we audition each pass and select the best one.

➡ *What Is MIDI? pp. 28–31; MIDI pp. 252–267; Sequencing pp. 288–305*

Part One: The Essentials

WHAT ARE VIRTUAL INSTRUMENTS?

How would you like to have an almost unlimited number of instrument sounds available at your fingertips to use with your multitrack MIDI recordings? Do you crave the sounds of vintage analogue synthesizers, samplers, electric pianos and tone-wheel organs, but you cannot afford them or you are wary of constant repairs? How about being able to add a new synthesizer or sampler to your studio without using any more space?

Nowhere has the computer music revolution had more impact than on synthesizers and samplers. Once considered a dream, computers now provide virtual instruments that rival hardware synthesizers and samplers and yet are nothing more than special programs. Even accurate-sounding imitations of vintage instruments are available inexpensively.

Virtual instruments are software programs that use the same principles as hardware instruments to create sound. Software calculations create digital audio that is played through the computer's sound card. Virtual instruments require no physical space. New instruments are added by installing software. When you upgrade your computer's capabilities you can play more simultaneous virtual instruments. It is like getting more synthesizers for free.

The computer's vast capabilities offer new opportunities for novel synthesizer designs. Since virtual instruments are less expensive to develop, designers can dare to try new approaches. Better yet, virtual instruments will only get better with every new generation of personal computer.

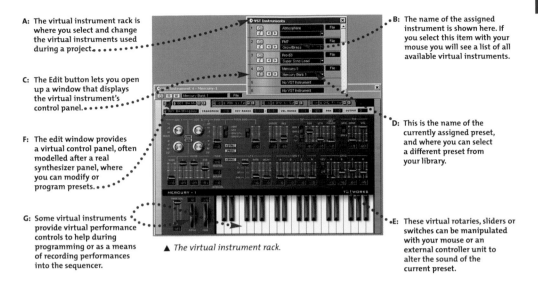

A: The virtual instrument rack is where you select and change the virtual instruments used during a project.

C: The Edit button lets you open up a window that displays the virtual instrument's control panel.

F: The edit window provides a virtual control panel, often modelled after a real synthesizer panel, where you can modify or program presets.

G: Some virtual instruments provide virtual performance controls to help during programming or as a means of recording performances into the sequencer.

B: The name of the assigned instrument is shown here. If you select this item with your mouse you will see a list of all available virtual instruments.

D: This is the name of the currently assigned preset, and where you can select a different preset from your library.

E: These virtual rotaries, sliders or switches can be manipulated with your mouse or an external controller unit to alter the sound of the current preset.

▲ *The virtual instrument rack.*

HOW DO I USE VIRTUAL INSTRUMENTS WITH MY SEQUENCER?

Many sequencers provide a type of virtual rack to contain the project's virtual instruments. You can choose any of the compatible instruments on your hard drive, usually placed in a special folder. Once you assign an instrument in the rack it is available as a destination for MIDI tracks and as an audio source for the sequencer's mixer. Each virtual instrument provides a number of preset sounds that you can select. You can use these as they are or modify them within the instrument's control panel. Presets that you create or change can be saved and used later on.

One of the best features of a virtual instrument is that all the instruments and settings can be saved as part of the project's file. This makes it easy to return to a project at a later date and pick up where you left off – something that has always been a challenge when using hardware synthesizers.

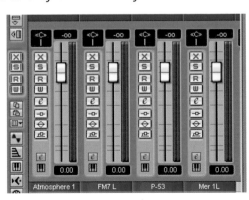

▲ *Once you have selected your virtual instruments in the virtual instrument rack, each will appear as another audio source in your sequencer's mixer, just like an external synthesizer in a "real" mixer.*

ARE VIRTUAL INSTRUMENTS AS GOOD AS REAL SYNTHESIZERS?

The simple answer is yes. Hardware and virtual instruments use the same synthesis principles. It is possible to equal or exceed hardware synthesizers with care and clever programming. In fact, many of today's hardware synthesizers use software-like methods to create their sound. You might even think of these as hardware virtual instruments.

Jargon Buster

LATENCY is the delay between the time that audio or MIDI data enters the computer and the time it is received at its destination after processing.

Classic analogue synthesizers remain somewhat elusive for software or hardware virtual instruments to convincingly imitate. There are a number of well-regarded hardware and software virtual analogue synthesizers, but the subtle difference between individual analogue instruments makes substituting a virtual analogue synthesizer a matter of individual taste.

Virtual instruments have continued to improve both in capabilities and sound quality as developers have honed their skills and computers have become increasingly powerful. Some virtual instruments are now considered superior to their hardware counterparts.

It is possible to use virtual instruments instead of hardware synthesizers and have a completely virtual studio. There are, however, limitations. When your computer crashes it takes your instruments with it – embarrassing if you were performing live. **Latency** may be a problem with certain instruments on slower computers.

Finally, software licensing agreements place limitations on the reselling and trading of your copy of a virtual instrument, so you might be stuck with it once you no longer need it.

◄ *A virtual studio can be as good as the real thing, and takes up a lot less space.*

WHAT ARE VSTI, DXI, RTAS, TDM, AUDIO UNITS, REWIRE AND STAND-ALONE INSTRUMENTS?

Virtual instruments conform to specific software conventions called **interfaces** (more commonly referred to in the US as **platforms**, **formats** or **application programming interface** – API). VSTi is the most popular and is widely used on both PCs and Macs. DXi is only for PCs. RTAS and TDM are specific to the Pro Tools software sequencer. Audio Units is the Apple standard for OS X. Some virtual instruments work alongside the sequencer or by themselves in a stand-alone fashion. ReWire is a special interface for stand-alone instruments that lets audio and MIDI information pass between your sequencer and the instrument.

Pro Tip

A PLUG-IN WRAPPER is a special program you can use to adapt a virtual instrument or plug-in effect from one type of interface (platform) to another, for example from VSTi to DXi.

VIRTUAL INSTRUMENTS WITHOUT A SEQUENCER?

With the right host software (a special program for this situation), or if stand-alone versions are available, virtual instruments can be used without a software sequencer. You can use your virtual instruments for practice or playing live without the trouble of running the sequencer. A laptop running a few stand-alone virtual instruments is a worthy replacement for a rack of hardware synthesizers for live performance, and is much more portable.

Should your studio needs ever outstrip one computer you can dedicate a second computer to providing virtual instruments. Most musicians will never use this much capability, but it is good to know it is there if needed.

▲ *Reason's rack provides a wide array of instruments and effects that can be used stand-alone or connected via ReWire to your sequencer.*

➡ *Software pp. 218–247; Synthesis pp. 268–287*

WHAT IS A SOFTWARE STUDIO?

Imagine that you could purchase a single software program that would provide a complete working studio of instruments, effects, a sequencer and even a rich library of preset sounds. Furthermore, the program is powerful yet easy to use because its all-inclusive capabilities work together seamlessly.

This is the software studio: a highly capable, yet affordable, musical tool. It promotes a smooth working environment so that ideas take root and develop more quickly.

A: The virtual mixer is used to adjust audio levels from the instruments and effects.

B: A virtual instrument shown with its control panel fully accessible for adjusting settings.

C: Virtual effects processors such as this reverb are an important component in a software studio.

D: This virtual instrument currently has its control panel closed to make a more compact rack.

E: The sequencer allows you to record and edit the music that plays the virtual instruments. You can also record changes to instrument and effects settings, as well as to the overall mix levels.

F: The transport bar is where you control, record and play, much like with a tape recorder or CD player.

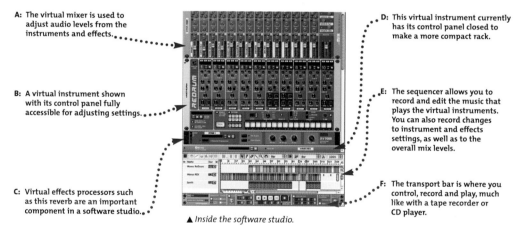

▲ *Inside the software studio.*

A complete software studio should offer:

- A collection of virtual instruments that provides you with a broad palette of sounds,
- Virtual effects for processing instrument sounds and polishing a final mix,
- A virtual mixer for combining the audio of each instrument,
- A sequencer to capture, edit and play your musical ideas.

Expansion is less important if the software studio has the right ingredients from the beginning. In fact, expansion can actually detract from the usability if not originally conceived to integrate with the rest of the software studio.

The better software studios allow you to change your studio's make-up if needed, so that you can choose the instruments and effects for each project. Not only is this a flexible way of working, but it also helps to ensure a long, useful life for the software studio, even as your needs and interests change.

NO AUDIO RECORDING?

Traditionally, software studios do not include any type of multitrack audio recording. A software studio is mainly concerned with using MIDI tracks to control virtual instruments, samples and loops. Virtual samplers, or sometimes a special "loop-player" instrument, are used to play the samples or loops. You can use some

▲ *Reason completes the illusion of a virtual rack of by allowing you to access the back of the rack. Here you can connect instruments and effects with cables to create interesting studio setups.*

clever techniques to work around the "no audio recording" limitation to incorporate audio parts such as vocals in your software studio-produced songs.

One benefit of the MIDI and sample focus is that software studio project files are usually much smaller than those of normal sequencer projects. Most software studios offer a way of packing up a song into a single computer file. Usually this file is small enough to exchange over the Internet, which can then open up a whole wealth of collaboration possibilities.

A software studio's included sound library is a very important element to be considered – it makes the difference between an inspiring software studio and one that is arduous to work with. There are a number of inexpensive sound-library expansions for the most popular software studios that can help keep your sounds fresh and inspiring. Of course, the best "future-proof" insurance you can have is being able to program your own sounds.

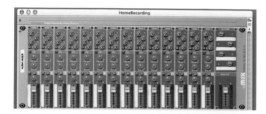

1. Your software studio project starts with a sparsely populated rack of equipment, featuring only the mixer and an empty sequencer.

2. Choose a drum machine loaded with a set of inspiring sounds and program a few patterns in its pattern sequencer. Trigger the patterns in the main sequencer.

3. Add a virtual analogue synthesizer and create a four-bar bassline part using the sequencer's Piano Roll Editor. Use Copy and Paste to repeat for 16 bars.

4. Load a sampler and select an electric piano preset. Program a four-bar chord progression using the Piano Roll Editor. Repeat over 16 bars.

5. A virtual reverb sweetens the electric piano's sound. Creating a 16-bar song was fast and easy!

SOFTWARE STUDIO VS SEQUENCER

How is a software studio different from a sequencer, and why not just replace the sequencer with a software studio? The lack of straightforward audio recording is one reason that a software studio does not replace a sequencer. Another limitation is that audio editing requires a separate program.

Illustrated Home Recording Handbook
Illustrated Home Recording Handbook

The software studio's MIDI sequencer is feature limited and not really designed for large, complex MIDI projects. Editing tools tend to be basic and serviceable, but lack the sophisticated features that are sometimes necessary. Most software studio sequencers are for use exclusively with their virtual instruments and have no provision to use external MIDI instruments or even virtual instruments running in other programs.

On the other hand, software studios cost less than a top sequencer and come equipped with a comparable complement of virtual instruments and plug-in effects. The most important benefit, though, is that the software studio is designed so that all its components mesh well. The tools tend to be simple so they are easier to master, yet they are deep enough for doing serious, non-trivial music work. Complex features are omitted in favour of keeping the software studio easy to use, with a fun and satisfying workflow. Using the studio correctly, you end up focusing more energy on the music and less on the tools.

HOW CAN I USE MY SOFTWARE STUDIO WITH A SEQUENCER?

At some point you will probably want to use a full sequencer to tackle the jobs done poorly by the software studio. One way to do this is to move the project from the software studio to the sequencer using one or more of the software studio's special export facilities. Another good way to combine the best of both is to use the software studio as a collection of virtual instruments and effects controlled from the sequencer. This is a nice way to expand a sequencer. Most software studios include a means of transmitting audio and MIDI information back and forth to a sequencer.

An alternative is to have the software studio play its portion of the song and use the sequencer for audio tracks, external MIDI tracks and virtual instruments that the software studio fails to offer. A good deal of collaboration is possible between the software studio and sequencer, but take care that you do not make things too complex to enjoy and use effectively.

➡ *What Is a Sequencer? pp. 44–47; What Are Virtual Instruments? pp. 48–51;*
Software Sequencers pp. 220–233

WHAT IS A CONTROLLER?

Computer-based recording is wonderful, but the computer user's input devices were not designed with music making in mind. The mouse and computer keyboard are not ideal ways of entering, or performing, musical passages in your sequencer, or of playing virtual instruments. There must be a better way!

Music controllers can improve your working methods and make your studio activities more enjoyable and inspirational. There are three broad types you will encounter.

◀ *A MIDI controller combines rotary and fader controllers. Sometimes called a fader box, it is good for adjusting synthesizer settings and effects. It can even serve as a poor-man's control surface for your sequencer.*

The first are controllers used to perform musical passages while recording into the sequencer. These music controllers are typically styled after a piano keyboard, though there are other types, too. If you do not play piano you will still find it easier to enter notes into the sequencer with a keyboard controller, even if it is just one note at a time.

Jargon Buster

SLIDERS are up-down or left-right controls, often found on mixers. **ROTARIES (KNOBS or POTS)** are similar to hi-fi volume controls and change their value depending on how much you rotate the control.

A second type of controller provides slider, rotary and switch controls. These MIDI controllers are often called **fader boxes** because the slider controls are reminiscent of the audio faders found on mixing consoles. MIDI controllers can adjust settings for virtual instruments and effects, making sound programming more enjoyable. The sliders also control the levels on the sequencer's mixer. To add automatic changes to your song you can "play" a MIDI controller while recording the MIDI data it puts out .

A third variety of controller provides a complete command centre for your sequencer, including sliders and rotaries to control the sequencer's mixer, and numerous buttons to control sequencer operation. These control surfaces look very much like an actual mixer. The sliders are motorized so that the sequencer can move them to indicate current settings. The rotaries, often endless, work in such a fashion that turning the control always properly affects its current assigned setting.

The control surface also has many control buttons that supplement the mouse and computer keyboard. This helps you to keep your focus on one type of input device instead of constantly switching between mouse, keyboard and controller. A control surface with well-integrated sequencer support makes using the sequencer a much more hands-on and enjoyable experience.

Regardless of the type of controller or controllers you choose for your studio, you will need to connect the controller to your computer. Modern controllers connect through USB or FireWire. Older controllers connect using MIDI, so your computer will require a separate MIDI interface.

Some USB-equipped controllers require their own power cable but many take their power directly from the USB connection. This is very convenient if you are trying to assemble a portable studio. A laptop, one of these USB-powered controllers and some good headphones make for a formidable mobile studio.

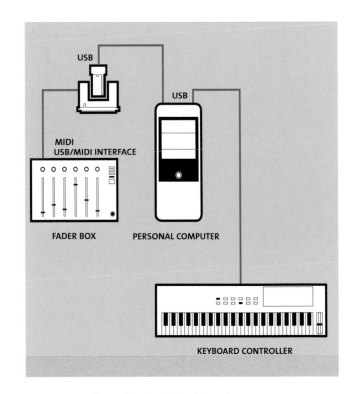

▲ *Recent controllers, such as the keyboard shown here, use USB to interface with the computer. Other controllers offer MIDI outputs. The fader box connects its MIDI output through a USB–MIDI interface.*

DO I REALLY NEED A CONTROLLER?

Controllers are very useful but hardly essential. Even for entering musical passages by hand, most sequencers work well with the mouse and computer keyboard. Many musicians who have learned to work this way now prefer it to using extra controllers. If your budget does not allow for a controller, consider trying it with the mouse and computer keyboard first. You may decide that you like that best.

The mouse and computer keyboard, however, are not the final answer; for some they even dampen music creativity. A simple two- or three-octave music keyboard that includes a few sliders and rotaries is an inexpensive way around this limitation. Having some type of physical controller lets you take more of a performance approach to recording your inspirations. Music is a form of intellectual, emotional and physical expression. Diminishing the physical aspect may well change your results in an undesirable way.

ARE THERE OTHER CONTROLLERS BESIDES KEYBOARDS?

Keyboards are the most popular, but there are other types of music controllers. These can offer drummers, guitarists and wind-instrument players a more natural way of recording MIDI.

◄ *Small multi-function controllers place a wide variety of controls at your fingertips while using little studio space. This model packs drum pads, a music keyboard, sliders and rotaries into a single compact controller.*

Drum parts can be played and recorded using a drum-pad controller. Some of these are sensors attached to actual drums, while others are special drumming surfaces struck with sticks, palm or finger. Table-top models designed for finger playing are useful, even if you do not play drums.

◄ *Special-purpose controllers such as this USB drum pad are useful for playing and performing the musical parts, rather than simply programming the music in the sequencer.*

Special guitar controllers convert normal guitar play into MIDI. Some adaptation of your playing technique is usually necessary to work around guitar controller limitations.

MIDI wind controllers use mouth and fingering methods familiar to those of sax, trumpet and flute players. They are much simpler to learn to play than a real wind or brass instrument. These are an often-overlooked alternative method of recording expressive MIDI performances that can be learned by almost anyone.

A number of special controllers – true instruments in their own right – offer familiar or exotic ways of playing music. If you are interested in exploring new performance and recording methods these may open up some new opportunities.

◄ The wind controller shown here provides a more natural way for non-keyboard players to perform and enter music into a sequencer.

► Alternative controllers, such as the Ztar shown here, offer a unique way of performing music for recording into a sequencer. The Ztar control looks like the familiar guitar but is a unique musical instrument in its own right.

➡ What Is MIDI? pp. 28–31;
What Is a Sequencer? pp. 44–47;
Hardware pp. 332–341

WHAT IS A SOFTWARE PLUG-IN?

In many ways, effects are as important to a song as the recorded audio itself. Effects can be used to alter a sound's character, either subtly or in a dramatic manner.

A proper home recording studio is incomplete without an assortment of audio effects processors. Like most other aspects of the computer-based studio, it is the computer itself, running software plug-ins, that will add these effects to your studio tool kit.

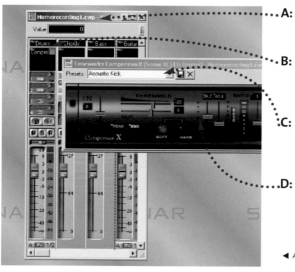

A: The sequencer virtual mixer display.

B: A plug-in slot where plug-ins are placed for that particular mixer channel.

C: A list of preset effects settings for quick access to a certain effect.

D: The plug-in's virtual front panel ready to be adjusted using your mouse.

◄ *A typical plug-in effect.*

In the past, sequencer companies looked for ways to include effects or for them to be added later, perhaps even provided by a different company. They created a standard way for the sequencer software to work with a software effect that adhered to a software interface designed for this purpose. Since different effects could be "plugged in", software effects became known as software plug-ins, or just plug-ins.

A software plug-in can also be called a virtual effect, since the software running on the computer creates the effects processor. This is analogous to virtual instruments. Both use computer software to perform the necessary calculations on the digital audio, recreating their hardware counterparts with dazzling accuracy. Software plug-ins and virtual instruments both use the computer's processing capabilities, so there are limits to how many effects and virtual instruments you can have operating at the same instant. Today's computers are capable of running many plug-ins, or sounding many software instrument notes. Eventually, though, your needs will exceed your computer's abilities, and you will find your system unable to cope with that one last plug-in you have called up, leading to a dramatic slowdown and possibly even a crash. You will have to learn how to manage and balance how your software plug-ins and virtual instruments are used, sometimes trading one effect for another.

WHAT ARE PLUG-IN PRESETS?

Once you find a combination of settings for a particular plug-in that works for you, you can save those settings as a **plug-in preset** so that they can be used again. Plug-in presets are similar to virtual instrument presets. These are useful when you wish to use the same type of effects processing on different tracks or even songs. Be careful, though, that you do not misuse this feature. Some effects require slightly different adjustments for each musical situation. It is best to view plug-in presets as a starting place and adjust the plug-in according to the song's needs, guided by your ear.

WHEN ARE PLUG-IN EFFECTS USED?

Plug-in effects are just another creative option, so you can employ them at almost any time during a song's production. You can use effects while recording external audio sources; adding some **compression** while recording a vocalist, for example, can help smooth out unnecessary volume changes. Guitars can be recorded using plug-in effects instead of the usual **stomp boxes**.

Virtual instruments are another good place to apply plug-in effects. You can use the effects as an additional synthesis option when creating your own sounds. Effects are often used towards the end of a project as a way of adding polish to the overall recording. This is often referred to as "sweetening" a track.

WHAT IS PLUG-IN AUTOMATION?

You can adjust plug-in settings during the course of a song and have those adjustments occur each time the song is played. This is known as **plug-in automation**, and it opens up exciting possibilities using software plug-in effects as a dynamic element of your compositions and productions.

Jargon Buster

DISTORTION alters a sound by contorting the audio, making the sound more harsh or edgy. Guitar fuzz-boxes produce a type of distortion – as heard on the Rolling Stones' '(I Can't Get No) Satisfaction'.

You could add a **distortion** plug-in to the main instrumental melody, for example, during a climactic section of the song to increase the drama, turning it off or decreasing its presence once the section has passed. Another example would be changing the setting of the **reverb** from a small room to a cavernous hall to impart a sense of the song's location having changed.

Plug-in adjustments can be recorded and edited. Sequencers offer automation drawing tools that are used to create and modify settings much like one uses a drawing program. Sequencers also let you assign external controllers such as a **fader** or rotary control, and record the adjustments you make as plug-in automation information in real-time.

▲ *This track display shows plug-in effects automation (the yellow dotted curve near the top) changing one of the effects settings over the course of 16 bars.*

WHAT IS SOUND MANGLING?

The availability of powerful software plug-in effects has made it possible to experiment with extreme audio processing. Taking audio and changing its character dramatically like this has become known as **sound mangling**.

Sound mangling is a wonderfully creative technique that can be used to transform ordinary sounds into your own unique sounds. The objective is to process a sound using one or more plug-ins until it is something entirely new. Sometimes the plug-ins are applied togther, one after

Illustrated Home Recording Handbook

the other, and this is called an **effects chain**. Another method is to process the audio repeatedly, taking the previous result and subjecting it to additional processing.

Many sequencers have special commands that let you apply one or more plug-ins to a section of an audio recording to make a new recording. These commands usually include a way of auditioning how the processing will sound. You can try different plug-in presets and settings to find exactly the sound you are seeking and then "print" the effect on to the audio so that it is permanently part of it, allowing you to unload the plug-in and reclaim valuable system resources.

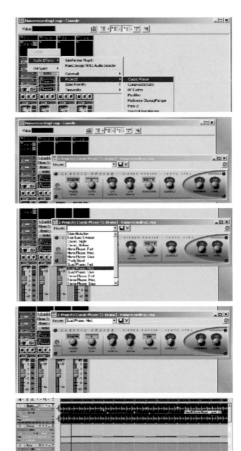

1. Add a plug-in effect to a track first by clicking on a plug-in slot. Choose one of the effects from the pop-up menu.

2. Open the plug-in's front panel so that you can select a preset and adjust some of its settings.

3. Play your song and audition a few presets until you find a promising candidate that you can further adjust to taste.

4. Keep the song playing and adjust the effect's front panel controls until you are happy with the sound.

5. You can control a plug-in using automation features to draw a curve for each setting (as in the red line shown), or use an external controller to record your adjustments while the music plays.

➡ *What Is an Effect? pp. 68–79; Effects and Processors pp. 306–331*

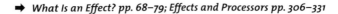

BUT I CAN'T READ MUSIC!

Do you have a burning passion for making your own music, but your only formal music education was music-appreciation class in primary school? Are your memories of instrument lessons filled with endless, boring and tiresome scale exercises? Do you feel your musical urges stifled because you cannot read sheet music?

Anyone with a love of music, and the desire to learn to compose and perform music can do so with the help of a computer-based home studio. You might be surprised at how many professional musicians are in the same boat.

CAN SOFTWARE HELP ME?

Music software makes songwriting and recording possible even without a formal music-theory background or instrument proficiency. Sequencers can be used to overcome some of the gaps in your musical training. Some musicians might even consider the mouse, keyboard and computer to be their musical instruments.

Recording your music using MIDI lets you work at the level of a single note, with full control over how it is played. Mistakes are readily fixed and alternatives easily tried. All this occurs while you hear the results in real-time. This is an unprecedented, interactive way to write your songs. Sequencers, MIDI, synthesizers and samplers can all work together to lessen the dependency on mastering the physical aspect of playing each instrument you wish to incorporate into a song.

Music training and education is beneficial, but do not let the fact that you lack formal training prevent you from enjoying the thrill of creating music and capturing your musical ideas. Assemble your own home recording studio today to start a lifetime of music creation!

I AM A COMPLETE BEGINNER

You can begin making your own songs by learning to work with sample loops (see p. 38). A special type of CD-ROM called a sample tool kit contains a number of related samples that can be used to make different songs. You can use these elements to assemble a complete song that reflects your sense of the music. It is a bit like being a band leader and directing what is to be played, but relying on each musician to interpret the music. You are free to embellish your own recorded parts and creatively apply software plug-ins to alter each part. The whole process is similar to a **remix**.

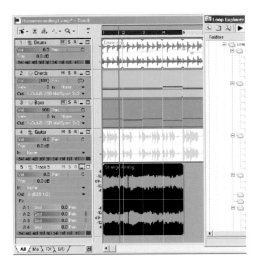

▲ Audio loop arranging can make it easy to get started when composing a song. You can audition new loops even while repeatedly playing a portion of the song.

Jargon Buster

A **REMIX** is where the audio tracks of one song are reused in a creative manner to fashion a new version or an entirely new song.

You can also find collections of MIDI drum patterns, instrument phrases (often called **riffs**), or even entire songs in MIDI format. These so-called MIDI loops can be a more flexible and satisfying way to assemble a song. It is easier to extract only a portion of each part if needed; you can edit it as music instead of sound and you can use different virtual instruments to achieve the instrument sound you are after.

You can combine both sample loops and MIDI loops in the same song. As you gain knowledge about your tools, musical skills and confidence, you will find yourself relying less on pre-recorded loops and more on making your own musical parts.

HOW CAN I MAKE MUSIC IF I CANNOT PLAY AN INSTRUMENT?

MIDI recording lets you work with music, much like a writer works with words. A poet who labours carefully over each word and syllable can create just as beautiful poetry as that rare poet who recites a new poem from the top of his or her head. MIDI lets you craft your song at your own pace using whatever works best. The fact that you cannot even play a short melody on an instrument is no longer reason to keep your music inside your head!

The **piano-roll editor** lets you paint your musical ideas one note at a time and see the composition at any time in an easy-to-understand pictorial fashion. A MIDI **drum grid editor** works in the same manner, so that you can craft rhythms, even though you can hardly keep time with a tambourine. In either case, you edit and make changes using simple visual techniques that are familiar, especially if you have used a computer painting or drawing program before. All the while you can let your ear guide you, since all this can be done while the music is playing.

◄ *Keyboards are the most common music controllers available. Some, like this model, feature a weighted playing feel comparable to an actual piano keyboard.*

A music keyboard controller and step editing allow you to record notes one-by-one. The software manages all the timing details so that the music plays properly. This can be a faster and more enjoyable alternative to painting notes with a mouse.

Pro Tip

If you use sample loops, MIDI loops or part (or all) of a MIDI song, consult an expert for advice about what legal permissions you need before offering your songs to others, even for free.

There are software musical gadgets that allow you to perform music in a fun and interactive way. **Arpeggiators** transform slowly played chords into melodies. Step-sequencers make it easy to create basslines and melodic phrases. There are even special MIDI processors that can take a MIDI recording and play it in different musical styles – like a guitar player strumming chords, for example.

➡ *What Is a Sample? pp. 36–39; What Is a Sequencer? pp. 44–47; Sequencing pp. 288–305; How to Read Music pp. 364–368*

1. If you can draw on the screen and you have a good ear, you can construct your own melodies and harmonies.

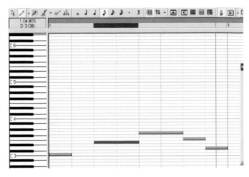

2. Tools such as this imitation of an old-school analogue step sequencer make creating MIDI parts easy, interactive and enjoyable.

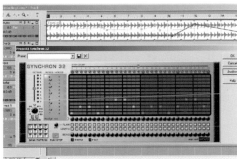

3. Another way to enter notes is to use step entry and play them from a keyboard controller one by one without regard to rhythm. Step-entry systems take care of all the rhythmic details.

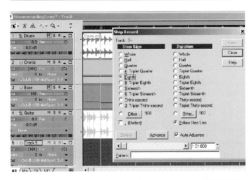

4. You can use the drum grid editor in your sequencer to paint drum rhythms while you listen.

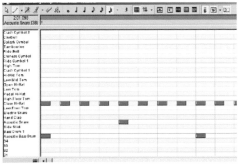

WHAT IS AN EFFECT?

WHAT ARE EFFECTS PROCESSORS?

One of the most exciting and creative parts of recording your own music is the way in which you can shape and transform the sound between the initial recording and the final mix. These manipulations are often the difference between a good song and a great one. One favourite tool used to perform this sonic metamorphosis is the effects processor.

◄ *Effects are available in a variety of types. A diverse collection provides you with numerous choices for colouring your recordings. Software plug-ins give you practically unlimited choices.*

An **effects processor** takes the input sound and alters it using various operations. The results of these alterations can be used by themselves or combined with the original source to produce the final output. Almost every effects processor has a setting, or **mix**, that controls how much of the output is from the original source audio and how much is from the effect. A mix setting of 75 per cent would mean that the output is three quarters processed, one quarter unaffected.

Effects are sometimes used on a single input source or recorded part. The effect is "inserted" between the signal source and its destination. Often this occurs in the mixer channel (virtual or otherwise). An effect used in this fashion is called an **insert effect**.

Alternatively, it may be desirable to apply a little of the same effect to a number of sources simultaneously. Effects used in this way are called **send effects**. A mixer control known as the **effects send** determines how much of each source is sent to the effects processor. Depending how they are connected to your mixer and sound sources, most effects processors can be used either as a send effect or an insert effect.

> ## Pro Tip
>
> **WET** is the processed portion of the signal, **DRY** is the unprocessed portion. The ratio of processed to unprocessed is "the wet/dry mix". If the output is all processed it is "100 per cent wet".

Effects can be used to subtly shade a sound or to create entirely new sounds. There are no rules other than your own aesthetic sensibilities. Beware, though, that there is a tendency to overuse an effect on the first few projects after becoming acquainted with it.

The computer-recording revolution has placed an almost unlimited variety of effects processors at your fingertips in the form of software plug-ins. Provided your computer is up to the task, you can use almost any combination of effects. You can use automation to record adjustments you

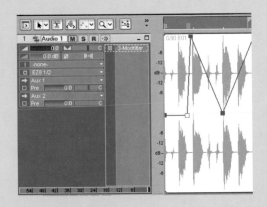

▲ *Effects automation is a powerful way for you to integrate effects into your music. This example shows a low-pass filter cutoff frequency being changed as part of the overall music. (A low-pass filter passes the low frequencies while stopping the upper frequencies.)*

make to effects settings while the music is playing. Effects processors can be "played" almost like a musical instrument by varying their settings as part of a musical performance. This is an exciting avenue in which to pursue new and unique musical expressions.

REVERB PROCESSORS

It is hard to forget the stunning sound of music performed in a great concert hall. The music is so alive and beautiful. Reverb processors were created to give your recordings the same sense of depth and space as recording in a fine acoustic space.

Natural reverberation is the total of all sound reflections arriving at your ear from walls, ceilings and other surfaces. These sonic bounces are known as **reverberant reflections** and they help the brain to perceive the size and shape of the acoustic space. They also help you to locate the sound's position and estimate its distance. A **reverb processor** adds an approximation of the reverberant reflections for a fictitious listening space that you select, like a club, concert hall, arena or canyon. This allows you to create the illusion that the recording was made in the selected venue. Other reverb settings determine the location's size and liveliness. You can alter the apparent location of a sound by using the reverb to take advantage of how the human brain processes aural clues. Adding reverb tends to push a sound to the back of the mix, making it seem distant and behind other instruments.

Reverb is sometimes used to make a sound bigger or more lush. Reverb transforms vocals, pianos, synthesizers and most instruments into majestic-sounding devices.

A: Selects the type of reverb, such as concert hall, small room or canyon.

B: Because reverbs are complex to set up, it is sometimes best to begin with a preset.

C: Decay controls how long the reverberation takes to die away.

E: Reverbs offer numerous settings and many possibilities, but you will need to learn what each setting controls.

D: The dry/wet (mix) adjustment determines how much of the output is made up of the reverb portion.

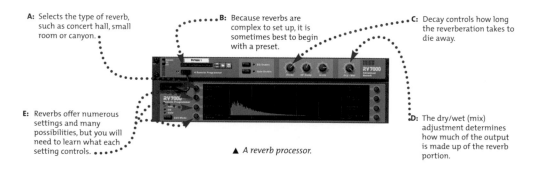

▲ *A reverb processor.*

Illustrated Home Recording Handbook

Almost everything sounds good on its own through a reverb, but be careful not to become too enamoured with its use, as too much reverb on every instrument in a mix will ultimately make a track sound smeared, overly distant and muddled.

Each reverb processor or plug-in has its own sound. Often particular models are coveted for a unique sound. Some reverbs emulate classic reverb processors, such as older devices like **spring reverbs** and **plate reverbs**. Spring reverb is a combination electrical and mechanical device that uses the sound properties of a metal spring to imitate reverberation. A plate reverb is similar except that a metal plate replaces the spring. Special reverb effects such as **gated reverbs** are very useful for processing drum sounds. Gated reverb is a special reverb process that turns the reverberation on or off,

▲ *Impulse response reverbs (IR), also called convolution reverb, use special recordings of actual acoustic spaces to create realistic reverberation effects. It is like playing your music in a famous concert hall!*

depending on the level of the input sound. A more recent innovation, the **convolution reverb**, can duplicate famous performance halls and nearly any acoustic space with uncanny accuracy.

As you gain experience using reverb you will need to learn moderation. What sounds great for a track played in isolation can sound muddy when mixed with other reverb-treated tracks. There is a tendency to use too much reverb (or make the setting too "wet") when listening to the part by itself. Even when you are applying reverb to the entire mix, it is better to add just enough so you sense it rather than overtly hear it. Think of reverb as the final elegant touch you can add to your recordings. You should aim for just enough to bring the music to life.

Pro Tip

You can sometimes make two recordings sound like they were recorded in the same location by adding a small amount of the same reverb to each one.

Part One: The Essentials

COMPRESSION: USE IT MORE

Sometimes, while you are watching television, the sound blares when sponsors shout their messages. Instinctively you reach for the remote control. Once the regular broadcast returns you turn the volume back up. You have just compressed the television's audio and you were the compressor.

Compression is a type of automatic level control. It is used to reduce the disparity between the highest and lowest levels in a recording. A recording's **dynamic range** is the difference between its loudest and quietest levels. Dynamic range contributes a great deal to a recording's vitality: a wide dynamic range is interesting and dramatic.

Consider the problem of trying to listen to the wide dynamic ranges in classical music. The softer passages are often too quiet to hear above the noise in a room or in a car. Loud passages may not be enjoyable. A compressor can be employed to restrict the dynamic range. You can also use compression on individual instruments or vocal parts to smooth out undesirable level changes. You can even use it to intentionally change the character of a sound.

Jargon Buster

ATTENUATION is a reduction in the level of an electrical signal.

Compressors measure the input signal level and progressively apply more **attenuation** as the level increases. This reduces the dynamic range of the output by an amount expressed by the **compression ratio**. This describes how much the input level must increase for each change in output level. Uncompressed is 1:1; a 1-dB increase in input level raises the output level 1 dB. A 4:1 compression will raise the output level only 1 dB for every 4 dB of additional input.

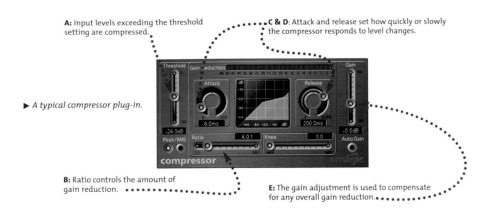

A: Input levels exceeding the threshold setting are compressed.

C & D: Attack and release set how quickly or slowly the compressor responds to level changes.

► A typical compressor plug-in.

B: Ratio controls the amount of gain reduction.

E: The gain adjustment is used to compensate for any overall gain reduction.

A compressor reduces the level when the sound is loud. This lets you raise the level of the sound after compressing it without making the loud parts too loud. The amount you raise the overall level is often adjustable with a setting usually known as **make-up gain**.

The compressor's **threshold setting** determines when compression is applied. Compression is used when the input level is above the threshold; below the threshold, the input signal passes unaffected. Levels can change very quickly, so it is important for the compressor to react appropriately; too quick and the tone colour is changed, too slow and a momentary level increase will inadvertently pass through. The **attack** setting controls how quickly the compressor responds. Higher attack values make the compressor less responsive. A similar setting, **release**, is used to keep the compression applied for an adjustable length of time after the level drops below the threshold.

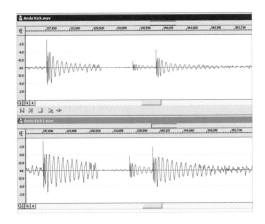

▲ A kick drum loop before (top) and after (bottom) compression. Notice how the overall level of the lower amplitude portions have been boosted up closer to the waveform peaks.

Compression strengthens the weak and tames the unruly, but like many effects it loses its power with overuse. Exercise care when applying compression or you can suck the life out of your music.

CHORUS: BEEF UP THAT SOUND

What happens when two or more musicians play the same music on the same type of instrument? Even fretted instruments like guitars that are "in tune" have barely perceptible pitch variations, and even the best musicians play each note on string, brass, and wind instruments with slightly different pitches.

A: Delay selects the starting delay.

B: Speed (rate) indicates how fast the delay time varies.

C: Depth selects how much the delay time varies.

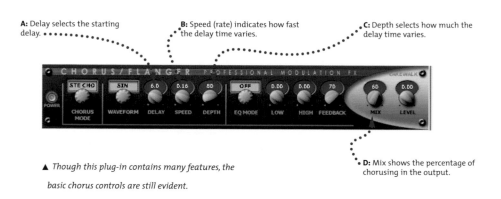

▲ *Though this plug-in contains many features, the basic chorus controls are still evident.*

D: Mix shows the percentage of chorusing in the output.

There is also a small variable delay between the notes. This is why an ensemble sounds fuller and richer than a solo instrument. Chorus effects processors were invented to mimic the effect of two or more musicians playing together. A **chorus effect** delays the input by about 10 to 20 milliseconds and adds it to the original signal. The delay time is slowly modulated above and below the initial setting. The rate of this variation and the depth are two important chorus settings. These are often called **modulation rate** and **modulation depth**. Some chorus processors also modulate the level of the input, and may add a little of the output back to the input. These alterations are not normally changeable by the user.

A low modulation rate and depth setting add a subtle change comparable to an ensemble. As you increase the depth, the effect is more pronounced and you begin to hear pitch warbling. A fast rate and high depth can be used for a special effect. Many chorus effects offer stereo outputs, so that you can use chorus to create the illusion of stereo with a mono source signal. It can also be used to increase the sense of stereo width in a stereo source signal. Too much chorus processing will, however, tend to push a sound further back in the mix.

▲ *The upper synthesizer waveform becomes the lower waveform with slowly varying pulse widths when treated by a chorus effect. The resulting sound is richer, similar to mixing two slightly detuned oscillators.*

FLANGING AND PHASING

Chorus is a special example of **delay modulation** processing. Two related effects are **flanging** and **phasing**.

Flanging is sometimes called a **jet sound** or the "whoosh" sound, because it reminds one of a jet plane passing overhead. It uses a

▲ *A delay modulator is a general-purpose effects processor that can be used to create chorus, flanging or phasing effects.*

short delay of about five milliseconds and an adjustable output amount is added back (called **feedback**) to the input. Flangers usually offer control over delay time, modulation rate, modulation depth, feedback amount and **input/output mix**, which is how much of the original input is mixed with the effect's output. A phaser, or phase shifter, is a more subtle form of flanging, with a delay time that is around two milliseconds and has much less delay modulation.

Flanging and phasing work best with complex or unpitched sounds. Drum sounds such as cymbals, hi-hats and snares are especially good candidates for flanging or phasing. Phasing can be used to impart an almost underwater feel to a sound. Extreme effects are possible by increasing feedback, modulation depth and modulation rate.

DELAY: A LIGHT DUSTING

Delay is one of the most versatile of all effects processors. It is at the heart of effects such as chorus and reverb. Delay can be used to thicken a sound, to create novel rhythmic echoes, or to impart a sense of distance and depth.

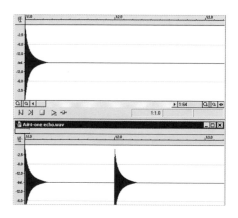

◄ *Delay in action. The synthesizer note in the upper picture is processed by a one-quarter note delay and added to the original; the result is shown in the lower picture.*

A **delay** sends the input signal to the output at a later time that is set by the **delay time**. This can be as little as a few milliseconds or as much as many seconds. The delayed signal is combined with the original in an amount set by input/output mix.

Slap-back delay is a delay effect used to create the illusion of a bigger sound. A short delay of a few milliseconds creates a result similar to that of two instruments played simultaneously. You have probably heard this effect on some bass guitar and vocal tracks. **Flamming**, named for the sound a drum makes when it is double-hit, is similar to slap-back, but the time difference is less. You may have heard this signature sound when a DJ creates it inadvertently while beat-matching two records.

The echoes heard in a large stairwell are caused by the time it takes for sound to travel to a distant surface, rebound and return. Each time the sound bounces off a surface, it drops in level, which is why echoes fade away. You can use a delay processor to manufacture echoes by adding the feedback to the input. Feedback determines how long the echoes take to die out. The more feedback, the longer they last. Too much feedback means the echoes never fade.

Illustrated Home Recording Handbook

DELAY PROCESSORS

Delay processors allow you to set the delay time as a rhythmic time value, such as a quarter note, based on your song's tempo. This type of echo can become an integral part of your music's rhythmic feel.

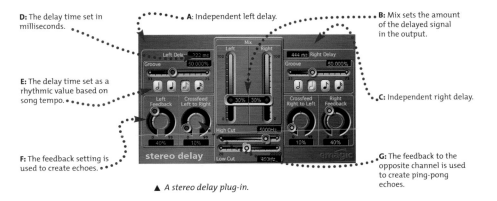

D: The delay time set in milliseconds.

A: Independent left delay.

B: Mix sets the amount of the delayed signal in the output.

E: The delay time set as a rhythmic value based on song tempo.

C: Independent right delay.

F: The feedback setting is used to create echoes.

G: The feedback to the opposite channel is used to create ping-pong echoes.

▲ *A stereo delay plug-in.*

Echoes are fairly dramatic and noticeable, so a little bit goes far. It is usually best to create a sense of echo rather than making it the dominant feature of the sound. Try keeping the delay mix setting low, in the 10 to 40 per cent range. Above 50 per cent, the sound becomes mainly echoes.

A **multitap delay processor** is used to create complex echoes and even to approximate reverb. The multitap delay offers two or more independent delays. Each delay can be positioned in the stereo output field, and become part of the feedback. With the right delay and feedback settings, a simple input can create fascinating textures of rhythms and echoes.

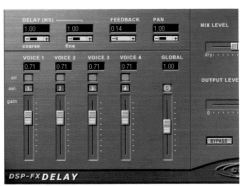

▲ *A multitap delay combines two or more independent delay sections to create complex rhythmic effects. This plug-in offers up to five delays, each with independent delay time, feedback and pan settings.*

FILTERS: USE THEM MORE

If shaping sound is like sculpting, then filters are your hammers and chisels. You may find yourself using filters more than other effects processors. A special type of filtering, equalization, is so useful that it has its own section in this book. Filters do not add to a sound, but work by selectively removing frequency components from it.

There are four common types of **filter: low-pass**, **high-pass**, **band-pass** and **band-reject**. Each is named for how it alters the frequency content. A low-pass filter passes the low frequencies while stopping (attenuating) the upper frequencies. A high-pass filter passes the high frequencies while stopping the lower ones. Band-pass filters pass frequencies in a narrow range; band-reject filters stop all frequencies within the same range.

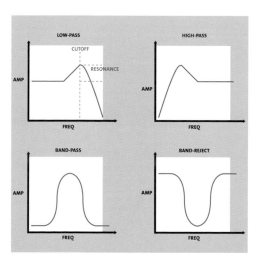

◀ There are four basic filters that you can use as effects: low-pass, high-pass, band-pass and band-reject. Each filter colours the sound in its own unique fashion.

The **cutoff frequency** determines the transition between passing and stopping. A low-pass filter, for example, passes frequencies below the cutoff frequency. Band-pass and band-reject are slightly different. The frequency setting of a band-pass or band-reject filter is commonly known as the **centre frequency**. An additional setting, **bandwidth**, determines the range above and below the centre frequency affected by the filter.

Illustrated Home Recording Handbook

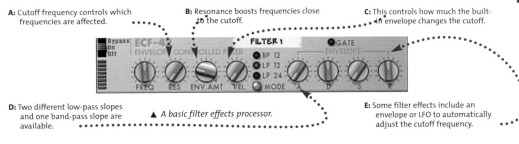

A: Cutoff frequency controls which frequencies are affected.

B: Resonance boosts frequencies close to the cutoff.

C: This controls how much the built-in envelope changes the cutoff.

D: Two different low-pass slopes and one band-pass slope are available.

▲ *A basic filter effects processor.*

E: Some filter effects include an envelope or LFO to automatically adjust the cutoff frequency.

The change from passing a frequency to stopping it is not immediate. The sharper the filter, the quicker this transition occurs. Filter sharpness is expressed as the rate at which the attenuation changes, expressed in **dB per octave**. A gentle filter will have a 6-dB per octave slope. A 24-dB per octave filter has a sharp slope.

Filters can amplify frequencies around the cutoff frequency. This is called **resonance**, or sometimes **Q** (see p. 83). High-resonance settings can dramatically emphasize those frequencies close to the cutoff frequency. Be careful with high resonance, as the sound can become loud and shrill. If you gradually change a high-resonance low-pass filter's cutoff frequency up or down, you will produce an effect cliché known as a **filter sweep**.

One exciting way in which to use a filter is to alter the cutoff frequency, or resonance, in time to the music. Some filter effects processors include a **low frequency oscillator** (LFO) or **envelope** that modulates the filter's cutoff frequency. The envelope can be triggered by the sound itself or even another track. Often, the LFO can be synchronized to the song's tempo.

A more general way to automatically control a filter is to use your sequencer's automation. This gives you almost limitless creative possibilities to sculpt the sound while the song plays.

➡ *What Is a Software Plug-in? pp. 60–63; How Do I Use EQ? pp. 80–87; Using Effects and Processing pp. 154–155; Synthesis pp. 268–287*

▲ *A low-pass filter plug-in with both adjustable (LFO) and envelope modulation. The LFO can even be set to follow the song's tempo.*

▲ *A filter bank is a special filter effect that combines two or more adjustable band-pass filters, plus low-pass and high-pass filters.*

WHAT IS EQ?

So you have recorded all your audio and MIDI parts, and you have picked out great sounds for all the synthesizers you are using. You have even added a dash of effects here and there. Now it is time to do some level matching and you are done, right? Yet somehow, as you listen to your mix, those great synthesizer sounds no longer sound so hot, and the vocals and other instruments sound muddy. Now what?

Sounds that worked well by themselves sometimes clash when combined. Each sound has a number of prominent and less-prominent **frequencies**. These frequencies are a big part of each instrument's tonal colour. Sometimes one sound's frequencies overpower another's, or the frequencies combine too strongly, making the sound boomy or shrill. Often, all the musical parts are lost in a sea of sound.

One remedy for these frequency conflicts is to use an **equalizer** (EQ). An equalizer lets you precisely alter the frequency content of any sound. Your first experience with EQ was probably with the tone controls on your television or stereo. These bass and treble

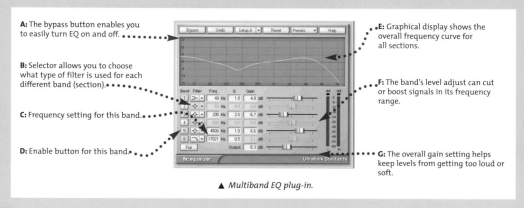

A: The bypass button enables you to easily turn EQ on and off.

B: Selector allows you to choose what type of filter is used for each different band (section).

C: Frequency setting for this band.

D: Enable button for this band.

E: Graphical display shows the overall frequency curve for all sections.

F: The band's level adjust can cut or boost signals in its frequency range.

G: The overall gain setting helps keep levels from getting too loud or soft.

▲ Multiband EQ plug-in.

controls are simple equalizers. You can make the walls shake by turning up the bass setting, and you can make the sound tinny by turning up the treble. Or you can make your expensive stereo sound like a cheap radio by turning both down!

WHERE DO YOU FIND EQ?

You will encounter EQ as a part of your synthesizers, your effects processors, your hardware mixer, and especially your sequencer's virtual mixer. Possibly the most commonly used equalizer in the computer-based studio is the EQ plug-in, a particular type of software plug-in. Let's spend a moment looking at these.

Different EQ plug-ins have different features and sounds. Most equalizers strive to be as transparent as possible but some actually colour the sound, either intentionally or inadvertently. Some EQ plug-ins offer a very high-quality sound, but this is usually at the expense of consuming a good deal of your computer's processing facilities.

Each EQ plug-in has a different "feel", so it helps to learn how they alter the sound and how each setting works. Once you have learned your EQ plug-in's behaviour and how different settings affect the sound, you will be able to quickly pick the right plug-in and set it up as required.

You should choose the right equalizer for the job at hand. For example, it makes little sense to use an eight-section EQ plug-in if you only need to boost your low frequencies. If you use only what you need, the EQ is easier to adjust and it will reduce the burden on your computer. Many EQ plug-ins offer a number of sections that can be individually turned on and off. It is helpful to start with only a few turned on, adding more sections as needed.

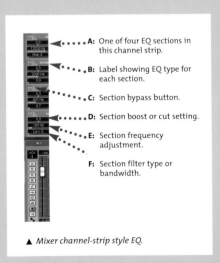

A: One of four EQ sections in this channel strip.

B: Label showing EQ type for each section.

C: Section bypass button.

D: Section boost or cut setting.

E: Section frequency adjustment.

F: Section filter type or bandwidth.

▲ *Mixer channel-strip style EQ.*

WHAT ARE THE VARIOUS TYPES OF EQ FILTERS?

Each equalizer section has a filter that is one of a handful of different types. Each filter type is designed to treat its frequency range in a particular fashion. EQ is much easier to master if you understand what each filter type is doing to your sound.

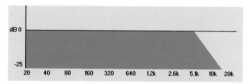

▲ *A low-pass EQ cutting frequencies above 5 kHz.*

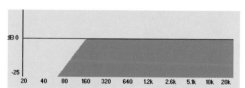

▲ *A high-pass EQ cutting frequencies below 160 Hz.*

▲ *A low-shelf EQ boosting frequencies below 160 Hz.*

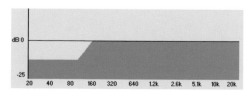

▲ *A low-shelf EQ cutting frequencies below 160 Hz.*

The simplest EQ filter types are the low-pass and high-pass filters. Low-pass attenuates the level of those frequencies above the EQ filter's frequency setting. The high-pass EQ does the same thing but attenuates the level of frequencies below the EQ filter frequency.

The **shelving filter** is related to the low-pass and high-pass filter. If you look at a graph of how the filter's gain or attenuation changes with frequency, you will notice that it drops down (or goes up) and then flattens, much like a plateau or shelf – hence the name.

The final type of EQ filter you will encounter is the **peak filter**. The peak filter either boosts or cuts the frequencies immediately around its frequency, usually called the **centre frequency**. The

Illustrated Home Recording Handbook
Illustrated Home Recording Handbook

range of frequencies cut or boosted is set by the bandwidth, also known as **Q**. Peak filters can either cut or boost, depending on the filter's gain adjustment.

Equalizers are created by combining two or more of these filters. Each is adjusted independently until the desired frequency shaping is realized. The diagram below shows a composite EQ frequency response for six sections.

Pro Tip

If you drew a graph of your EQ you would see humps or dips where the signal was boosted or reduced. The width of these humps or dips is set by the Q control.

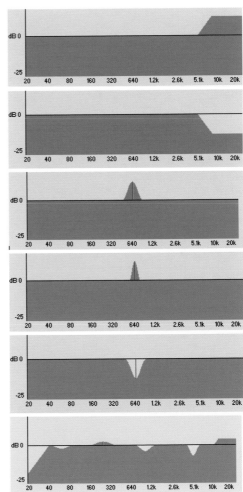

▶ A high-shelf EQ boosting frequencies above 5 kHz.

▶ A high-shelf EQ cutting frequencies above 5 kHz.

▶ A peak filter boosting frequencies around 640 Hz.

▶ Another peak filter boosting frequencies around 640 Hz but in a narrower range (bandwidth) than the previous illustration. Bandwidth is often referred to as Q.

▶ A peak filter cutting frequencies around 640 Hz.

▶ A typical composite EQ frequency response assembled from four peak filters, a high-shelf filter and a high-pass filter.

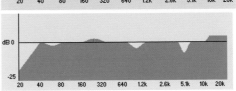

WHAT ARE PARAMETRIC AND GRAPHIC EQUALIZERS?

Here we will take a closer look at two types of equalizer.

▲ *A simple four-band parametric EQ. Note how each vertical section provides independent adjustment for the section's boost or cut amount (Gain), centre frequency (Freq), and filter bandwidth (Q).*

PARAMETRIC EQUALIZERS

A common type of equalizer offers a number of fully adjustable filter sections. Each section's frequency, gain and bandwidth are independently adjustable.

A filter's settings are sometimes called **parameters**, so this type of equalizer is known as a parametric equalizer. These usually include a low-pass or low-shelf section, a high-pass or high-shelf section, and then one or more peak sections. Since all the frequency settings are adjustable, this equalizer is very flexible. You can do extremely precise sound shaping with a few parametric sections. It is a little harder to use because of all the settings, but with practice you will find this to be the sharpest scalpel in your surgeon's bag!

GRAPHIC EQUALIZERS

One special type of EQ that you may already have encountered in your home stereo is known as a **graphic equalizer**. This has a certain number of individual sections called **bands**, each operating at a fixed frequency. Each band allows you to boost or cut a range of frequencies.

The band's **gain** level is set by a slider arranged in an up-and-down orientation. All the band gain controls are arranged in a column with the centre frequency increasing from left to right. When the slider is positioned above the centre line, that band is boosting its frequencies; below the centre line, the band is cutting its frequencies. If you look at the arrangement of the sliders, it resembles a graph of the equalizer's frequency response. This is why it is called a graphic equalizer.

Jargon Buster

GAIN is the amount by which a signal is amplified.

Graphic equalizers are handy when you need to affect a wide range of frequencies with a decent amount of detail. The more bands the equalizer has the more control you have over the frequency response. Most graphic equalizers include a low-shelf and high-shelf filter so that you can boost or cut frequencies above or below the extremes of the frequency range.

One popular scheme for selecting the frequencies of each section is to double the frequency between each succeeding band. So, for example, the bands might be 50 Hz, 100 Hz, 200 Hz and so on. This is called an **octave-band equalizer**. A more refined and detailed version, found in many studio and live performance venues, is the **one-third octave equalizer**. This divides the equalizer's frequency range from 20 Hz to 20 kHz into 31 bands. The frequency doubles every three bands.

One popular application of graphic equalizers is to compensate for frequency response deficiencies in a monitoring system and studio room. A graphic equalizer is used to boost and cut frequencies to smooth out and flatten the overall response. The graphic equalizer is not the best way to fix acoustic problems, but it is often the most expedient.

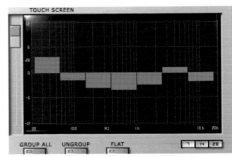

▲ *A graphic equalizer allows you to boost or cut a specified number of fixed frequency bands. A seven-band equalizer is shown. Using more bands gives you finer control over the EQ.*

Part One: The Essentials

SHOULD I RECORD WITH EQUALIZATION?

You might wonder when it is best to use equalization during the course of recording a song. Do you use equalization to adjust the sound prior to recording a track, or is it best to leave all the equalization work until it is time to create a finished mix?

Like using many devices in the studio, there is no single correct method. Pros use any of a number of approaches. It depends on the situation and how you like to work.

◄ *Performers such as Sheryl Crow use EQ to improve parts of their recording once it is completed.*

Sometimes the equalization is thought of as part of the sound. When recording a vocal part, for example, you may desire a certain sound. The singer and the microphone may require some frequency shaping in order to get the best overall tone. Guitars, bass, drums and almost any instrument are good candidates for EQ processing while recording. Some synthesizer presets incorporate EQ as a part of the total sound, making the EQ as essential as the other synthesizer elements used in the preset. All these examples share a common thread in that the original sound incorporates the equalizer as an integral part of its total tone colour.

The other side of the coin, however, is that equalization is often used as a means of making each of the separate instrument parts and tracks fit together. This is one of the most important aspects of creating a satisfying mix. When you use EQ in this manner it is best not to record the equalization until the last possible moment.

Unfortunately, these two approaches can sometimes be at cross-purposes. Any EQ that you use on the source while recording may need "undoing" once the track is heard in the song's final context. On the other hand, waiting to "nail down" the EQ may result in your losing that tone completely.

▲ *B.T. is a great advocate of computer music, and all manner of effects can be heard in his work.*

This is something you will learn with experience. The general rule is to defer EQ decisions until as late in the project as you can. One possible way to do this is to record any sound that relies on EQ with the EQ disabled. When the track is recorded, approximate the original EQ settings using the mixer EQ or a plug-in. This makes it easy to alter the EQ later on as the mix requires. This is another instance where a virtual studio really shines. The EQ settings are saved as part of the project, so you do not need to worry about losing that great instrument sound.

➡ *Finishing Off pp. 144–161; Projects pp. 162–209*

SAMPLES

In this section we begin to explore the world of samples in greater detail.

Samples can be divided into two kinds: **individual sounds** and **rhythmic loops**. An individual sound may be a single note on a piano, for example, or it could be part of a collection of related samples, known as multisamples, in which several (or all) notes on the piano were sampled. Loops, usually in the form of drum patterns, may be repeated to form the rhythmic backbone of your composition.

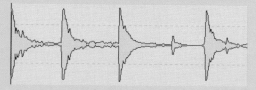

▲ *A single electric piano note. Notice the abrupt beginning (attack) and gradual falling away of the sound (decay). Individual vibrations are visible.*

▲ *A typical drum loop. No vibrations are seen here; the loop consists of "noise" rather than pitched sounds, although the individual drum "hits" are clearly visible.*

Jargon Buster

Professional samples will be recorded in .WAV or .AIF formats to at least commercial CD quality.

WHERE DO SAMPLES COME FROM?

First we will look at three major sources of samples created by other people and then see how you might start making your own.

THE INTERNET

Individual samples, multisamples and loops are available in many places on the Internet. Enthusiastic amateurs often make their own samples available as free downloads, and commercial companies will usually market their products (samples on CD) by offering a free trial selection. Some companies may deal mainly or entirely on the Internet. Sometimes you can listen to samples in MP3 format first, to decide whether you like them enough to bother downloading the sounds as **.wav** or **.aif** files.

The Internet changes rapidly, so this book could never direct you to all that is currently available (see p. 376 for a small selection). Use your favourite web browser and search for yourself, using phrases such as "sample", "loop" and "download".

Be aware that high-quality samples are large files and may take quite a long time to download. A stereo CD-quality sound file requires approximately 10 MB of storage per minute. High-speed Internet

▲ *You can download samples from web sites like this one ...*

▲ *... or like this one.*

connections have made download times a marginal concern for most people, and higher-quality compressed audio formats, like .AAC and .MP4 mean that you can get good-sounding samples in much smaller file sizes, including in some cases the popular .MP3 format.

SAMPLES ON COMMERCIAL CDS

Orchestral libraries are recorded under pristine studio conditions; each section of the orchestra and individual instruments from the various families are sampled at different pitches and dynamics. Additional files of ornamental features, such as trills, may also be included. These collections, aimed at professional film composers, come in multi-CD packs and will cost you hundreds of pounds or dollars.

Many CDs focus on one instrument or family – piano, for example – where you might get one top-flight instrument multisampled in meticulous detail, and perhaps a few others with contrasting tones.

Traditional acoustic instruments are not the only sounds available on sample CDs; you can also find samples from vintage synthesizers, many not readily available any more. Because a sample sounds the same every time you play it, many exacting analogue synthesizer enthusiasts prefer the slight unpredictability of the original hardware. If you are less demanding, a sampled synthesizer is a good compromise between authenticity and price.

Many CDs contain loops – mostly drums or percussion, though some feature bass, guitar or keyboard. These may be as short as a single bar/measure or as long as eight or 16 bars. Often **fills** (the bits at the end that lead into the next section) are included to mark ends of sections, and loops may be broken down into constituent parts – hi-hat, snare, kick, etc. – on different tracks, which will play together to give you the full pattern. Some CDs contain "kits" of percussive and instrumental loops and multisamples, all aimed at a particular genre and at the same tempo.

LOOP, SAMPLE, AND AUDIO FORMATS

Rex (REX2) Files and Refills: Rex files are loops split up into separate hits (single drum sounds) so that the tempo can be adjusted without changing the pitch of the loop. These are especially useful for users of Reason software, but can also be used with many other applications. Collections of loops or sampler patches that may only be used in Reason are called ReFills.

▲ ACID loops are found on the Internet, as well as on CDs.

"**Acidized" Files**: Named after Sony'sACID sequencer, these files have tempo and pitch information embedded within them and, with suitable software (e.g., ACID itself, Cakewalk SONAR, Cubase SX3/SL3, GarageBand 2 and others), can be played back at virtually any pitch or tempo.

Apple Loops: Apple Loops work with Apple's Garage Band, Logic Pro and Logic Express applications and can be time stretched and pitch shifted in real time.

NN-XT (.SXT): These files are for Reason's advanced sampler. The format allows for high-quality samples but is incompatible with other samplers.

GIGA (.GIG): Giga files work with Gigastudio (PC only) and were the first that could be streamed from a hard drive in real time.

KONTAKT (.NKI): Kontakt files were designed by Native Instruments (NI) and work with the company's Kontakt, Kompakt and Intakt programs. Many commercial CDs provide them as Instrument files with "mini player" versions of the NI programs included on the CD.

BATTERY: This format is optimized for Native Instrument's drum software sampler Battery. The files also work with Kontakt, Kompakt, and Intakt.

EXS24 (.EXS): EXS files were developed for Apple's Emagic line of samplers, including the EXS24, EXSP24 and EXS24 MK-2, as well as Logic and HALion 2.0.

HALION (.FXP): These files are designed for Steinberg's HALion sampler. Integrates well with Steinberg's Cubase.

MACHFIVE: A format for developed for MOTU's software sampler MachFive, the files also work with NI Kontakt2.

AKAI (.AKP): Once highly popular because of Akai's hardware samplers, the files are compatible with most samplers; however, the can't generally be browsed in software waveform editors or sequencers, and Akai-formatted discs won't mount on a Macintosh.

WAV (.WAV): Originally a Windows format, .WAV files offer uncompressed (full-resolution) audio. The files can be used by most hardware and software samplers, are compatible with Macs, and can hold loop information.

AIFF (.aif or .aiff): Originally Apple Audio Interchange File Format, it is still used for full-resolution audio files, can be used by most hardware and software samplers, and can hold loop information.

SD2 (Sound Designer File): Originally for Digidesign's Sound Designer 2, Sound Tools, and ultimately Pro Tools programs, these were the primary formats used for pro audio on a Mac.

Audio: This is the standard audio from a CD or other source that must be sampled to create a digital audio file.

"FREE" SAMPLES

Some music magazines, particularly in the UK, provide loops and samples on their cover CDs, and so are "free" (you have to buy the magazine, of course!). This would be a good place for the less-experienced artist to start looking, as the magazines also contain articles and tutorials on creating music. Two excellent publications (UK-based but available throughout the world) are *Future Music* and *Computer Music*.

RECORD YOUR OWN SAMPLES

This may seem like a daunting task if you have not tried it before. Obviously, for samples intended to sound like real instruments you will need access to those instruments, but sampling can also be a creative process. So keep your ears attuned to all the noises around you, searching for that unexpected thump, knock or ping!

Whatever your goal, you will need a reasonable-quality microphone (though for a "lo-fi" sound anything will do), some portable means of recording the sound – such as a MiniDisc or DAT (digital audio tape) recorder – and some software for editing your sounds once they are inside your computer.

If possible, spend some time experimenting with microphone placement around your source, whether it is a grand piano or a spoon hitting a coffee cup. Varying angles and distances can make a vast difference in the signal the microphone picks up.

If you are recording a pitched instrument, do not content yourself with the first note you hear. Record notes in all registers and keep a written record of what they are.

Transfer the recordings to your computer hard drive via the inputs on the audio interface; the method of doing this will vary according to your recording device.

EDITING YOUR SAMPLES

Now you have an audio recording of, say, six different notes from your aunt's grand piano and you transfer them from your MiniDisc to your computer's hard drive. What comes next?

You will need some kind of sample-editing software, such as Steinberg's PC-only WaveLab, Sony's Sound Forge, or the Mac-only BIAS Peak. There are also freeware or shareware editors out there such as EZ Editor for the PC and Amadeus Pro for Mac OS X.

At the very least, your string of notes will need to be chopped up and trimmed so that each one occupies a separate file with the sound starting right at the beginning of the file, preventing what is known as **dead air**.

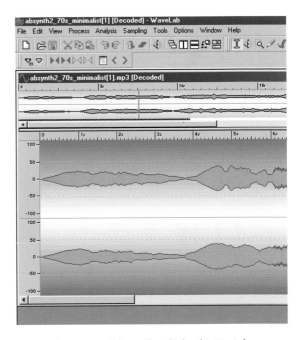

▲ *Part of a stereo sample's wave form displayed in WaveLab.*

As you save each sample, make sure that you check which note it is and include that information in the file name, e.g., "PianoC3.wav", so that you will know which key to assign it to later on. There are various conventions used in naming notes on electronic musical instruments (which includes computers). Here we are using C3 to indicate middle C, which is moderately high in most male voices, but middle to low for female voices. C2 and C4 would be an octave lower and higher, respectively.

Pro Tip

Further refinements at this stage might include checking and correcting the tuning of the sample, if your software allows, and normalizing the volume – raising it to the maximum allowable in the digital domain, which is known as 0 Db, or zero decibels.

TURNING YOUR SAMPLES INTO INSTRUMENTS

Software samplers load a sample, assign it to a note – for example C3 (MIDI note 60) – and then replay it when that key is pressed. When a different key is played, the sample is sped up or slowed down to produce the required pitch.

This works well, up to a point, but transpose some samples too far away from their natural pitch and they begin to sound grotesque or comic. The voices of 1950s pop act the Chipmunks were normal voices sped up.

The solution to this restriction is to take multisamples, sampling the instrument at more-or-less regular intervals (several per octave) and assigning them all to corresponding sampler notes. Three piano samples of A2, C3 and D#3 are three semitones (half-steps) apart, so each sample only needs to be stretched by one semitone each way to fill in the gaps.

For many instruments, a more realistic effect will be achieved if the samples are played back more loudly as the keys are struck more quickly – this is known as velocity sensitivity.

◄ *Part of an electric piano instrument loaded into Reason's NN-XT sampler. Each light-blue rectangle represents a sample stretched over a short range on the keyboard.*

HOW DO I ASSIGN DRUM SOUNDS?

Here we are not using drum loops, but simulating a drum kit using separate notes on the MIDI keyboard.

Samples containing single drum hits are assigned to adjacent MIDI notes, resulting in an instrument very unlike a conventional keyboard. Familiar scales and chords make no sense whatsoever, as each key has a completely different sound from its neighbour – a snare drum on one, a cymbal on the next, and so on.

You can arrange your samples in a way that makes sense to you, but certain conventions prevail. The principle convention is **General MIDI Drum Mapping** (GM); this is based on conventional acoustic drum and percussion sounds.

GM ensures that all MIDI drum devices keep their individual drum sounds assigned to the same notes, for consistency between manufacturers. For example, the main bass (kick) drum is assigned to C1; the closed hi-hat to F#1, and so on. This has many advantages – for example, you instantly know where you are with GM mapping – but it may also stifle creativity, driving your thinking about percussion along all-too-familiar lines.

All the same, even purely electronic percussive sounds will probably be heard in terms of familiar acoustic ones. It helps, therefore, to know the GM drum map. Some of the main key assignments are listed on the right.

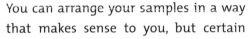

D#2 ......ride cymbal
D2 ....highest tom
C#2 ......crash cymbal
C2..........high tom (MIDI note 48)
B1..........upper mid tom
A#1 ......open hi-hat
A1..........low mid tom
G#1 ......hi-hat closed with foot
G1..........low tom
F#1........closed hi-hat hit with stick
F1..........lowest tom
E1..........alternative snare
D#1 ......clap
D1..........snare drum
C# 1 ......stick across snare rim
C1 ....main bass drum (MIDI note 36)
B0 ....alternative bass drum

➡ *Drum Loops and Grooves pp. 99–101*

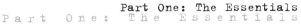

HOW TO MAKE SAMPLES SOUND LIKE THE REAL THING

The easiest real instruments to deal with are synthesizers. Some might argue that they are not entirely "real" instruments, but have been around in their hardware form for decades... anyway, we are not going to get lost in a semantic argument.

To match the functionality of a synthesizer as closely as possible, use samples that have been recorded at maximum volume (an **on-off envelope**) and with no filtering so that the sound is as bright as possible. Use at least one sample per octave.

Use the sampler's own envelope shaper and filter to "sculpt" the sound as you would in a synthesizer. Apply velocity sensitivity to the amplitude and filter cutoff as necessary for the kind of sound you envisage. These last two points will make the resulting instrument more responsive to variation in playing "touch", if that is what you require.

Organ samples can be treated similarly except that organs are not traditionally velocity sensitive.

Pianos generally come next in terms of "realism". Well-sampled acoustic and electric pianos can work sufficiently, provided nothing extreme is done with the filter or envelope. Listen carefully to a held note: does it die away at the rate you would expect? Adjust the amplitude decay parameter if not. This, and velocity sensitivity (amplitude and filter), are probably the most crucial aspects to get right.

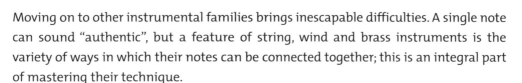

Moving on to other instrumental families brings inescapable difficulties. A single note can sound "authentic", but a feature of string, wind and brass instruments is the variety of ways in which their notes can be connected together; this is an integral part of mastering their technique.

It goes without saying that a single instrument such as a trumpet can only play one note at a time. An immediate beginner's mistake can be avoided, therefore, either by making sure the recorded MIDI notes do not overlap, or by making the sampler monophonic – capable of playing only one note at a time.

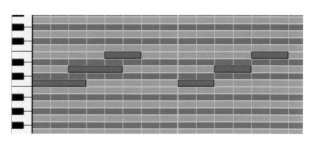

▲ *Overlapping and corrected notes for a sampled trumpet.*

If you record a passage for a section of three trumpets, three monophonic samplers will give a slightly more authentic sound than one playing all three notes. You will also be able to pan the outputs slightly to place the "players" in space.

ARTICULATION

For authenticity, you must pay close attention to how close adjacent notes in a phrase are to each other. Generally, musicians will instinctively group all the notes in a riff together and leave a gap before the next phrase, but some of the notes, especially accented ones, may be played **staccato** – cut short and with a tiny gap before the next one. You will need to develop an analytical ear for how a passage is phrased and make sure, either by your MIDI entry or by editing the notes subsequently, that you have recorded exactly what is required.

STEREO PLACEMENT

Realistic panning of instruments will help, too. For example, it may seem exciting to use the **pan controls** in your drum machine to spread the drum samples right across the stereo stage, but the drummer then sounds as wide as the entire band.

Jargon Buster

The **PAN CONTROL** moves a signal between the right and left stereo extremes.

In mixing generally – using the main mixer in your application of choice – keep essential parts at or near the centre (bass and lead vocals especially) and group similar instruments, such as a brass section, together but panned slightly away from each other. String orchestras take up a lot of room, so spread them out across the stage: first violins, second violins, violas and cellos from left to right. Double basses can be "behind" the cellos or mid-stage – this is because deeper sounds are less directional.

KNOW YOUR INSTRUMENTS

Even though you are using sampled virtual instruments, you should, for authenticity, still write for them as if they were the real thing. This means not including notes that are off-range or playing two notes on a monophonic instrument (for example, all the wind instruments).

The same goes for drum parts; if you are using a sequencer, you could easily layer more and more patterns over each other until you would have to employ an octopus to play it. Even (or especially) if you do not play them yourself, learn to "think drums" and only write what can be played with four limbs. A very fast hi-hat passage, for example, would be played with both sticks in alternation, so a hit on snare or tom toms would require the drummer to move one hand away from the hi-hat and then back again. Therefore, do not overlap the two sounds.

There is simply not enough space here to give a tutorial on every orchestral and band instrument, but many useful books on instrumentation are widely available.

DRUM LOOPS AND GROOVES

In the fields of pop and dance music, choosing or creating a good drum groove is almost certainly the most crucial factor in making the track work. For beginners, the easiest approach would be to choose the loop that is closest to your conception and then fit the other parts around it.

First, we are going to consider using off-the-shelf grooves in the form of audio loops. These may be recordings of real drummers, hitting real drums, or sounds generated by drum machines or other synthetic means. They may also be presented "clean" or have had effects applied to them; compression is the most likely, but flanging, reverb and **vocoding** (using the voice as an oscillator) are not unknown.

Given the dance and pop genres, most of the loops will be in 4/4 time and usually in lengths that are multiples of two measures. If you have an audio editor they may easily be trimmed to a

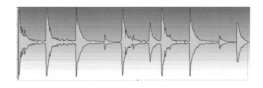

▲ *A representation of a drum loop. The individual hits can be clearly seen. Can you work out the rhythm?*

shorter length, or even have sections removed or repeated to create a different time signature. Occasionally, you may need to tidy up a loop if it has any unwanted silence at the beginning or end that prevents it from looping evenly.

REARRANGING HITS IN A DRUM LOOP

Here is a musical problem: we have a march loop (in 4/4 time) but we want to record a waltz (in 3/4 time). Can we use this loop?

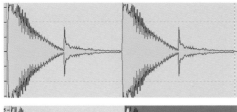

1. Here is the march loop, "dum-tah-dum-tah", loaded into a sound editor.

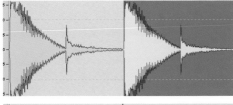

2. Select the last two hits by dragging over them.

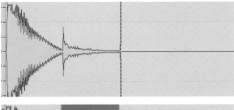

3. Hit Delete and now we have just "dum-tah".

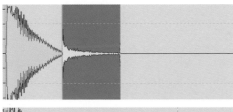

4. Select the last "tah" and then, clicking in the selection, drag it right ...

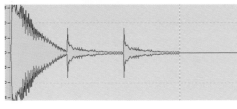

5. ... and drop it on to the end of the loop. Voilà! We now have waltz time, or "dum-tah-tah".

Of course, a very simple example was chosen so that you could readily see the rhythm change before your eyes. In creating a real-life waltz loop, we would have to take great care over the precise length of the sections that were deleted and copied, otherwise the waltz would probably be out of time.

REARRANGING HITS IN REX FILES

Rex files, a development of the Swedish firm Propellerhead Software, are audio loops with markers placed to slice the loop where audible attacks occur. These may be played in dedicated Rex file players such as Reason's Dr.Rex, though some sequencers (for example, Cubase) will allow you to place them directly on audio tracks. Dr.Rex assigns the slices to consecutive notes from C1 upwards, and a MIDI file that captures the exact timing of the original loop is placed on its track. When played through in the original tempo the file sounds exactly like the original, but if the tempo is changed the slices are spread apart or squashed together, keeping the same relative distance from each other and preserving the rhythm.

Pro Tip

Also consider pHATmatik PRO (Windows and Mac), a plug-in loop player that will slice up, rearrange and play plain .wav or .aif files in much the same way as Rex files.

But the notes in the MIDI file can be adjusted as much as you like; the "march-to-waltz" transformation shown opposite only requires a few mouse drags with a Rex file. Drum patterns can be radically altered or subtly tweaked to suit your track.

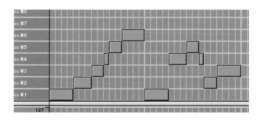

▲ *The original pattern from the Rex file and a variation.*

ARE DRUM LOOPS SUCH A GOOD THING?

Certainly for beginners and less-experienced producers, finding strong loops can transform early efforts into driving tracks; it would be mean-spirited to take away such immediate gratification. Then too, at any level of experience, if a particular loop is just right for your current track (or style generally) then it would be unnecessarily austere to shun it.

Relying totally on off-the-shelf loops to power your tracks, however, removes the possibility of creating something yourself, something new and original. Just avoiding the use of loops does not guarantee originality, but if a loop downloaded from the Internet tempts you, just reflect on how many hundreds, if not thousands, of other musicians have already used it.

MORE ON SAMPLES

Samples take up a lot of space. Although the capacity of hard drives keeps increasing, it is remarkably easy for your samples to start occupying rather a lot of gigabytes on your computer.

If you buy your samples on CD then there is no need to keep them permanently on your hard drive – just while you are using them for a particular project, perhaps. If you do have sufficient storage space and want to amass a library of samples it is best practice to save them in an orderly fashion and with meaningful file names. We have already suggested naming individual notes in multisamples; you should also keep them in an appropriately named folder. Any rhythmic files should be named with their tempo in BPM (beats per minute) and some indication of style: "110 dist hiphop.wav", for example, tells you something about the loop before you hear it, whereas, "loop 59A-f.wav" is meaningless. Again, collect loops that have something in common in folders – all of a similar tempo or style. Give some thought to the structure of your library, so that you do not have to reorganize it too often and waste a lot of valuable music-making time searching for missing files.

Once you have gathered together your valuable hand-picked or self-created samples, you will not want to lose them. You will be upset if you discover your hard drive has irrevocably died with several years of work on it. So remember the motto (and act upon it): **BACK IT UP OR LOSE IT.**

▲ *External hard drives are convenient ways to keep your data backed up. Newer models like this Freecom drive have Ethernet built in, so that all computers in your home or studio network can access it directly. Some models also provide automatic backup software.*

FURTHER THOUGHTS ON SAMPLES AND SAMPLERS

Probably the most common single purpose that samples are used for is the emulation of "real" instruments, from string sections to electric pianos to synthesizers. With attention to detail, a fair degree of realism can be obtained in the simulation of real-world instruments, if that is what you require (although some instruments, especially solo strings and saxophones, defy convincing duplication because of the extreme flexibility of their sound and the variety of possible articulations).

A comprehensive sampler, particularly some of the more recent software samplers making it on to the market, is not restricted merely to playing back samples in as pristine and "authentic" a way as possible. The sample can be used simply as the starting point for sculpting the sound you want, by using the sampler's filters and envelopes. Some samplers will allow you to change the starting point of the sample so that, for example, a guitar sample with a sharp attack may be played in its entirety when the MIDI key is struck sharply, but with a softer stroke the sample is played from a little way in, omitting the attack portion of the sound. Once you begin to make your own samples and sample your own work, the possibilities are endless.

If there is a particular bass-drum sound you like but you find that you are always giving it a little boost at a certain frequency, sample it boosted and you have the sound you want right away. Similarly, if you have a particular favourite snare-and-reverberation combination, sample it (but make sure you include all of the reverb **tail**, or end). You could record the snare with varying degrees of reverb and select whichever one is right for a particular song, or even for a particular moment in that song.

A complex, multi-layered pad sound that requires several different synthesizers to be set up and played simultaneously can be sampled and reproduced exactly, though here the limitation of sampling begins to become apparent. Your synthesizer patch may be set up so that each instrument responds differently depending on how you are playing it, yet the sampled sound will be the same each time.

Use samples for their strengths and do not expect them to be what they are not; sampling is only one of many ways of making music on a computer.

➡ *Samples: Advanced pp. 248–251; Synthesis pp. 268–287; Internet Sites pp. 376–378*

PLUG-INS
WHAT IS A PLUG-IN?

In the same way that your computer can emulate the multitrack recorder and mixing deck of a real recording studio, plug-ins emulate the racks of effects and equipment that are used to bring all the recorded and sequenced parts to life.

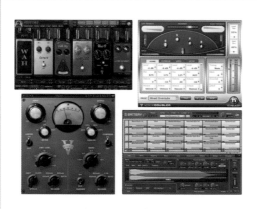

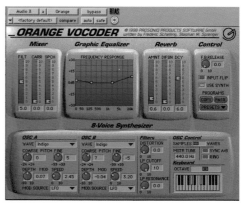

▲ *Examples of modern plug-ins: AmpliTube Jimi Hendrix Edition, TC Helicon Voice Doubler, Waves V-Comp, Native Instruments Battery 3.*

A **plug-in** is a mini processor that sits on a channel of your virtual mixer and alters the sound coming from that channel. Plug-ins offer a huge palette of sounds and effects; most desirable studio equipment has been lovingly re-modelled as plug-ins, and will fit into one of the following categories:

Compressors even out the volume of sounds. They are essential to vocals and can make anything sound more punchy and focused.

▲ CamelCrusher is a free multi-effects plug-in, one of the many available for download on the Internet.

Gates are useful for getting rid of background noise or reducing microphone spills, and can be used more creatively with **side-chains** (see p. 114).

EQs and **filters** will help you to balance the high, mid and low frequencies; when used together with filters they offer unlimited scope for tonally shaping the sound.

Delays and **reverbs** will make artificial space around your sounds to help make your mix more "three-dimensional".

Intonation correction plug-ins, such as Antares AutoTune, can correct an out-of-tone vocal.

Then there are the vocoders, phasers, flangers, chorus, pitch-shifters, distortion, **amp** and **effects modelling**, spatial and stereo effects, etc.

These are just the effects. Software synthesizers and samplers also come in plug-in form and offer you a potentially limitless library of sounds.

> ## Jargon Buster
>
> **AMP and EFFECTS MODELLING** are plug-ins that model the sonic characteristics of guitar amplifiers and effects. These plug-ins makes it possible to plug your guitar straight into your computer and get great sounds immediately.

HOW DO YOU MAKE THE MOST OF PLUG-INS?

Jargon Buster

An **AUXILIARY SEND** is a way of sending identical signals from one channel of your virtual mixer to another destination.

DON'T WASTE CPU POWER

Each time you call up a plug-in, you put more pressure on your computer's **central processing unit** (CPU). Eventually, if you attempt to overburden your poor CPU, your computer will refuse to open any more plug-ins – so you need to find a way around the problem. One way is to use **auxiliary sends** on your virtual mixer. This means that just one reverb plug-in can be opened (on an auxiliary return channel of your virtual mixer), but lots of different sounds from different channels can be sent to it – and you will not need a separate reverb plug-in for each sound you want reverb on.

◀ *Here is Audio Ease Altiverb over an auxiliary input, being fed from auxilliary sends*

Several audio applications have "**freeze**" functions, which makes a temporary audio file of a channel and its plug-ins, and then disables the plug-ins until you wish to alter them. This saves a lot of CPU power.

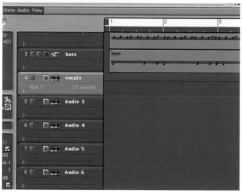

◀ *Logic Audio's freeze function.*

GROUPS AND BUSSES

The trick to making your plug-ins sound great is to use them in the same way you would have used the equipment that they are emulating, so the more you can find out about studio practice, the better.

Here is an example: in an analogue studio, there may be 10 channels of drums from all the different microphones. By sending the output of these channels to a

▲ Placing a plug-in compressor over one auxillary channel through which all the drums are being channelled has a dramatic effect on the sound.

bus (an empty sound pathway within a mixer that can be used to route signals) and connecting that bus to the input of an **auxiliary channel**, you can effectively have all the drums emerging from that one auxiliary channel elsewhere on the

mixer. Therefore, by putting a plug-in compressor over this auxiliary channel, you are using a single compressor to compress the entire drum kit. Experiment with the order of plug-ins. Swapping the order of reverb and compression on loops or drums will have a very noticeable effect.

AUTOMATION

The ability to automate the parameters of plug-ins offers some great opportunities for bringing delays in and out or performing big filter sweeps (these are a kind of automated EQ; think of a wah-wah pedal for a

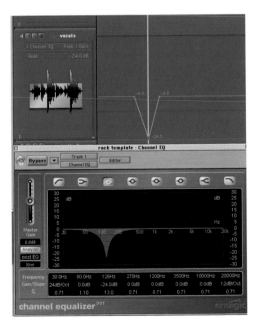

▲ Here is some automation information for Logic Audio's Channel EQ plug-in.

guitar), but it also transforms your plug-ins into useful tools for solving problems with recorded audio. For example, if you have a vocal that has a big popping sound of a "b" or a "p" right in the middle of an important line, you can put an EQ plug-in over it and automate the low frequency cut to remove the offending sound at just the right moment.

SIDE-CHAINS

Side-chains are a hidden way of unlocking the power of compressor and gate plug-ins. These plug-ins have a detector that reacts to the signals you pass through them, but you can send other signals direct to that detector via the side-chain input. A common example can be heard on the radio when a DJ talks over music and the music lowers in volume automatically – here the DJ's microphone is connected to the compressor's side-chain input. Try using a gate plug-in over a big, sustained chordal sound, while sending a hi-hat to the side-chain input. The big chord will only be allowed through the gate when the hi-hat plays, making your sustained chord into a highly musical percussive part instead.

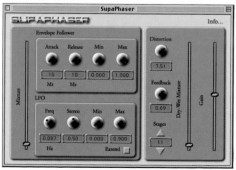

EXPERIMENT...

Using several ordinary plug-ins in a row can produce unpredictable and often exciting results. Try mixing gates, filters, delays, pitch-shifters and distortions for some really out-there sound mangling. Bring some order to your chaos, though, and make sure that any good sounds you make are saved in an organized way so that you can find them again easily. You will thank yourself later, when you can instantly call up some amazing sounds you created months ago, just when they are needed.

◀ *Reaktor is a respected plug-in that can be combined with a range of other effects, such as the SupaPhaser, to produce some great new sounds.*

FREE PLUG-INS

It will not have escaped your notice that many of these plug-ins cost a lot of your hard-earned money, but all sequencers will have a few basics of their own.

You may also be aware that it is possible to get hold of cracked plug-ins from various dubious web sites, but these have been illegally "cracked" (a hacker term for bypassing a copy protection system) and rob the industry of further research and development funds, so please do not go there.

But why steal them when so many excellent freeware plug-ins are out there? A quick web search will reveal countless libraries of free plug-ins made by major developers and independents. Some of the best are made by Ohm Force (ohmforce.com) and include the awesome filter Frohmage. Audio Melody (audiomelody.com) makes the superb Freeverb, and a trip to www.freeloops.com will earn you software synthesizers, drum machines and another free reverb. Smartelectronix.com and digitalfishphones.com are good places to find some high-quality compressors, gates and other oddities. Be vigilant when downloading freeware, but as far as the plug-ins go, the quality can be very high, and you can equip yourself with a good working collection of plug-ins for absolutely nothing!

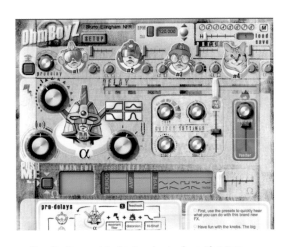

▲ *Thee OhmBoyz and Predatohm plug-ins from Ohm Force.*

Pro Tip

With Apple's development of the audio programs Soundtrack Pro and GarageBand and the AppleLoops format, a wide variety of free loops can be found for Mac OS X users. See thegaragedoor.com for links to loops.

ROOM ACOUSTICS

One of the most critical aspects of achieving a professional-sounding result is also one of the most commonly overlooked: acoustics. Whether you are operating with a modest setup or the most elaborate world-class equipment, it will amount to little if the environment suffers from poor acoustics. Fortunately, there are many inexpensive things you can do to tame the room and, in turn, produce better recordings and mixes.

To address possible problem areas, it is necessary to understand a little about how sound interacts with your recording and mixing environments. As you may already know, sound is created by vibrations in the air. These sound waves react differently to different materials in the room. You have probably noticed that your tiled bathroom provides a good environment for singing. This is because of the tiled walls and floor, which reflect the frequencies of your voice and bounce them about the room. Your ears are not met solely by the unadulterated sound of your voice, but by these multitudinous reflections, which all arrive at different amplitudes and times. While this might be desirable for recording a rich vocal track, it is a less than perfect environment for other sources, and certainly not great for reference listening or mixing.

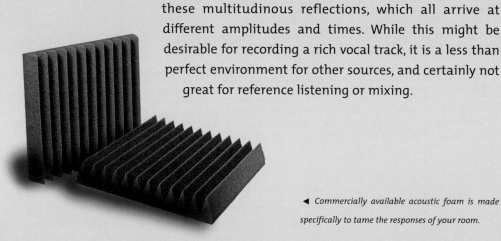

◄ *Commercially available acoustic foam is made specifically to tame the responses of your room.*

Of course, no one would ever suggest that you build your studio in a bathroom. You may not be aware, however, that every room will have its own particular acoustic trouble spots, and these need to be addressed before doing any serious recording work. For instance, if the acoustics in your room swallow up the bass frequencies, you could find that you overcompensate for that loss of signal by emphasizing those frequencies in your mixes. Your tracks will then sound too bass heavy when listened to outside your studio.

▶ *Low-frequency sound waves are so long – and strong – they are the toughest to control. Bass traps, as shown here, can tame any overwhelming bass frequencies you might encounter.*

To test the acoustic properties of your studio, play a test tone through your system. This should be an unadorned **sine wave** at anywhere from 4 to 6 kHz. You can use a readily available test disk, or you can produce one from a software synthesizer. Do not worry; it need not be exact. While the sound is playing, turn your head. You will hear the sound fluctuate in volume. In some positions in your room the sound may seem to nearly disappear, while in others, reflections may reinforce the original frequency, causing it to seem louder. As you can see, this can make accurate monitoring a tricky process.

Pro studio owners spend incredible amounts of time and money tuning their rooms. Obviously, the average home recordist cannot afford such luxuries, but there are steps you can take. Hanging carpeting on the walls or introducing plush furnishings can help to absorb wayward reflections, as can objects such as bookcases and wall-mounted CD racks. Over time, you will find the proper balance and your efforts will be repaid with better mixes.

▲ *You can perform a basic test of the acoustics of your room with a sine-wave generator such as this one.*

KEEPING THE NOISE DOWN

Noise is the ultimate nemesis of any recording studio, whether it is housed in a corner of your living room or in a world-class facility. Noise is everywhere, even if you are unaware of it. There is noise from passing traffic, from your neighbours' stereos and from your own equipment.

It can be a real chore to track down and eliminate all that wayward cacophony. You may have even become so accustomed to the din that you have tuned it out.

WHERE DOES THE SOUND COME FROM?

You cannot, however, tune unwanted sound out of your recordings. From the start, you must make sure it never creeps into your tracks. An air conditioner or heater kicking in during a critical vocal recording spells disaster, particularly if you do not even notice it until the tracks are recorded and the vocalist has left. How about creaking doors or water running through the pipes? Precaution is the name of the game here.

◄ *Do not take the risk and let the sound of your neighbour's television ruin your vocalist's best efforts. Look around you and soundproof your workspace before it is too late!*

SOUNDPROOFING

You may have heard people discussing soundproofing; we need to address this issue right from the start. Hanging up empty egg cartons is not going to make a lot of difference, and even expensive acoustic treatments will not help. Many people are under the mistaken impression that these precautions will keep the sound contained within the confines of their studios, but this just is not the case. These are simply solutions for taming acoustics, and are not meant to keep your neighbours from being disturbed and pounding on your door when you are toiling away at 3 a.m. The only thing that will truly contain the sound is mass: concrete, insulation and other costly and weighty types of material that are not likely to be at the disposal of a bedroom engineer.

Professional studios have the luxury of being able to afford insulated dual walls, suspended ceilings and floating floors to aid in isolating them from the outside world. You will probably have to make arrangements with neighbours so that you can work without causing a disturbance or being disturbed in turn. The only recourse is to do the best you can within the limitations of your immediate environment, and to try to isolate the individual instruments that you are intending to record. Needless to say, if you never intend to record a full drum kit or guitar amps with their levels cranked up high, you have a lot more freedom, although – at least in the case of the latter – there are methods that will help you accomplish the task.

▲ *Although you will not have the resources of a pro studio to invest in all the latest in soundproofing, you can take steps to ensure that the neighbours will not be round when you are in the middle of your recording session.*

KEEPING UNWANTED SOUND OUT

Once you have soundproofed your studio as best you can, you must turn to the job of keeping the outside world out of your recordings.

If your studio is entirely software or MIDI based, and you never plan to use a microphone, you are ahead of the game. Your sound will be transmitted digitally or through line-level connections and will never be exposed to the harsh and noisy intrusions of urban life.

A VOCAL BOOTH

If you plan to record guitars, vocals, percussion or any other sounds that need to travel through the air, you will have to give considerable thought to isolation. This involves isolating the microphone and the instruments, thereby preventing leakage from unwanted sounds. You have almost certainly seen performers on television or in the media with one hand cupped to the headphones, wailing away into a microphone in a studio's isolation booth or vocal booth. These are usually small rooms built specifically for the purpose of recording vocalists without picking up any other sounds. Your home studio will probably possess no such recording booth, but a walk-in closet can serve the same purpose.

If your studio is literally in your bedroom, then the clothes hanging in the closet can actually serve to absorb reflections. This can make for a dead space, which is ideal for artificial treatment during mixing. If a dead space is not required, the tiled bathroom and long microphone and headphone cables can provide a very lively sound that may need no additional reverberation. Either way, outside interference can be kept to a minimum.

GOBOS

If you have no such space available to you, or more room is required, you can make use of a commercial or homemade **gobo**. Gobos are portable walls that can be positioned around the

◄ *A gobo will help reduce the amount of sound that can escape and the amount of sound that comes in while you are making your recording.*

instruments and the performer to tame reflections and prevent undesirable leakage. They can be easily constructed if your budget is tight. They need to be at least a metre (three feet) in width and equally tall, if not taller. If they are too small, the low frequencies will simply sidestep the gobos. If you desire a deadened sound, they should be padded. Gobos with smooth surfaces are excellent for capturing a lively recording, and with a combination of the two types you can really tailor your sound. If your budget is especially restrictive, hanging heavy blankets from a clothesline can do a decent job of keeping signals in and noise out.

➡ MIDI pp. 252–265

▲ *A thick rug, some foam rubber and a walk-in closet or cupboard can be fashioned into a makeshift vocal booth.*

▲ *Wynton and Branford Marsalis using commercially available gobos. You can make your own out of foam, heavy blankets or any other thick material.*

EXTERNAL HARD DISKS

Depending on the speed and performance of the hard drive or drives inside the computer you use as your DAW, you may want to invest in one or more external hard drives.

With newer, faster standards such as FireWire 800 and USB 2, external hard drives are a viable option for both tracking and backup purposes. But are they really necessary? Probably not. The fact is that internal hard-drive performance, which in most cases today is based on the serial ATA (SATA) standard, matches the performance of SCSI (small computer system interface) drives, which were popular during the early days of disk-based audio recording. These days, the drives on board your modern PC or Mac offer plenty of speed and can handle high track counts.

WHY IS IT USEFUL?

On the other hand, the external drive can be a useful option for a lot of reasons. First, there is backup. External drives offer a fairly inexpensive way to back up your system and your work offline. It is never a bad idea to keep multiple backup copies of your most valuable work in more than one location for safekeeping. An external drive makes this prospect easy and less costly than in the past.

Today, however, DVD drives are capable of storing vast amounts of data on a very inexpensive medium, which makes them a more cost-effective solution.

▲ *Despite advances in internal hard-drive performance, external hard drives are still useful for transporting projects to other studios and migrating applications to upgraded systems.*

▲ *A DVD drive is a cost-effective solution to backing up and transporting your data without breaking the bank.*

One viable reason for considering an external, removable drive is the increasing popularity of challenge/ response-based copy protection, in which the software generates a special code based on your computer setup. This will not help a bit if the challenge is based on an overall system ID number rather than just an ID based on your hard drive and, sadly, those types of copy-protection schemes have become more and more popular. If, however, you have a number of products that do generate their codes from your disk drive's ID, then an external drive can save you a lot of headaches when the time comes to upgrade your system.

▶ *USB Flash Memory drives, which come in many forms, had reached capacities as high as 8 GB by early 2007, and became popular for transporting smaller projects to remote locations.*

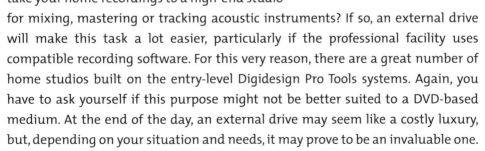

PORTABILITY

Another benefit of a high-speed external drive is portability. Do you plan to record on more than one computer? Do you intend to take your home recordings to a high-end studio for mixing, mastering or tracking acoustic instruments? If so, an external drive will make this task a lot easier, particularly if the professional facility uses compatible recording software. For this very reason, there are a great number of home studios built on the entry-level Digidesign Pro Tools systems. Again, you have to ask yourself if this purpose might not be better suited to a DVD-based medium. At the end of the day, an external drive may seem like a costly luxury, but, depending on your situation and needs, it may prove to be an invaluable one.

➡ *Software Sequencers pp. 230–233; Hardware pp. 332–341*

CHOOSING AND USING MICROPHONES

If you are going to be recording any acoustic sources at all, the importance of the humble microphone cannot be exaggerated.

Mention the subject of microphones to any professional engineer and his or her eyes are likely to glaze over as he or she waxes long and wistfully about the merits and attributes of some long-discontinued classic valve model. The subject stirs up passions and controversies and is not to be taken lightly, particularly if you are on a budget.

Jargon Buster

Any microphone with a diaphragm including and larger than 3/4 inch is considered to be a LARGE DIAPHRAGM MICROPHONE.

WHAT IS THE BEST MICROPHONE FOR ME?

Depending on your needs, one good, relatively inexpensive **large-diaphragm condenser microphone** will serve you infinitely better than a dozen lower-cost **dynamic microphones** or a couple of poorly made bargain-basement **condenser microphones**. You would also be wise to be wary of some of the recent large-diaphragm condenser microphones that promise world-class performance for the price of a cheap dynamic microphone. There is no guarantee that a high-end condenser microphone is going to make your projects sound professional, but it is almost certain that inferior microphones will make your home studio tracks sound like home studio tracks

Dynamic microphones are the most common type of microphone and they are reasonably inexpensive. They require no electrical power to operate, making them popular for home recording.

▲ *The versatility of the large diaphragm microphone means it will quickly become the mainstay of your collection.*

Condenser (or capacitator) microphones are far more sensitive than dynamic microphones, and so are often used to record distant and quiet sounds. A condenser microphone contains a thin diaphragm, which is situated very close to an electrically charged metal backplate. When sound waves strike this diaphragm, the resulting vibrations cause the voltage to vary, and that varying electrical signal, when sufficiently amplified, can be recorded. The diaphragm within them can vary in size and thickness.

▲ *Used for recording more sensitive sounds, there are more affordable condenser microphones on the market than ever before.*

USE YOUR MICROPHONE

Even if you never plan to do any acoustic recordings, you may still need to look at a good microphone for capturing samples or as an alternative to direct-injecting a guitar (that is, taking its output directly to tape). You can also bring a great deal of life to a synthesizer track by routing the signal through a small amplifier and placing a microphone in front of it. In this case, it need not

be a costly condenser microphone, but might simply be a versatile dynamic model such as the ubiquitous Shure SM57. The microphone will then record the airwaves between it and the speaker, and from the space around them.

This is sound at its best: chaotic, unpredictable and utterly alive, something that cannot be reproduced in the software domain. This one simple and inexpensive technique can bring a mix to full, vibrant life in ways that cannot be matched by any amount of artificial reverberation or amp simulation. "All digital" does not always equal higher sound quality; your mix could end up sounding flat and lifeless.

◀ *You cannot go wrong with a versatile industry standard dynamic microphone like the Shure SM57.*

WHAT TO LOOK FOR IN A MICROPHONE

Obviously, the main reason for using a microphone is to capture an acoustic source, such as a human voice, a drum, a guitar or any other instrument that is struck, plucked, blown or bowed. The microphone that you choose will depend on the source material you wish to capture, though for some it may come down to budgetary factors. As luck would have it, good-quality microphones are getting less expensive at an exponential rate these days. You can find decent large-diaphragm condenser microphones for a price similar to a quality dynamic microphone of 10 years ago, although both types still have a place in your recording arsenal.

THE DYNAMIC MICROPHONE

If you have very little money to spend, you may find that your choice is limited to a dynamic microphone. These handheld microphones are seen on many stages the world over, and some good ones are available at very reasonable prices. If you make the right choice, a good dynamic microphone can remain an important and useful tool long after you have added more expensive microphones.

A good case in point is the aforementioned Shure SM57. This classic dynamic has a fairly detailed response and is well suited to a variety of tasks, including recording guitar cabinets, horns and some vocalists. It is especially good for tracking snare drums and has achieved "industry standard" status in this field. Take a peek into any professional studio's microphone locker and it is a safe bet that you will see at least one of these little fellows. This microphone represents excellent value for a first-time buyer, since it is virtually impossible to outgrow and can always be pressed into service for one purpose or another even when more expensive microphones have been acquired alongside it.

▲ *Even high-end companies like Neumann offer affordable large diaphragm microphones these days, including the fabulous-sounding TLM 103.*

In looking for a microphone, you may come across dynamic models that are designed specifically for vocals. If you are on a tight budget, you should think twice about such a microphone. These are more often than not designed for use in a concert environment, and are engineered to reject feedback, not necessarily for the best or most accurate

Illustrated Home Recording Handbook
Illustrated Home Recording Handbook

response. They are also tailored for the voice and are often good for little else. Having said that, there are some big-name singers who enjoy the sound of these microphones and track their vocals with them in the studio.

THE CONDENSER MICROPHONE

If your primary instrument is the human voice, it would be a good idea to look into a large diaphragm condenser model. These are typically **side address** units, meaning that you sing into the side of the microphone. Where once they cost thousands of pounds or dollars, low-cost models from manufacturers such as CAD, Rode and Blue have begun to stream into the marketplace. While these models are actually quite serviceable, they have been accompanied by a veritable flood of cheaply made copycat models of varying quality and dubious origins.

Research your needs carefully before settling for any microphone and be aware that, in most cases, you really do get what you pay for. If you can afford to spend a little more, you may want to do so to assure quality. Keep in mind that a condenser microphone is going to require a power source, usually in the form of **phantom power**, and this could add to the cost. This is a power source that is often supplied to the microphone via the pre-amp or mixer. It travels from the pre-amp to the microphone via one of the pins in the **XLR cable** that is plugged into the microphone. Dynamic microphones require no such power supply, but the trade-off comes in the form of detail and accuracy.

> ## Jargon Buster
>
> **XLR CABLE is most often used with a professional microphone and pre-amp. Its connectors have three conductors. The female end fits into the three-pin connection on your microphone while the male end connects to an XLR input connector on a mixer, stand-alone mic preamp, or audio interface.**

◄ *XLR cables are robust cables carefully designed to reduce noise.*

CONDENSER MICROPHONE RESPONSE PATTERNS

Condenser microphones are extremely versatile and often come with a variety of options and extras. Many of the affordable models have a "fixed" **cardioid response pattern**, although some units also feature **figure-of-eight** or **omni** modes. What is meant by response pattern? This is simply the directional attribute of the microphone's response.

A cardioid response means that the microphone picks up what is directly in front of it, while rejecting to various degrees the sounds from the rear or the sides. A figure-of-eight response means that it will pick up what is directly in front and directly behind, while rejecting the sounds off to either side of the microphone. An omni response is designed to pick up the sound from all directions at once, hence the name. This is ideal for capturing the sound of the room.

For most purposes you will probably use the cardioid pattern, and it is for this reason that so many cardioid-only microphones are on the market. There may be times, however, when an omni or figure-of-eight pattern could be beneficial (such as when you would like to include the natural ambience of the room), so if you can afford it, a more flexible model is worth considering. One thing to note about cardioid microphones is that they often suffer from a **proximity effect**. This produces an exaggerated low end in the signal when the subject is too near the microphone capsule.

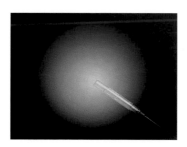

▲ *An omni pick-up pattern. The area around the microphone shown here is the area in which sound is picked up by the microphone. Although these microphones pick up sound equally well in all directions, you are also likely to pick up unwanted noise.*

Other features you may find on a good microphone include a pad switch, which will reduce the overall level of the signal. This is a must for tracking percussive sounds such as a drum being struck, as using a pad protects you from accidental clipping (where the signal exceeds a certain volume, causing bad distortion) during recording. You might also find a low-frequency roll off switch for reducing vibration-induced rumble from the microphone stand or excessive "boominess".

Illustrated Home Recording Handbook

SMALL DIAPHRAGM MICROPHONE

If you are planning on recording stringed instruments regularly, or intend to mic a drum kit, you might want to consider a small diaphragm microphone. These microphones are very similar to large diaphragm microphones in

▲ *A few small diaphragm condenser microphones can really add to your collection.*

design and function but often possess a pronounced high-end response. As such, they make an ideal choice for cymbals, hi-hats and guitars. Like their bigger siblings, small diaphragm condensers require power – sometimes phantom, at other times from an onboard battery or from an **electret**, which carries a permanent charge. An electret microphone is a type of condenser microphone that does not require an external power supply such as phantom power; it has an electret built into it. Like other condenser microphones, electrets require some sort of pre-amplification as their signal output is very low.

Pressure Zone Microphones (PZMs), are some of the less common microphones, as well as the most recently invented. Technically speaking, PZMs are actually a form of condenser microphone, but bear little resemblance to the vocal microphones you might be used to seeing. Looking something like a big square plate, they can be affixed to a

▲ *A PZM, or boundary microphone.*

surface such as a wall or a piano's cabinet, and work on the principle that acoustic pressures are built up on a surface as sound waves strike that surface. They are sometimes referred to as boundary microphones. PZMs can be extremely clear and detailed and can reproduce bass frequencies quite well (the larger the surface to which the microphone is attached, the more low frequencies will be heard). They make a great choice for picking up a room's acoustic "sound".

➡ *Special Issues pp. 136–143; Projects pp. 162–209*

CHOOSING AND USING MONITORS

It is an old but true axiom that the two most important links in your studio signal chain are the first and the last, in other words the microphone and the monitors.

By **monitors**, we are not speaking of the CRT or LCD screen glowing warmly above your QWERTY keyboard. No, we are talking about the speakers that are responsible for playing back and monitoring your recordings.

CAN'T I JUST USE MY HI-FI SPEAKERS?

Initially, many neophytes will be under the impression that they can use their expensive hi-fi system for monitoring their work. After all, some consumer hi-fi equipment costs far more than pro-studio gear. However, there is a problem with this approach, as consumer gear is specifically tailored to make pre-recorded music sound good, not to present it accurately.

Most consumer systems have built-in equalization curves to add a desirable sheen to the sound. On the other hand, professional studio monitors are

engineered to present the material with the utmost accuracy, regardless of perceived quality. There is no colouration here (well, there is not supposed to be, but no monitor is perfect) and the signal is unadorned by any artificial attempts to boost, cut, blur or otherwise compromise or "improve" the

◀ *The Event 20/20 series of nearfield monitors offers full sound at a budget price.*

material. The fact is, if you are monitoring your tracks via your home stereo, then you are simply not hearing an honest reproduction of your work, and your mixes will not translate well to other systems. A good set of professional monitors is a must.

▲ *The aim of studio monitoring is to provide an accurate reference to judge your work; using speakers such as these can help you do that.*

TYPES OF MONITORS

In the professional studio you will often see a variety of monitors. Some are huge, wall-mounted affairs, while others are as small as the most modest bookshelf speaker. Surprisingly, the latter usually gets as much of a workout as the huge speakers behind the console. These smaller speakers are what are known as **nearfield** monitors. You have probably seen the seemingly ubiquitous white-coned Yamaha NS-10M monitors perched atop many a mixer in pictures of professional control rooms. While not wholly accurate (they tend to be a bit shrill), the NS-10Ms have become the industry standard simply because mixes played through them tend to translate well to other speakers.

NEARFIELD MONITORS

These have many advantages over larger monitors. First, they are portable and an engineer can drag them along wherever he or she needs to mix. Second, they tend to promote less ear fatigue than their larger cousins do, simply because they cannot reach the same ear-shredding **decibel** levels. Importantly for the home studio owner, they are

Jargon Buster

The NEARFIELD monitor is designed to be used when the listener is close to the speakers. Monitors should be placed on a shelf or speaker stand and placed so that an equilateral triangle is formed with vertices at the listener's head and at each monitor.

Jargon Buster

A DECIBEL (abbreviation: dB) is a measurement used to describe sound pressure levels or amplitude. In digital recordings, any signal over 0 dB will result in distortion.

invariably less expensive and can get you into professional monitoring on a budget. This never used to be the case, but as with all things in music technology the prices of nearfield monitors have plummeted during the home recording boom of the last decade.

Another benefit to the home studio engineer is the fact that these smaller speakers are less dependent on the acoustics of the control room. They have a much smaller optimum position, which is usually aimed at the seat in front of the console or computer.

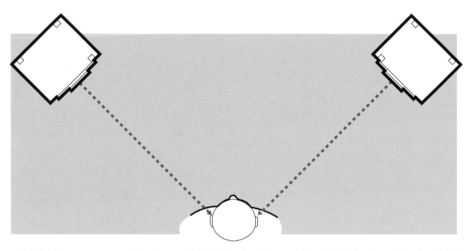

▲ *You should arrange your monitors in an equilateral triangle with your seat, keeping the tweeters at about ear level.*

ACTIVE AND PASSIVE MONITORS

A cursory glance at the various nearfield monitors available on the market will reveal two distinctly different types. The first is the more traditional **passive monitor**, which requires a separate amplifier. This allows the buyer to determine the brand and model of amplifier he or she prefers. This can be advantageous if in the future you plan to upgrade either the speaker or the amplifier, but does require a little more thought as it is imperative that amplifier and speakers be a good match. Depending on the amp driving it, the same set of monitors can sound quite different.

The other types of monitors on the market are **active monitors**. These come with a built-in amplifier or amplifiers, depending on the model. Once the sole purview of high-end studios, these speakers have several advantages over their passive counterparts. The amplifier is always a good match, for instance, as it has been specifically designed for that particular speaker. Additionally, housing the amplifier makes no demands on your precious rack space. It is right inside the unit. Furthermore, there is no chance of damaging the speaker due to a mismatch between amp and monitor. One disadvantage of these monitors, however, is their substantial weight, which can leave flimsy speaker stands straining.

TRY THEM OUT!

Once you have found a pair of monitors that suits your needs and budget, it is crucial that you get used to them before attempting any critical mixes or tracking. Carefully follow any instructions on speaker placement that may come with them. Some monitors need to be positioned away from the wall behind them, while others may not. The ideal position for speakers is in an equilateral triangle with your seat providing one of the points (see the diagram left). Your ears should be level with the **tweeters** (the small cone or dome). Play CDs on them that you know well. This will train your ear and you will make better mixing decisions. It can take time to grow accustomed to your new speakers, so do not give up if your first few mixes do not sound like a commercial recording by your favourite artist.

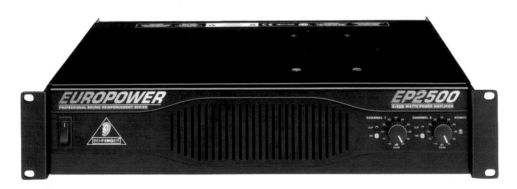

▲   *A power amplifier will be required if you choose passive monitors.*

WHAT SORT OF HEADPHONES DO I NEED?

Let us get one fact straight right from the start: under no circumstances should you make alterations to your mix based on what you hear in your headphones.

It does not matter how expensive they are or what claims the manufacturer makes, you will not get acceptable results, as headphones will not present an accurate representation of the frequencies or noise levels. During the mixdown process, you might use headphones to check stereo balance, for example, but even so, a good pair of nearfield monitors will be much better suited to the task.

WHY DO YOU NEED HEADPHONES IN THE STUDIO?

The answer to this question is that they serve a number of vital purposes, particularly if you will be recording vocals or acoustic instruments. If you try to use a microphone while monitoring through your amplifier and speakers, you are going to wind up generating a deafening feedback loop. Alternatively, you may introduce phase problems from the signal leakage produced by the monitors. This means that you will want to be monitoring any acoustic recordings via headphones. The type of headphones you need will depend on your intended application.

OPEN EAR HEADPHONES

The **open ear** type of headphone is a lot lighter than the **closed ear** type, so if you are planning to don them for any extended sessions they will prove to be a far more comfortable option. If you have the budget, it would be advisable to go with an established brand, such as those from AKG or Sennheiser.

▲ *Open-style headphones are lighter weight and more comfortable for long periods of time when leakage is not an issue.*

CLOSED EAR HEADPHONES

For tracking vocals or other critical acoustic material, you will want a closed ear type. This sort of headphone fits over the ear and reduces any leakage that might be picked up by the microphone, thereby allowing the singer to monitor a higher signal level. The same goes for acoustic guitar, violin and other instruments.

JACKS

You should give some consideration to the available connectivity. Initially, all headphones came with 1/2-inch TRS-style plugs, but in these days of portable CD players and laptop interfaces, the smaller stereo mini-jack connections have become increasingly prevalent. There is a myth that these mini-jacks

▲ *Closed ear headphones are ideal when recording acoustic sources, as they reduce leakage of the playback signal into the microphone.*

are inferior in sound quality, but this is, of course, a fallacy. The build quality of the larger jacks may be more robust, but this has no effect whatsoever on the signal integrity, assuming that the connection is secure and resistant to corrosion.

For the most part, professional and semi-pro mixers and recorders use the 1/4-inch variety, so it may be wise to take this into consideration. If, however, you are particularly fond of one specific set of headphones and its connectors are incompatible with your mixer's, an appropriate adapter may be used.

OTHER EQUIPMENT

The equipment list for your studio will obviously depend on the style of music that you intend to record and the recording methods you prefer.

Pro Tip

In a typical **UNBALANCED** audio cable, the signal is carried by two conductors, one of which is the **EARTH**, or **GROUND**. In longer cable runs, the ground can transmit noise. In a **BALANCED** cable, a set of three wires is used, the third of which is the shield, and carries no signal, but is used to prevent any unwanted interference from reaching the conductors.

Even if you are constructing a modest system, you will need many ancillary items that might not become obvious until the moment they are needed. It is no good getting the band in for the recording only to find out that you have no way to distribute the signal to their individual sets of headphones. You need to do some planning for whatever situations could arise, particularly if you intend to do any sort of commercial work, or you will be facing the ticking clock of a deadline.

CABLES

In any studio, no matter how big or small, one common denominator is the ever-present network of **cables**. There are MIDI cables for stringing together outboard gear, and audio cables for routing your signal in, out and around your equipment. There are also all the normal sorts of cables involved in using your computer, such as those required by any USB or FireWire devices. In addition, you will need any specific adapters for correcting mismatched connections, and

◄ *Even with the wonders of modern plug-ins, you may find a need for some outboard equipment, such as a pre-amp, patch bay or line conditioner.*

you may need a USB or FireWire hub for distributing signals to and from the computer.

Do cables affect sound quality? The answer is an undeniable, unequivocal "yes". You should get the best cables you can afford. Cheap Radio Shack audio cables will not do the job as well as a professional-quality cable from Proel or Canari. It really will make a difference. Also, a high-quality cable will be sturdier and less likely to short out. It will not take too long digging around behind your computer or your rack, searching for a bad cable, before you will wish you had gone with the high-end cables.

CABLE RUNS

When purchasing cables, it is imperative that you give careful thought and consideration to your cable runs. The ramifications of buying cables that are too short are obvious, but you may also find that overly long cables are just as problematic as they will inevitably wind up in a tangled mess. Moreover, longer cables are more likely to introduce troublesome hums, pops and interference into your signal. In addition to the cables, you may want to invest in some cable ties or cable harnesses to keep your cables tidy. Be sure to get Velcro ties, as twist ties sometimes have metal inside and this could result in RF (radio frequency) interference.

When setting up your studio, you should take extra care in cabling the gear together. Power cables and audio cables can make for a troublesome combination. If it is not possible to keep them separated, they should only cross each other at right angles. Under no circumstances should they run parallel with one another.

▶ *The ubiquitous unbalanced instrument cable is a staple of every studio. Keeping the cables in a tangle will cause unwanted and unnecessary noise on a recording.*

HARDWARE

It will be obvious to anyone reading this book that many genres of music can be composed, recorded and produced entirely within the computer with little need for any external hardware.

This is true, but you may still need a way to get audio and MIDI signals into and out of the computer. These tasks can be handled by a variety of interfaces. There are dedicated devices to deal with both audio and MIDI duties, and some that can perform both tasks. These are often in the form of FireWire or USB devices. There are even a few devices, such as M-Audio's Ozone, which combine audio, MIDI and a keyboard controller.

The audio devices, especially when used with PCs, include a variety of **drivers**, which offer different levels of performance. A driver is a piece of software that tells any hardware connected to your computer how to function. The quality of your audio driver will determine how well your audio interface performs in terms of latency and functionality, although the actual sound quality entirely comes down to the hardware itself. If you wish to play virtual musical instruments or use virtual effects plug-ins in real-time on a PC, you will need an audio interface with low-latency ASIO or WDM drivers. The development of Mac OS X's built-in audio environment, Core Audio, has meant that drivers are rarely needed for basic Macintosh audio interfaces. The recently released Windows Vista may require new versions of drivers that ran under Windows XP.

HARDWARE MIXER

Depending on the amount of inputs you will be needing and how much outboard equipment you will be using, you could find yourself in need of a **hardware mixer**. A mixer does exactly what the name suggests: it takes multiple inputs and mixes them together at the outputs. Some mixers provide equalization, built-in effects or effects busses, microphone pre-amps and phantom power. Their prices can run the gamut from a few hundred to hundreds of thousands of pounds or dollars. Do remember that every bit of hardware the signal passes through will add noise to that signal, particularly if the hardware is of the active variety, as is most studio equipment.

PATCH BAY

One passive device you may find indispensable is an audio **patch bay**. This is especially useful if you have a lot of outboard equipment, such as synthesizers or effects, and a finite number of inputs on your audio interface. A patch bay usually contains two rows of jacks at the front and two at the back, with all your hardware "permanently" connected at the back and temporary connections made between it all at the front. One row of jacks is for the incoming signals, and one is for outgoing signals. Patching a short patch cable from the incoming jacks to the outgoing jacks makes a connection from one device to another.

◀ You cannot go wrong with a MIDI interface such as this USB MIDIsport 8x8/S.

Other types of patch bays that might find their way into your rack are MIDI and digital types. A MIDI patch bay performs the same function for outboard MIDI equipment that an audio patch bay does for audio signals,

▲ M-Audio's keyboard, audio and MIDI controller in one unit: the Oxygen 8.

letting you quickly patchsignals between your connected equipment as required. Some models offer myriad other useful functions, such as MIDI merging, MIDI delay and filtering of the MIDI data stream. If you have a great number of synthesizers or MIDI-endowed effects, such a device is well worth your consideration.

A digital audio patch bay behaves exactly as its analogue cousin does, but for digital audio signals. These devices often have multiple input and output types for the different available digital standards, as well as word-clock outputs for making sure all digital audio is synchronized to the same clock source. With an increasing amount of low-cost equipment being manufactured with some form of digital connectivity, there is every reason to suspect that the digital patch bay will eventually become as ubiquitous as its analogue forebear has been.

▲ *Small studios with even a modest amount of outboard equipment may need a patch bay for routing signals.*

PRE-AMPLIFIER AND CHANNEL STRIP

If you are going to be recording any acoustic sources, a good **pre-amplifier** or **channel strip** may be in order. Sure, you may already have a built-in pre-amp on your mixer or your audio interface, but a high-quality, dedicated device can make the difference between an amateur and a professional sound. We don't need to reiterate the fact that the cost of quality recording gearhas been in a free fall, but rest assured that excellent pre-amps are available at unprecedented price points. Even some of the big-name, high-end manufacturers such as dbx and Focusrite have entered the home studio market, offering superb units such as the Focusrite TrackMaster Pro at prices that are very "project-studio friendly".

Jargon Buster

DE-ESSING is the term used to describe reducing the effect of sibilance (hiss) in vocal signals.

▲ *The Focusrite TrackMaster Pro is a good bet as it possesses both pre-amplifier and channel strip functions.*

The TrackMaster Pro might actually be considered a channel strip, as it has EQ, compression, phantom power and **de-essing** built in. What is a channel strip? As the name might suggest, it is essentially a single, high-quality input and EQ channel, such as those found on world-class consoles. The idea is that the home studio owner has no need (and probably cannot justify the cost) for a huge mixing desk sporting 24 channels, yet would probably welcome a single channel or two of high-quality pre-amplification and EQ. By concentrating on a single channel at a time, the manufacturer can offer all the quality of the big desk without the price tag usually associated with it. This has been a major boon for the project and home studio owner, who can now access a pristine, top-class signal path without breaking the bank.

➡ *Hardware pp. 332–341*

▲ *Although your studio does not have to have as much hardware as percussionist Evelyn Glennie uses, there is some kit that will really come in handy.*

Part One: The Essentials

RECORDING GUITARS

It is obvious that the guitarist's role is vital to so many styles of music; therefore, capturing that singular sound as a stream of bits is critical.

THE ELECTRIC GUITAR

You may think that recording the electric guitar is as simple as running a cable from the guitar's output into your computer's audio interface. Well, yes – and no.

Guitars have a very low-level output and the signal needs to be brought up to **line level**. This can be accomplished by using either a **direct box** or, in some cases, your microphone pre-amp. If you do this, however, the sound will likely be dull and lifeless.

When you hear an electric guitar on your favourite records, you are probably also hearing the sound of the amplifier it is plugged into, which has been expertly miked up to capture the sound of all of the air being pushed around by the speaker. This has a considerable impact on the quality of tone. Many guitarists are as particular about their amps as they are about their guitars, and they will want you to capture their distinctive sounds. There is really no substitute for the real thing, so you owe it to yourself, and to your listeners, at least to give it a try.

▲ *Although not in the public eye as much as lead singers like Eddie van Halen, it is often the guitarist who provides the rock upon which the success of a band is built.*

Jargon Buster

LINE LEVEL signals are the levels your recording system likes to hear and are typically calibrated from 0 dB to +4 dB.

THE RIGHT MICROPHONE

Miking up a guitar amp could not be simpler. You can grab your trusty Shure SM57 (we told you it was a versatile microphone), put it on a boom stand and angle it towards the speaker cone. Do not point it directly at the centre of the cone, but rather off-axis, towards a place between the centre and the outer edge of the speaker cone. Keep it at a distance of at least six inches. If you have a decent large diaphragm condenser microphone, then you might consider setting that up in the same room, but farther from the speaker. Use your ears and experiment with microphone placement until you get the desired sound. You may find it best to place the amplifier on a padded chair or stool.

CONSIDER THE NEIGHBOURS

Obviously, miking up your amp may be out of the question if you live in a flat with paper-thin walls and neighbours who cringe at the slightest peep. What can you do? Fortunately, there are a number of devices on the market designed to simulate the sound of various guitar amplifiers and speakers.

Line 6's popular POD is one such device and there are others from Johnson, Behringer and Yamaha, to name but a few. These usually have a lot of flexibility and allow you to dial up an assortment of combinations, some of which may not even be possible (or at the very least, affordable) in the real world. While they will be no replacement for the sound of real air molecules getting tossed about, they do a very good job and allow lots of control after the fact. After all, when using a real amp and speaker, once it is tracked it is written in stone.

With an amp simulator, if you decide during mixdown that the Marshall Stack is better than a VOX amp, it is simply a matter of dialling in a new setting. You may not even need to use an outboard device. There are several software plug-ins these days that do the same sort of job. IK Multimedia's AmpliTube springs to mind, as does Native Instruments' Guitar Rig and Line 6's Gear Box. The latter comes with a USB interface module especially designed for guitar. Waves' Guitar Tool Rack comes in a native version and one for Digidesign Pro Tools TDM hardware. Universal Audio's Nigel is bundled with the UAD-1 powered processor PCI card.

THE ACOUSTIC OR SPANISH GUITAR

Tracking an acoustic guitar is a completely different discipline. Unlike the electric guitar, an acoustic guitar is not amplified, which means that the player (and all the noise he or she makes) cannot be separated from the recording. If your guitarist moves about a lot while playing, all that hustle and bustle will end up on the track, along with string squeaks, pick noises and all manner of other aural intrusions. Depending on the sound you are going for, this can lend an air of intimacy or prove to be an annoying obstacle. The string squeaks can be tamed by applying specialist products, or even a fine layer of vegetable oil, to the strings. The rest is up to the guitarist to control.

Since in this case you cannot just put an amplifier in a cupboard, the sound of the room becomes all-important. You can create a sonically dead environment by hanging blankets around the guitarist, creating a sort of "baffle tent". Alternatively, you can purposefully go for a "live" sound by tracking in a pleasant-sounding room or hall. If you plan to use artificial reverberation in the mix, you might prefer the former method.

THE RIGHT MICROPHONE

When it comes to miking up the acoustic guitar, use the best quality microphones you can afford. While the dynamic microphone may be great for

◄ *The ambient sound from the room you are recording in can be as much or as little a part of the recording as you choose (pictured: Paul Simon).*

capturing an amplified guitar signal, it will not fare as well with the subtle delicacies of the acoustic guitar. In this case, you will want to use at least one condenser microphone – a pair would be better still. There are a lot of inexpensive small diaphragm condenser microphones on the market, and these can prove most useful for this task.

At the lower end of the budgetary scale, the Oktava MK 012 is a good choice, providing a crystalline high end. If you are not too financially restricted, the Neumann KM184 is an excellent choice. Of course, if you have a good large diaphragm condenser model, this can be called into play here, too.

Traditionally, the acoustic guitar is miked in two places. For a full, round tone, the first microphone is aimed at the sound hole, at a distance of six or seven inches. You might also choose to mic the fretboard. This is conventionally done by aiming a second microphone off-axis at the 11th fret. Finally, if you are in a live room, set up a room microphone three feet away. As always, experiment with placement and trust your ears. These techniques are not gospel, but simply suggestions. Only your ears will give you the answers.

Pro Tip

When recording an instrument such as a guitar, you can often enable **INPUT MONITORING** in your DAW software, assuming that your audio interface's latency is low enough. This will allow you to hear the signal going in through the effects plug-ins. The real treat lies in the fact that these effects are not actually applied to the signal, so you can alter them later if necessary.

▶ *Your ear will be the best judge to decide how an acoustic guitar should be miked. Here, a large diaphragm condenser is positioned to pick up the sound hole and the frets.*

RECORDING BRASS AND WOODWIND

Depending on the styles of music you wish to record, you may well be called upon to capture the sound of brass or woodwind instruments at some stage.

At the very least, you might find yourself recording a saxophone or flute at some point and, when the time comes, if you are limited by space you will probably need to close-mike the instruments. However, if you have the space and your landlord or neighbours do not mind, you will almost certainly get better results from putting some distance between the microphone and the instrument. As always, a combination of microphone placements will probably produce the best results.

With the following examples, your best bet will be your finest large diaphragm condenser microphone; a Neumann TLM 103, for instance, would be a superb choice.

THE RIGHT MICROPHONE

When close-miking woodwinds or brass, some of the same precautions must be taken that you observe with guitars and vocalists. Watch out for the rustle of clothing, microphone-stand rumble and all the mechanical sounds produced by the instrument. A saxophone, for instance, is laden with myriad finger valves, all of which clatter away like chattering teeth on a cold day. Obviously, great care must be taken to avoid too much of this leaking into your recording.

SAX AND OTHER WOODWIND

For saxophones, you want to get as much of the instrument's sound as possible, so you have to be aware that the sound does not emanate solely from the bell, but from the area of the keys as well. Point the microphone at an angle

◀ *The keys and valves of many woodwinds can cause a mighty din. It takes good microphone technique to find the right balance.*

Illustrated Home Recording Handbook

▶ *A good choice for flutes and higher-pitched winds might be a small diaphragm condenser microphone.*

towards the upper ring of bell and keys, at a distance of at least four or five inches. Use your ear to determine the best placement for capturing both sound sources; your particular taste will obviously determine the right combination of bell and key noise for your recordings. Other woodwind instruments with bells should be miked in a similar fashion. Flutes are generally miked from above and in front of the keys.

BRASS

For a trumpet, or a multitude of trumpets such as a brass section, you might try placing the microphone at a distance of five feet or more. This will allow the full sound of the trumpet to blossom and, if you are tracking a section, it will allow for a natural blending of tones.

For a brass section, the best results can be obtained by miking in stereo. A simple **X-Y** miking technique can work wonders here (see the diagram right). This is where the microphones are positioned close together but angled away from each other towards either side of the sound field. Using this technique offers a lot of control, while simultaneously providing a rich, full stereo image, but bear in mind phase coherency when using dual microphones in acoustic recording.

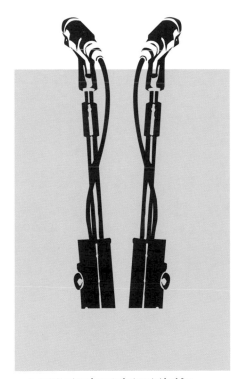

▲ *An X-Y microphone technique is ideal for capturing a brass section.*

RECORDING VOICES

Capturing the human voice as a stream of cascading electrons is not an easy art to master, but if you follow some basic rules you should be able to create vocal tracks that compete with the pros.

THE RIGHT MICROPHONE

Your choice of microphone is a crucial element in getting a good vocal sound. Every voice is different, so it is worth experimenting with different microphones. However, your best choice for a lead vocal recording is probably one of the many large-diaphragm condenser microphones available (some are specifically tailored to vocals). A "budget" condenser microphone will provide good results, but some less-expensive models from big names – such as the Neumann TLM 103 or the AKG C 414 – will meet the most demanding pro standards when plugged into a decent pre-amp or channel strip.

PLOSIVES

You will need to control **plosives** – the loud, exaggerated sounds that occur when the letters "p" or "b" are pronounced, caused by the sudden rush of air from the singer's mouth hitting the sensitive microphone capsule. You can prevent them by using a pop filter, consisting of closely woven fabric stretched over a hoop and placed between the vocalist and the microphone. If you are on a tight budget, make one out of some hosiery and a wire coat hanger. Alternatively, tape a pencil vertically down the front of the microphone, which will cause the air molecules to split before hitting the capsule and help to prevent plosives from occurring.

You may need to address rumble from the microphone stand. Engaging a high-pass filter, which will roll off excessive low frequencies in the signal, can eliminate this. Your microphone may have a built in high-pass filter, as might your pre-amp. If not, you can do the job yourself with a bit of equalization after the track has been recorded.

◀ *The microphone should be placed higher than the vocalist's mouth, so that he or she is forced to sing up into it, as Sam Cooke is doing here.*

MICROPHONE TECHNIQUE

The human voice is a fragile performer, and you must make sure that your vocalist is comfortable. Place the mic higher than the vocalist's mouth. This will cause them to sing upward, opening the throat more. Check that the singer is not too close to the microphone and ensure that the headphone mix is comfortable for the performer, but is not so loud that the sound leaks into the microphone.

One more thing to be aware of is that vocalists often provide their best performances in the first couple of takes. Make sure that you are recording everything. You may find that the most inspired performance comes when the singer is unaware that he or she is "live", and is therefore more relaxed.

BACKUP VOCALS

It might be best to record multiple singers or background vocals simultaneously. There are a number of ways in which they might be tracked; if there are two vocalists, the figure-of-eight microphone pattern may allow each of them to sing directly into the microphone's capsule. Another option is to track them all in omni mode, capturing a bit of the room in the process. The benefit of recording these vocalists simultaneously is that they will be able to perform the song as they are accustomed to singing it. The drawback is that you cannot then separate each vocal for individual treatment, so unless they are experienced and "together", you may want to record each singer to a separate track.

Record as many takes as you can, so that you can go on to create a **vocal comp track** made up from the best vocal performances cut and spliced together. It is now easy, using software tools, to carefully build the perfect vocal performance.

➡ *Choosing and Using Microphones pp. 118–123; Projects pp. 162–209; De-essers p. 318*

MIX IT LIKE A PRO

After all the tunes are arranged, and all the tracks are recorded, comes the most crucial (and possibly the most difficult) step in the engineering process. We are, of course, referring to the mixdown. You can use all the best gear, but it will not be worth anything if the mix is not up to scratch. Unfortunately, learning the skills of an expert mixing engineer takes years of hands-on experience.

WHAT IS MIXING?

Mixing is the process of adjusting the volumes, pan positions and frequency spectra of all of your recorded tracks. In the pro studios, this is achieved with one of those huge, slider- and knob-laden mixing desks (or consoles). The tracks are individually fed from the multitrack recorder into the console and are mixed down to yet another recorder, this one with only two tracks, often a **DAT** (digital audio tape) machine. Along the way, any number of signals might be bussed into effects processors, such as reverbs, delays and more, and then returned to the mixer. This final mix will then be sent to a professional mastering house to add the extra lustre that brings a track to life. The job of the mixing engineer is to ensure that the tape presented to the mastering engineer meets the professional standard of sound quality, while also getting the artist's message and personality across to the listener.

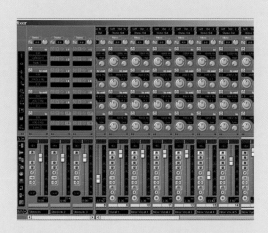

▲ *A mixer, hard or soft, can be intimidating. Nuendo's mixer allows the user to configure it to his or her own needs.*

Today's project studio looks very different from its past incarnations. Many home and project studios do not even have or need a mixing desk. With modern software DAWs, the mixer is often built in and, more often than not, it looks very much like its hardware counterpart. The software mixer, however, is infinitely more flexible, as it is not (for the most part) tied down to a handful of EQ parameters and effects, thanks to the brave new world of plug-ins. The variety and power available to the desktop engineer of today is, quite frankly, far beyond what was available to the most costly studios of days gone by.

▲ It might be hard to do, but reduce all those levels and start your mix fresh.

Pro Tip

Often when we compose, we adjust the mix as we add new tracks. It can be a good idea, when beginning a mixdown session, to start fresh. Take a deep breath and reduce the levels to silence, then bring your most significant signal up to somewhere under 6 dB. Mix the other tracks relative to the first.

EXPERIMENT

Of all the material covered in this book, mixing is one of the most abstract and subjective areas. What works well for one artist in one genre may be totally inappropriate for another performer in his or her chosen style. You will not, in all likelihood, produce a perfect mix in your first attempts, but you can still do a good job by using your ears, your brain and your experiences listening to professionally mixed songs.

◄ Try listening to the mix with the master volume reduced a bit. It can reveal certain flaws in the overall image that may have escaped your notice.

WHAT IS A GOOD MIX?

A good mix is a perfect balance of instrument levels, stereo space and frequency ranges. The music must be perceived as a complete entity with all the instruments blending together to form one cohesive, yet complex and many-faceted sound.

The listener's ear and attention should be drawn to the appropriate focal points at any given time, and change focus when the dynamic of the song changes. In other words, if there is a vocal with lyrics, the listener should be compelled to listen to those words, to sing along, and to switch focus to, for example, a guitar solo in the middle eight. The listener should be immersed in a three-dimensional space.

THE POWER OF MUSIC

Music is one of the very few art forms that allows the artwork to encompass the listener entirely. You are not creating a mere two-dimensional image for the spectator to glance at in passing, but are instead taking control of that listener's very environment. You are not weaving a tapestry of illusion, but are actually

moving and controlling the air molecules in his or her particular environment. Heady stuff, admittedly, but you have certainly experienced the fantastic psychological power of a great song, mixed to perfection.

MIXMASTERS

Close your eyes and you can easily envisage the performers in their own designated space. This is the mixing engineer's ultimate

◀ Roxy Music's Avalon: *a classic example of transparency can be heard in the superb mixing on this album.*

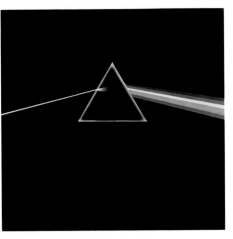

◀ Pink Floyd's Dark Side of the Moon: *unprecedented track counts and production values make this album a tour-de-force for the mix-savvy listener.*

task: the illusion of distance and depth from the listener's imagined vantage point. The best mixes from masters such as Bob Clearmounta in (Bryan Ferry, Roxy Music) or Tony Visconti (David Bowie, T-Rex) allow the listener to hear every single instrument with crystal-clear transparency, yet still perceive the song as a unified whole. The vocals are so clear and present that you can almost hear the expression on the singer's face, yet they never drown out the percolating percussion or pulsing basslines. This sort of thing only comes with a mastery of the art of equalization and gain staging, not to mention a mature and well-honed talent for processing.

One of the best things you can do is to listen for good mixes in your CD collection and examine them closely on your monitoring system. This will not only give you a clue as to how the engineers achieved their sound, but will also get you accustomed to your own speakers and amps. Listen to how every instrument sits in the stereo panorama, and how each instrument's frequencies are tailored to allow the other instruments to be heard. Hear how each instrument seems to have a clearly defined depth and distance from the listener. These are the same qualities you will want to achieve in your own mixes.

➡ *Profiles pp. 210–215*

▶ *Intricate performances and tight hand-spliced editing on Yes's* Close to the Edge *helped define a genre. It is a good lesson for our hard-disk-based modern productions.*

TEST DRIVE

Now that you have all your studio gear set up and you have recorded a few tracks, it might be a good time to put your equipment to the test.

How many tracks can your hard drive support? How many channels of EQ and reverb plug-ins can your **RAM** (Random Access Memory) handle without keeling over? Can your system deal with as many simultaneous synthesizer and effects plug-ins as you think you might need? This is the time to find out, before you are under the threat of a looming deadline, or before someone paying you for your studio time is left tapping their toes while you try to figure out what made your computer reboot.

CHECK IT OUT

It is also a good time to check out all your cable connections. Are they in working order? Are there any mysterious clicks, pops or buzzes? Does your halogen lamp introduce a hum in the signal path every time you turn it on? Are the patch bays all routing your various signals as they ought to? It is crucial that you investigate any potential for trouble before that first big mixdown.

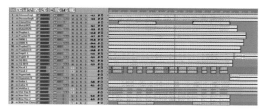

◄ *Try pushing your track count to the edge to see what you can expect from your hard drive. SONAR can deal with far more than any reasonable recording would need and it will warn you if you exceed the limits of your CPU.*

HOW MUCH CAN IT TAKE?

The hardest task will be to figure out exactly what your computer can handle without buckling. Check out your disk streaming capability by loading in any audio tracks you have recorded, or copying some to as many tracks as you can, all the while watching the CPU and hard-drive meters. You may want to use your computer's CPU meter rather than the one that came with your sequencer.

That one may not take into account the overhead required by your operating system and idle system processes. Keep piling on the tracks until the computer just cannot take it any longer, or until you know you have more than you will ever use. It will probably be a very high number. Can you imagine that musicians were once forced to spend small fortunes for even a fraction of what you have available right inside your desktop computer?

▶ *You can use Steinberg's VST performance meter to keep an eye on performance.*

WHAT WILL YOUR PROJECT ENTAIL?

Will you regularly be recording 24 tracks or more? Perhaps 48? Now, reduce the number of tracks you have loaded in to that amount. Throw in a couple of your best and most CPU-intensive reverbs. How does that CPU look? Fire up an EQ on each channel. Can you get one on each? How about software instruments? These all vary in DSP consumption, but you can get a rough idea of how many you can use by opening a few instances while your audio is running.

▶ *Windows users can use Ctrl-Alt-Del to call up their performance meter while the track is running to get an idea of how much CPU is being devoured.*

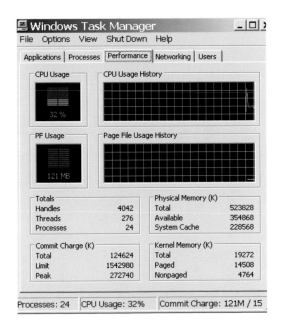

Did you try the various drivers that came with your audio card? If so, did you experiment with your audio interface and test the overall latency (the time it takes between playing a key on your keyboard and hearing the results)? Will that be acceptable? These tests will give you a good idea of what you can expect, and whether you need to make any changes to your system.

➡ *How Do I Set Up My Home Studio? pp. 110–135*

CLEAN TRACKS

In this digital age, it is common to take a cavalier approach to noise management. Many budding recording engineers are under the false impression that because the signal is digital it will be free of the noise levels of the analogue gear of past eras.

While it is true that the recording medium itself is no longer of concern, all the old bugbears still exist, and there are even some new ones we never expected.

DIGITAL RECORDING: AN UNFORGIVING MEDIUM

Anyone who has ever worked with tape can tell you that tape **noise** and compression can hide all kinds of other noises present in our signal path. This includes the ambient noises in the room, noise from the microphone or pre-amp circuitry and more. People who made the switch from analogue to digital media were often shocked by just how much noise there was that went unnoticed in their studios. Fortunately, manufacturers have risen to the occasion, producing equipment with lower noise levels, but you may still need to do some clean-up work in your tracks, particularly any that involve microphones or pre-amplifiers.

REMOVING EXCESSIVE NOISE

After the microphone or the electric guitar, the biggest culprit for adding noise is the audio interface. Though you may be tempted to use an internal sound card that has "professional CD quality sound" emblazoned all over it, it may not actually be as clean as all that. If you are using a built-in sound card or a gamer's card, you might as well face up to the fact that it is not going to be up to scratch. Many relatively inexpensive audio interfaces with pro-level digital resolution (up to 24-bit, 96 kHz) are available. These interfaces will almost always give you better results than a consumer sound card.

If, however, noise still creeps into your system, there are ways to remove it. A variety of "smart" noise-reduction plug-ins are out there. These applications examine a segment of isolated noise and then proceed to strip that noise out of your tracks. They work miracles when it comes to cleaning up old tape recordings, and are well worth seeking out. Mind you, if you are meticulous about your recordings from the start, you may never have to use them.

Another sort of noise to concern yourself with is **ambient** or **incidental noise**: the intake of breath just before the vocalist sings, or the buzzes and hums of an electric guitar when the guitarist is idle. These used to be a real pain to edit out, but modern DAWs make it a snap to snip out such intrusions. It will be to your benefit to adopt an obsessive attitude about such things; your mixes will sound better for the effort.

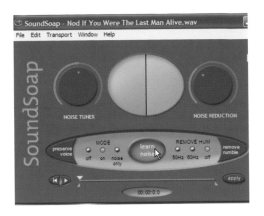

▲ *SoundSoap is a cross-platform plug-in that analyzes the noise in a signal and removes it.*

▲ *Putting a simple noise gate on a signal, such as a guitar, when it is being recorded can prevent noise before it hits the recording.*

▲ *Your host sequencer may have a noise-reduction plug-in built right in. Steinberg includes this one with Nuendo 2.*

EQUALIZATION

The applied art of equalization is one of the most daunting skills to master in all the recording sciences. The approach has changed little with advances in technology, although modern equalizers are far more advanced and capable than ever before.

Where once we might have had only a few bands per channel on even the most sophisticated mixing consoles, today's software equalizer often has an unlimited number of bands, all fully parametric or "sweepable". (A **parametric EQ** is one in which the frequencies that can be adjusted are not fixed.) At the very least, your EQ should have parametric mid-range frequencies. Some EQs even possess the ability to examine the frequency content of two separate recordings and apply an EQ curve based on one to another.

TYPES OF EQUALIZER

Equalizers generally come in one of two types. First, you have the familiar **graphic** variety. This is the sort commonly seen on consumer hi-fi systems, with dedicated sliders for each adjustable band. These bands are predetermined and fixed by the manufacturers, thereby not offering a great deal of flexibility to the recording engineer. Still, they can be quite useful and their ease of use gives them a certain amount of appeal.

▲ All Steinberg's products have dedicated parametric EQs on each mixer channel.

The other type is called a parametric equalizer and is the sort most commonly seen on mixing desks. This one usually has a few knobs representing the frequency bands, and each one can be adjusted to the frequency you need to attenuate or boost.

Furthermore, some of these have a control for Q, which determines the amount of effect your adjustments will have on the frequencies surrounding the band you are cutting or boosting. In other words, if you are boosting, for example, 3 kHz, the Q controls how much gain is applied to 2.9 kHz, 3.1 kHz and so on. This offers a flexibility that can be critical in nailing a good mix.

EQUALIZING DURING THE MIX

When it comes to equalization, it is best to adhere to the "less is more" school of thought. As we have already discussed, you can avoid excessive equalization at mixdown by thinking ahead during the recording and arrangement stages. It would be nothing short of miraculous, however, if you did not need to equalize a little during the mix. When you do, there are a number of guidelines to follow.

It is always best to attenuate a signal rather than boost it. In the days of analogue tape and solid-state circuitry, any gain stage added noise, and equalizers were some of the worst culprits. Obviously, our digital software EQ will not be raising your noise floor, but you will still be better off if you avoid boosting any given frequencies, as you could end up clipping the signal. Instead, if a track needs to stand out more, try cutting the frequencies of other tracks that are stepping on it. Just a very little bit often does the trick, and will help focus the listener's ear on the appropriate instruments.

➡ *How Do I Use EQ? pp. 80–87*

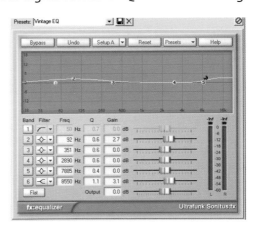

▲ *Included with Cakewalk's SONAR Producer package, the Sonitus parametric EQ is flexible and sounds great.*

> ### Jargon Buster
>
> **HERTZ is the standard and agreed-upon measurement of frequencies in cycles per second. One hertz is exactly that: one cycle per second. A KILOHERTZ, then, is 1,000 cycles per second.**

USING EFFECTS AND PROCESSING

Pro Tip

It is customary to compress the vocal on input, but with careful attention it is often unnecessary in the world of digital audio. However, if you do choose to compress the vocal on input, try using the compression sparingly and add more to the recorded track.

From subtle to extreme, effects can be that extra touch that transforms a song into something special. Conversely, poor judgement in using effects processing can result in a bland, lifeless mush, robbing the song of the dynamics and presence that it might once have had.

VARIETIES OF EFFECT

Effects come mainly in two basic varieties. **Dynamic effects**, such as compressors, limiters, equalizers and filters, affect the perceived volume of a given sound or frequency. These are used when you want to add or detract from an instrument's presence in the mix. They can also be used as special effects, as in the case of a filtered drum loop.

The other class of signal processors works within the time and pitch domain. These effects include delay, reverberation, chorus, phasing and more. They are used for myriad

◄ *Proper use of reverberation is an essential part of getting a good mix. Lexicon has been producing excellent reverbs for years, and has now started producing plug-ins.*

reasons, from adding a sense of depth (reverb and delay), to fattening up a thin sound (chorus). Many effects contain a combination of processes. A good reverb effect, for instance, will not only use time- and pitch-based processing to create the artificial reflections of the signal, but also a filter for controlling the frequency levels of those reflections.

APPLYING EFFECTS

Effects are generally applied in one of two ways. First, there are the insert effects that are applied before the gain controls of a given track. This is usually where effects such as compressors and equalizers are applied, as we want to hear only the affected signal at the output.

▲ *When the effects sound as good as those that are included with ReFX's Slayer 2, it can be tempting to overdo them. Use caution, and apply them sparingly.*

The other way to apply an effect is to route the dry (meaning there is no effects processing) signal through some sort of auxiliary bus or effects send, which is then sent to the processor. This sort of routing is used when you intend to send more than one track through the effects, but wish to control how much signal processing is applied to each of them.

Reverbs and delays are usually applied to sends. When using an effect on a send, you will want to set the wet/dry level of the effect to 100 per cent wet and manage how much is applied to each track via that track's send level.

Like equalization, effects are best used sparingly. Less is always more, unless you are attempting to create a special effect. One of the most common flaws in home studio mixes is the overuse of reverb. Apply it sparingly and exercise good judgement. Remember, the more reverb you have on a track, the further away that instrument will sound.

➡ *What Is an Effect? pp. 68–79; Effects and Processors pp. 306–331*

MASTER IT LIKE A MASTER!

Mastering is the final stage in a musical recording. This is when the final mixes of the songs are arranged in the order in which they will appear on your album, and some amount of effects processing may be applied to bring it all together.

Mastering engineers spend ages honing their craft and training their ears. They have at their disposal prohibitively expensive monitoring systems and high-end signal processors. It would be a mistake to think that you can achieve at home what the professional mastering houses can do.

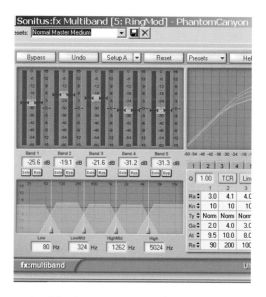

▲ *A multiband compressor is a must for mastering. This one is available from Cakewalk.*

However, the tools are readily available to the desktop recording engineer, and there is no reason to suggest that you cannot come very close, and for a lot less money than a professional mastering job will cost. If you do decide to master at home, keep a pre-mastered version of your mix backed up, so that you can choose to re-master it again at a later date.

WHAT DOES MASTERING ENTAIL?

As stated above, you will be choosing the order of the material and preparing it for final release.

The mastered project is what is presented to the CD replicators; what appears on the master will appear on the final release. All incidental pops and clicks should be removed from the spaces between songs, and the length of those spaces determined. Any fade-ins or fade-outs of the songs themselves are performed in mastering.

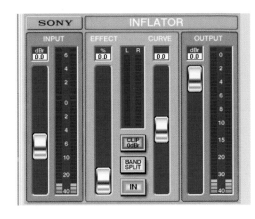

▲ Sony's Oxford Inflator plug-in for TC Electronics' Powercore will pump up the perceived volume.

You may also be using some gentle compression to manage the overall dynamics, and some equalization to bring all the songs together and make them sound as if they belong on the same record. Overall levels are addressed at the mastering stage. You want the quiet songs to sound quiet, and the loud songs to have a certain consistency. What you want to do is create a cohesive album, with no unintentional jumps in volume levels or awkward shifts in frequency content. Mastering is also a time when minor changes in frequency can be made, such as boosting or tightening up the high or low end of a track or tracks.

Plenty of standalone and plug-in mastering suites are available from developers such as iZotope, PSP and IK Multimedia. These applications contain all the effects you might need for any signal processing that is required, and usually have a brace of presets designed to handle different musical styles.

➡ Plug-ins pp. 104–109

▶ PSP's VintageWarmer adds a professional-sounding vintage feeling to your final tracks.

HOW DO I MAKE MY OWN CDS?

After all the work and the final mastering, your album will, at long last, be ready to be immortalized. But in what form? If you have an album's worth of material and intend to distribute it physically, you will probably want to make a master CD to duplicate yourself or have professionally duplicated.

These days of course, so many people listen to music on portable players like iPods, and the distribution of new music over the Internet has grown so popular, that you might just keep your songs in MP3 (or Apple's AAC) format for distribution online (see p.172-173). Whatever you intend to do with your songs, you will need to get them into your desired format and out of your computer. Audio CDs like the ones you buy in stores conform to an industry standard called **Red Book**, and the ones you make must conform to this standard to ensure that they'll play in all CD players, especially older ones.

▲ *Dirt cheap, but with some nice features, Steinberg's Clean! can be used to burn discs, clean up recordings and more.*

WHAT DO I NEED?

The first requirement for burning your own CDs is a CD writer. Unless you're using an ancient computer (in computer years that would be one manufactured more than about five years ago) your computer came with a CD-R, or quite possibly a DVD-R, built in. If not, both are now inexpensive to add to your setup and usually come bundled with the appropriate software for burning both data and audio discs.

Illustrated Home Recording Handbook

(With recordable DVDs you can store more of your songs and project files, and create multichannel surround mixes of your recordings.)

For standard audio CDs, you will need appropriate software for arranging and converting your files to the Red Book standard. These applications can run from the very basic and inexpensive, such as Cakewalk's Pyro, to more elaborate and professional solutions like Roxio's Toast Titanium and Sony's CD Architect. Some blur the distinction between mastering and CD-burning software, while many, such as Roxio's Jam and Nero Inc.'s Nero, have rudimentary audio editors built in or have a basic audio editor included in the package. Some audio editors have CD-burning functions, but only allow you to burn "track-at-once" (one track at a time) and are, therefore, of no use for a complete disc.

Pro Tip
You can burn audio CDs directly from Apple's iTunes program on a PC or Mac, but remember to use the original full-resolution .WAV, .AIF, or .SD2 files you recorded and not compressed formats (MP3 or AAC), unless you're satisfied with their sound.

FLAGS

You may have noticed that the commercial music CDs you buy all have "indexed" track counts. Did you ever wonder how they got there? Someone like you had to put them there. These are **flags** that are placed at the start of each tune to tell the CD which track number is given to that particular track. Many CD-burning applications will attach these flags automatically, but you may still need to move them about if you have arbitrary track indexes, such as when one song segues into another.

▲ You can create CD projects, edit, add markers and perform all the essential functions to prepare a CD with WaveLab.

Once you have set your flags, done any last-minute editing and given it a few listens, you will have only to tell the software to burn your disc. You may need to experiment with disc-burning speeds, but there should be a default speed deemed "safe" for your particular CD writer. Be sure to save the playlist for future discs.

➜ Projects pp. 162–209

FINISHING OFF

HOW DO I PREPARE MY MUSIC FOR THE INTERNET?

The landscape has certainly changed in recent years when it comes to getting your music heard. Once, the only way to get your music into the public's hands was to press a record, do a show or get radio airplay.

Now, of course, those methods represent the costliest, least convenient ways to put your tunes into the hands of your adoring fans. The fact is that the Internet has forever changed the way music is heard.

MP3 FILES

The previously strange new world of making your music available on the Internet is now the first option for most home recordists, as budding producers create their own web sites, prepare albums and Podcasts for the iTunes store, and upload music and videos to sharing sites such as YouTube and social networking sites like MySpace and Friendster.

The most popular audio file formats on the Internet are the MP3 (or MPEG 3) file and the more advanced and audibly superior AAC (part of the MPEG 4 multimedia format) file used by Apple's QuickTime and iTunes. You no doubt have many such files on your hard drive from other artists. These files employ a type of data compression that reduces

◄ With Apple's free iTunes application, Mac and PC users can easily convert full-resolution audio files they've recorded to MP3 or AAC format for sharing on the Internet.

the file size of audio and video files. CD-quality digital audio files are huge and, as such, take up far too much space and bandwidth to be easily traded online. MP3 and AAC files are small and convenient. Even a high-quality MP3 is up to 10 times smaller than uncompressed digital audio. Such compression comes at a price. MP3 files can lack the high-end lustre of a CD-quality file. Most listeners, however, can't distinguish a difference between a properly encoded AAC file and the original CD audio. Also, when you create an MP3 file, you usually have some amount of control over how much compression is applied.

HOW DO YOU CREATE THESE FILES?

It is almost a given that you have some sort of software installed on your computer that will allow you to convert or save audio as an MP3, or AAC file. Even the most inexpensive DAW software allows you to do so, as will the latest media players built into operating systems such as Windows XP and Mac OS X. ITunes, of course, has conversion options built in, but can also play your original uncompressed audio files and can burn CDs of those files.

A good compromise between size and sound quality is 16 bit, stereo, 128 kbps (kilobits per second), although you could easily go lower or higher. Many MP3s available online are only 64 kbps, while some artists choose to host higher rates of 192 kbps. What you do will depend on your audience as well as the available web space.

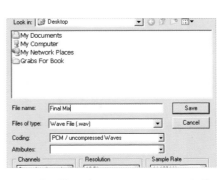

▲ *Nuendo will happily export your song as an MP3 file.*

➡ *Projects pp. 162–209;*
Getting Your Music Out There pp. 369–372

▶ *Steinberg's WaveLab will perform batch conversions of multiple files to MP3.*

PROJECTS

USE THE COMPUTER AS A SKETCHPAD

The best ideas are usually the ones that come in a flash of inspiration, often when you are in the shower or miles away from your computer! Wherever you are, it is vital to capture as many ideas as possible – otherwise you might stop having them.

In order to do this, you need a system in place that is quick and functional. When you go to your studio, you do not want to spend half an hour creating sessions and finding drum sounds – you want to get that idea down. Fortunately, modern computer technology makes this very easy.

A good first step is to buy a personal tape recorder or dictaphone small enough to keep on you at all times (many mobile/cell phones and MP3 players now offer this facility). This way, you have a fighting chance of remembering the idea when you get home. Set up a template session on your sequencer that contains the basic elements of a song, that is, drums, bass, piano **pad**, and some kind of synthesizer. It does not matter if the sounds are horrible and tinny, as long as you can access them quickly – you can worry about sound quality later. Keep an alias or shortcut to this template session on your desktop, so that it can be called up immediately with the click of a mouse.

Jargon Buster

A PAD is a smooth sound that is held for the entire length of a chord, like a piano sound, rather than being played percussively.

GET ORGANIZED

When the template session loads up, the first thing you need to do is to name the idea and make sure that any audio you record is stored in its own appropriate folder where it can easily be found later. Countless great ideas have been lost in piles of unnamed files and folders – it only takes 10 seconds to name and save one. If you tend to flit between genres, make sure that you have several different templates that will load up with suitable sounds or beats, for example, rock, hip-hop, R&B or house.

▲ *A Logic template session.*

SING IT

Always have a microphone set up on a stand and, if possible, plugged into a compressor ready to record, with a pair of headphones also ready to go. As soon as you have the metronome clicking away, you can start singing. Do not get bogged down with details; remember it is just a sketch. Even if you can hear a peculiar noise in your head that is the exact sound you are looking for, do not spend ages trying to make it now – just sing it! Get the idea down; you can work on the finer details later.

▲ *With the necessary preparations, your computer will be ready to save the bare bones of your knockout track!*

Pro Tip

Keep your computer on but asleep. This will save time when you decide to start working.

If you're a guitar or bass player, make sure that you have an instrument plugged in and ready to go at all times – just like the microphone. It does not matter which type of guitar you use, as long as it is always there and always set up to record.

➡ *What Is an Effect? pp. 68–79*

Part One: The Essentials

WRITE AND RECORD YOUR OWN SONG

For the purposes of this exercise, we will take the traditional view of a "pop" song: the three-and-a-half minute piece with a catchy chorus and a foot-tapping groove.

There is an established, tried-and-tested formula for a pop song that is based around the following structure:

Introduction ➡ Verse ➡ Bridge (connecting hook) ➡ Chorus ➡ Verse ➡ Bridge ➡ Chorus ➡ Middle eight ➡ Re-intro ➡ Chorus ➡ Chorus ➡ End

The introduction is the exciting "fingerprint" of the song. The verse establishes the rhythm of the song, setting the scene for the chorus. The bridge (usually called the "B section" or "prechorus" in the US) takes the song up a gear and lets you know that the chorus is coming. The chorus resolves all the tension that has been building up in the verse and bridge. The middle eight (usually called the "bridge" in the US) provides a little respite and sets the scene for the exciting introduction to appear again, while the final choruses and end section nail the point home.

Songs never arrive the same way twice; sometimes you will have a lyric first, sometimes a melody, and sometimes both will come to you at once. When you have an idea of the chorus melody, make sure that you are working in a key that suits whoever will be singing – a good and well-recorded song must never sound like it was hard work.

▲ *Some artists have learned how to create the perfect pop song – there is no reason why you cannot.*

TIPS FOR WRITING LYRICS

- A lyric is not a poem. Make sure that the words work well with the music rather than worrying about whether Shakespeare would approve.
- Be careful to keep the tenses, viewpoint and tone of the lyrics the same throughout the song.
- Write from the heart. Sincerity can make the difference between a mediocre and a great song.

Pro Tip

Keep your introduction snappy, try to hit the first chorus around the 1-minute mark, and try to hit the last chorus around 2 mins 40 secs – this is the perfect radio formula.

STUCK?

If you have a killer beat but cannot get a tune going, try using a basic chord sequence. Get up a bass sound or a pad sound and play a bar each of C, F, G and C or C, A minor, F and G. Sometimes a good bass line can form the backbone of an entire song, for example, Michael Jackson's 'Billie Jean', in which the chordal structure only changes briefly as a bridge before each chorus. A good riff can work for a whole song too, for example, Led Zeppelin's 'Whole Lotta Love'. The backing track to your song should sound complete and satisfying in its own right, yet still be sympathetic to the dynamics of the lead vocal. If you are stuck for a lyric, write about something everyone can relate to, for example falling in love, hating work, ending a relationship.

KEEP IT SIMPLE

Beware of attempting to cram all your ideas into one song. Too many elements, however good, will dilute the power of the whole piece. This kind of self-censorship is not easy, so think about working with a writing partner. Bouncing ideas around can be a great way of filtering out the mediocre stuff.

DO NOT BE PRECIOUS

Even though it is your song, you may not be the best person to sing it. It is a real treat to hear singers who know what they are doing bring your song to life. If they do things differently, do not try to correct them instantly – give it time. Sometimes singers have an instinct for knowing how things should be sung.

➡ *Samples And The Law pp. 373–374*

RECORD AN EXISTING SONG

Once you have decided to record your own version of someone else's song you have a choice. Do you try to recreate the sound of the original mix and simply insert your vocals, or do you want to put your own spin on the song and create a radical new version, maybe with a new, dance-floor-friendly groove?

Many artists simply borrow a section of someone else's song to use alongside their own raps, for example, Coolio's 1995 hit 'Gangsta's Paradise', which draws from Stevie Wonder's 'Pastime Paradise' (from his 1976 album *Songs in the Key of Life*). Whichever of these options you choose, you are still going to have to identify and recreate some key elements of the song.

▲ *Many top artists use portions of other artists' work to enhance their own, so you are in good company if this is the route you decide to take.*

THE ESSENCE OF A SONG

The lyrics are often the first port of call. If you are covering a Radiohead song, you may have to resort to the liner notes or the Internet to decipher the vocals, but whatever you do, don't guess. If you get it wrong, you will instantly annoy and alienate everyone who liked the song in the first place.

There is also the relationship between the melody, the chords and the bass to consider. Within these elements are the unique musical moments that make the song what it is. Even if you want to change some elements, it is still a good idea to nail exactly what happens on the original

Illustrated Home Recording Handbook

record before adapting it. Sometimes what seems like a fleeting passing chord can turn out to be a crucial harmonic element. The Internet is a great place for tracking down **TAB** and MIDI files. You can also check a CD's liner notes to find out who publishes the song, as sheet music is still published for most tunes. Even if you do not read music, you can make use of the chord boxes and lyrics.

> **Jargon Buster**
>
> **TAB** is short for **TABLATURE**, which is a graphic guitar-notation system.

TRANSPOSING

To ensure that no notes are beyond your reach, you may have to adjust the key of the song. If you play the guitar or keyboards, go through the song trying various chords until you get an idea of a good key for your voice. If you are not that hot on your notes and theory but have general MIDI files of the song, it should be easy enough to find the key by globally transposing the MIDI sound source you are using. This may throw all the drum sounds out of whack, but once you know the amount of transposition required you can go back and repeat the process more carefully, one part at a time.

DO NOT BREAK THE LAW

It is not against the law to record an existing song, but if you are planning to sell your efforts you will need to establish who owns the publishing rights to the original recording (the record) and the underlying work (the song), and ensure that the proper credits are observed. The publishing rights will encompass not only the lyrics and melody, but also any instrumental parts and samples, which contain recorded performances and therefore are subject to further copyright laws. Fortunately, publishing and copyright can often be cleared for a set fee.

The moment you commit any of your ideas to tape, hard disk or paper, they become your copyright-protected property. If you decide to add some rapping to a Beatles song, you may one day find the publishing credits reading "Lennon, McCartney, Your Name Here".

➡ *MIDI pp. 252–267; How to Read Music pp. 364–368; Samples And The Law pp. 373–374*

Part One: The Essentials

PUT YOUR SONG ON THE INTERNET

As connection speeds have increased, the Internet has become a key part of the audiovisual content distribution infrastructure, as well as an increasingly important shop window for music.

Most people today are able to download audio and at least view streaming video files without regard to connection speed.

SHRINK YOUR FILES

A big reason for this is encoding technology that makes finished audio files much smaller than they were when you first recorded them.

What you require is a small file that can be downloaded quickly, so you need to convert the files of your mix (typically WAVs, SDIIs or AIFFs) into MP3 or AAC format (see p. 172-173), which are about one tenth the size of the original files. MP3 is a codec, a word derived from the words "compress" and "decompress".

◀ Web sites such as these allow you to download MP3 files by your favourite band – and maybe by you one day!

Codecs use a special process to remove unnecessary information from your original files, without any apparent loss of sound quality or information.

BUT MY BEAUTIFUL MIX ...

Do not panic! The MP3 codec is so successful because it is able to identify elements of a sound file that we are unable to hear. Under normal circumstances, the brain filters out the vast majority of the sensory information we receive all the time – it decides what the important bits are and discards everything else.

MP3 does exactly the same and strips away the sounds that we cannot hear. These are sounds that are:

• Similar to other sounds happening at the same time.

• Quieter than a sound happening at almost the same point in time.

The brain naturally masks these sounds out anyway, so there is no need to record them. Once this reductive or **lossy** process has occurred, a second process compresses the remaining data in a more conventional way, completing the compression process.

The bit rate of an MP3 can be set to a constant or to vary according to the complexity of the source

▲ *There are sites on the Internet to which you can upload your music for others to hear, such as this Internet radio station.*

audio. As you can imagine, the encoding system requires a lot of computer muscle, but fortunately the system is designed so a fraction of that power is required at the decompression or playback stage. A slight amount of audio quality will be lost, but this is a small price to pay for the overall convenience.

HOW DO I CONVERT MY FILES TO MP3?

Many digital audio workstations and programs include a utility for converting mix files into MP3 format. These functions are usually found in the File/Export menus. If your system is lacking an MP3 compressor you can find free software on the Internet.

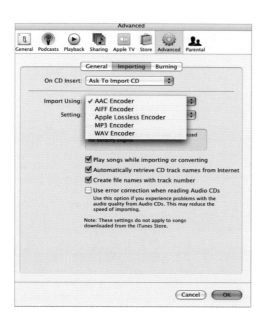

▲ Apple's iTunes lets you convert incoming audio to Internet friendly formats like .MP3 and AAC.

Because of its smooth integration with the iPod music player (not to mention the fact that it's free), Apple's iTunes has become a standard on Macs and PCs for creating AAC audio files as well as organizing your personal music library. Many other commercial and shareware audio programs for ripping and compressing audio exist for both platforms.

Among the more expensive but full-featured audio editors are Peak and Adobe Audition (formerly Cool Edit Pro) for Mac OS and Windows, respectively. You will find the full range of export options here so the MP3 file will be suitable for looping on your web site, streaming or downloading. The highest resolution compression is 320 kbps at 44.1 kHz in stereo, the lowest is 8 kbps at 11.025 kHz in mono. A good starting point for conversion is 128 kbps at 44.1 kHz in stereo with **variable bit rate** (VBR).

◄ Adobe Audition (formerly Cool Edit Pro) offers Windows users a host of pro audio features.

ON THE WEB

After making your MP3, you will need to distribute it to the rest of the world. Many sites today will give you web space for your music. Some like CD Baby and even Amazon give you the chance to make money from your music. Others offer mainly exposure. It is pretty straightforward to make your own web site, and most Internet service providers will supply a small amount of space for a basic site.

If you want a site that is capable of dealing with your music, you will probably need to buy a domain and rent enough space on a server to hold your files. This also gives you the chance to own a ".com" or ".tv" of your own. If you shop around, you can find domains and server space in all price ranges, but remember to check that the servers can support the necessary formats (like streaming audio) and file sizes.

You need to put your MP3s on your server. It is a good idea to use an FTP (file transfer protocol) program, such as Fetch or 3DFTP (freeware), to move the files from your computer to the server. With this you will have access to the server with a password, and transferring files is as easy as copying them from window to window. Once they are on the server, all you need to do is create a button that points the browser at the MP3 on the server, and the computer's media player will automatically identify the file type and play it.

If you want to provide a downloadable file on the server, you will need to make sure that it is **zipped**, or compressed. Use any zip compression program to zip the files and they will be downloadable in both Windows and Mac OS formats. Windows users may have just such a utility built into the operating system, in the shape of "compressed folders".

Take some time to research carefully all of the latest options for selling and distributing your music online, as the number of sites making such opportunities available has exploded in recent years.

➡ *Getting Your Music Out There pp. 369–371*

PODCASTING: HOME RECORDING EXCLUSIVELY FOR THE INTERNET

While home recording enthusiasts have understandably been focused on making records for the last 30 years, a bold new outlet for creative producers has been growing exponentially. Just open Apple's free iTunes program, select iTunes Store, and click on Podcasts to see what we mean.

Many may think of podcasts as simply commercials for big companies or the ravings of some egotist with a microphone in his basement. But the Internet offers a wealth of interesting programs as well, and the flexibility of the web means that your

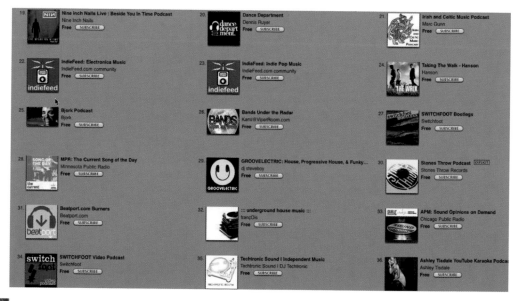

172   **Illustrated Home Recording Handbook**

home-produced creation could take the form of a radio station as well as a simple podcast, not to mention serving as a showcase for your songwriting or band's performance skills. (And besides, that loon in the basement might be willing to pay you to record his ravings.)

Even if you don't have any interest in producing a podcast yourself, you will likely find sources of entertainment and information you weren't aware of. There are podcasts for almost every form of music along with comedy, technical videos, politics and just about any kind of information you could want. You can share your mix tapes with the world, voice your opinions on the state of the world, or even just make a recording of the kids for grandma to hear. After all, an audio podcast is just an audio recording. It doesn't have to be available at the iTunes store; it can be stored on your own web site or emailed directly to other persons (presumably ones that have asked to receive it).

CREATING THE SHOW

Podcasts don't have to be produced with the skill of a professional radio or television program – some of the most popular ones, like some CDs, revel in their grittiness and lack of "slick" quality – but experienced home recordists will have the necessary tools to produce one that sounds good. Some podcasts with good-quality writing and announcing are surprisingly amateurish in their technical execution, with high distortion and uneven volume levels. Understanding compression, ducking, noise reduction, digital editing and other standard studio processes will help you record a better show.

Just as with any session, good preparation is essential. A well-written script, like memorized song lyrics, is an essential part of the recording. Try to

▲ Broadcast mics like the Electro-Voice RE20 are optimal choices for live voice recording, but with care you can create a technically good podcast with home studio gear.

create a beginning, middle, and ending. Read the script several times and edit ruthlessly, until you are reading only the most important pieces of information. That doesn't mean editing out the creativity. Just as you would with a music production, compare your recording with other podcasts many times before you even consider posting it on the web.

PROJECTS

If you're using several music passages, compare them carefully, not only for technical qualities like volume levels and frequency characteristics, but also for mood and tone. Do your selections really fit the text you're reading? Pay particular attention to the volume levels of music playing alone or when someone is speaking (underscoring). Use the sidechain feature of your compressor for ducking (automatic reduction of music levels when a speaker takes over).

Also choose your mics carefully. There's a reason radio DJs use certain mics like the Neumann BCM 104. A classic broadcast mic like the Electro-Voice RE20, a cardioid condenser, is designed to eliminate proximity effect, the tendency to produce excessive bass when a human speaker gets too close.

PODCAST RULES

When your show is ready you'll need to be aware of technical considerations relating to its publishing on the Internet. Podcasts consist of the episode files that you download, and an XML file that lists all the episodes. (XML files are the ones used by newsreader, or RSS, programs to make long lists of news headlines from several web sites.) When you subscribe to a podcast at the iTunes store, iTunes reads the XML file and downloads the latest episode. Each day, iTunes rereads the XML file. If a new episode is available, iTunes downloads it automatically.

Your podcast can be in any one of the following formats: .m4a, .mp3, .mov, .mp4, .m4v, and .pdf (yes, a podcast can be not only audio or video, but also a text file.) You have to post your episode file(s) on a server with a publicly accessible URL. You must create an RSS feed (the

◀ *Scores of podcasts like this one about roots rock are posted every day and available on the web.*

◀ ▶ ⌂ Podcasts ▷ ROOTS ROCK RADIO SHOW

ROOTS ROCK RADIO SHOW

RICHARD TAYLOR
Category: Music
Language: English
Total: 6 episodes

Free SUBSCRIBE

PODCAST DESCRIPTION

ROOTS ROCK RADIO SHOW–the best indie ROOTS ROCK/POP, alt COUNTRY/AMERICANA, BLUES/ROCKABILL the globe. © 2005 & 2006 RICHARD TAYLOR

CUSTOMER REVIEWS

Average Rating: ★★★★½

Awesome cast ★★★★★
by David from TN
This is one of the best podcasts out there now and still will be when there are many more added. The selec downloading and listening to every available episode now!

The Best on Planet Earth ★★★★★
by Marvelous Marv
You don't get better than this for roots rock and indie music. Don't subscribe for the usual radio stuff beca and alive. These tunes are new and vibrant from worthy composers and performers. ... **More**

XML file) that conforms to certain standards, post it to your server, and then let the iTunes store know where the information is. For complete information, see the Learn More files at the bottom of the Podcast home page at the iTunes store.

REMOTE RECORDING

Besides the gear in your home studio, you may find that a field recorder would make creating podcasts handy. Of course a laptop system might do the trick if you wish to, say, interview a person at a fixed location. But some podcasts originate from clubs, concerts, and businesses or even in the street. In mid-2007, several handheld hard disc or memory card recorders had taken over the field once dominated by microcassette recorders.

The Zoom H4 allowed you to record 24-bit, 96 kHz digital audio or MP3s with bit rates up to 320 kbps. The H4 featured two studio-quality electret condenser microphones and recorded onto Secure Digital (SD) cards.

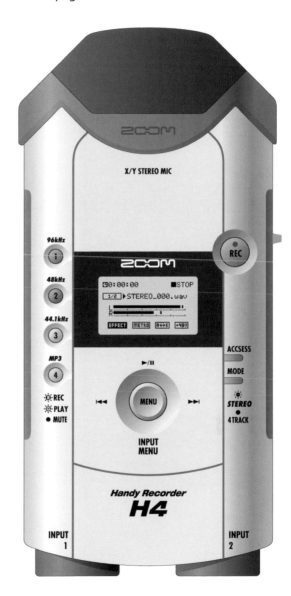

➡ *How Do I Prepare My Music for the Internet? pp. 160–161; Put Your Song on the Internet pp. 168–171*

▲ *The Zoom H4 handheld recorder could be a good choice for recording remote interviews for podcasts.*

MAKE A DEMO FOR YOUR BAND

If you have only a half-formed idea, it is sometimes best to play it to your fellow band members at a rehearsal and let their interpretations and ideas help the music to evolve naturally.

On the other hand, if you have a very specific vision of how the parts of a song should work together, it can save a lot of time and heartache if you record a demo of your ideas to play to your band. This helps to prevent a situation in which the band members play the first two bars of a song you show them and then go off on their own tangents, resulting in a completely different track than the one you originally envisaged.

You must remember, though, that unless you are paying wages it is unreasonable to expect other musicians to do exactly what you want them to do. When you are recording the parts for the demo, do not go into too much detail or get hung up on nuances of performance. Block in the major notes and demonstrate **syncopation** (where the accent moves to the weak beat) and any stops and starts, but leave any ornamentation to the other players. Do not let yourself get too attached to it – they will probably change it.

◄ *Nitin Sawhney plays to friends Julian Joseph and Jools Holland. Sharing thoughts in this way can help cement an idea in your mind.*

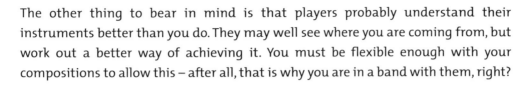
The other thing to bear in mind is that players probably understand their instruments better than you do. They may well see where you are coming from, but work out a better way of achieving it. You must be flexible enough with your compositions to allow this – after all, that is why you are in a band with them, right?

CLARITY

What you need to end up with is a simple session with a basic drum pattern at the right tempo, plus simple versions of the other parts that clearly show the chords, simple lead parts, stops and starts. Make sure that the vocal is loud and clear, as that is what the band is supposed to be supporting.

As well as doing a mix with everything in balance, make each band member a CD with his or her own instrument turned up loud in the mix, so that everyone can easily distinguish their parts. It is also a good idea to include any tracks that inspired your idea or that have a similar sound to the one you are after. If it is a bass sound you like, put it on the bassist's CD, as it saves a lot of time and long-drawn-out descriptions; the bassist may only need to hear one bar to know exactly what you mean. It is also a good idea to give the other musicians your session's audio and MIDI files, so they can have a look for themselves.

Finally, be prepared for the worst: when you turn up for the rehearsal expecting everyone to know their parts, bring along big chord sheets for everyone, because they probably listened to their CDs once and then lost them.

▶ *Nothing is more frustrating than people with no idea of what is going on in rehearsal, so come prepared for the worst by bringing spare copies of your music.*

RECORDING ON A LAPTOP

Over the past few years, huge leaps in processing power, storage capacity and data transfer capabilities have created a situation in which the laptop computers of today can totally outperform the desktop towers of yesterday. The compact size and sheer portability of laptops makes them a welcome addition to your life, regardless of any recording needs.

◄ *When you start thinking about laptops as being the heart of a mobile recording studio, they become irresistible.*

WHY HAVE A DESKTOP AT ALL?

Up until recently, the only option for incorporating a multi-channel audio interface into your computer was to actually open it up and put an audio card into one of the slots on the motherboard. These cards (PCI cards) would have a multi-pin connector of some kind, which would hook up to a bundle of audio plugs or a box (breakout box) with a selection of standard audio connection sockets to connect the computer to a mixing desk. To use a microphone you generally needed to use the microphone amps on a separate mixing desk and send the signal to the computer using the bundle of plugs or the breakout box. These PCI cards were the only way of moving bulky audio data around the computer at a high enough speed.

The other factor was data storage. There was room for extra disk drives inside desktops, but until recently the standard computer hard drives were not fast

Illustrated Home Recording Handbook

enough to record audio, so more expensive SCSI drives were used. However, these drives needed an extra PCI card in the computer itself.

WHY HAS IT ALL CHANGED?

It all comes down to FireWire and USB. Prior to the arrival of these two protocols, the only means of getting audio in and out of a laptop was via a PCMCIA (personal computer memory card international association). This enabled you to record high-quality stereo, but meant that you had a tangle of XLR microphone connectors hanging off the side of your computer.

These new data-transfer formats have speeded things up and made things cheaper. They are both used to connect all sorts of peripherals to your computer and are **hot-swappable**, which means that drives and interfaces can be switched around while the computer is still turned on (old SCSI technology required a restart).

USB was the slower of the two connections but with the USB 2 standard transfer speeds have improved dramatically, allowing for higher track counts at increased resolution.

External FireWire audio interfaces typically use the original FireWire 400 standard, capable of recording as many as six inputs while playing back ten outputs at 24-bit/96 kHz resolution. The newer FireWire 800 standard is available on some more expensive interfaces. It's capable of recording as many as 28 tracks at 24-bit/192 kHz resolution

These interfaces come in a wide range of specifications: some with microphone pre-amps, some with MIDI and some with digital-only options. Think carefully about what capabilities you need. There is a list of interfaces at the end of this section.

▲ *Digidesign's 003 Factory is a FireWire-based interface/control surface for Pro Tools LE.*

Part One: The Essentials

DRIVES

IDE hard drives inside a laptop tend to run at 5400 rpm. It is possible to record audio to this internal drive, as long as you have room. Usually, especially if you are multitrack recording, it is a bad idea to record on to your system drive; desktop users generally install extra drives specifically for audio. IDE 100 drives are now fast enough to cope with multi-track audio if they run at a minimum of 7200 rpm, so the answer is to use external FireWire drives such as those from LaCie and Glyph.

▲ *The LaCie d2 external FireWire drive.*

LATENCY AND MONITORING

The advantage of some of these new interfaces is that they have built-in microphone and line inputs, so you can operate without a mixing desk. However, there can be a problem with latency, which is a delay caused by the processing carried out by your audio card and computer. If you plug in a microphone and set up a track on your sequencer to record yourself singing, there will be a slight delay between when you make a noise and when you hear it back through the computer. As technology advances, of course, this problem is growing increasingly irrelevant. Even so, latency can make playing along with a track difficult, so some interface makers have devised a way around it.

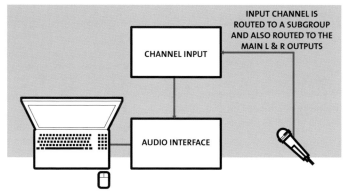

▲ *This is how to achieve no latency monitoring with a mixer.*

On some interfaces the input is split at the interface and routed both to the computer and to the headphones (or monitors) at the same time. If you turn down that track's volume on the computer, you will hear the rest of the backing track plus the input signal that is taken straight from the input, with no latency.

MIDI

Many audio interfaces also have MIDI onboard. If they do not, you will have to obtain a USB MIDI interface of some kind or a USB controller keyboard. The controller keyboard option means one less box to cart around. The more advanced ones will have MIDI input and output sockets so you can hook up your external MIDI gear or send and receive MTC for synchronization purposes.

▲ *The Korg microKONTROL*
MIDI controller keyboard.

These master keyboards often come with a series of assignable knobs and sliders for MIDI controller purposes. Some of them have preset configurations to fit any applications and software synthesizers you might be running. More and more effort is being made in this direction, with some well-thought-out and multifunctional controllers emerging that are well inside price band D (see p. 11). The Korg microKONTROL is a case in point, with a compact three-and-a-half octave mini-keyboard and assignable knobs, sliders and trigger pads, plus a librarian software program to manage your "scenes".

POWER

Forget about sitting on the beach and running everything from a computer battery. Even though some of the MIDI and audio interfaces will draw power from the USB port, they all come with their own power supplies and you will need to use them or your laptop battery will barely last as long as the average pop song!

➡ *Digital Recording pp. 346–353; Studio Layouts pp. 354–363*

RECORD YOURSELF SING

The vocal is the most important element of a song. Recording someone else singing is easier than recording your own singing because you can be more objective about the performance and the sound – the two key factors of a good lead vocal.

PERFORMANCE FIRST

A poor take recorded in crystal-clear Dolby Surround is still a poor take, and will let the song down. It is far better to have a great performance with an inferior sound. One of a producer's most useful skills is the ability to get good performances from people in what are not usually the most inspiring surroundings. It is hard to give a stadium-sized performance in a cramped room, while keeping an eye on the recording levels and singing into a pair of old tights, but sometimes it is the only choice available.

Experiment with sitting, standing, lying, hand-held and stand-mounted microphones until you find the most relaxed system. Bear in mind that you need to get to the mouse and keyboard easily, without interrupting your flow.

Try to arrange to record the vocals when the house is empty. Then you can disappear into your own little world and experiment with interesting vocal ideas without fear of siblings secretly recording your noises for blackmail purposes!

Once you have the sound levels sorted out, start recording all your run-throughs and practices. This will accustom you to the red lights being on, besides which early takes and experiments often end up in the finished mix.

HOW DO I GET A GOOD SOUND?

If you are using a dynamic microphone, you should be between three inches and 12 inches away from it, and up to double those distances for a condenser. If the environment sounds boxy or unpleasantly boomy, a dynamic microphone recorded up close will catch less of the ambient room sound. Experimentation will reveal the microphone that is best for you.

Using a pop filter will prevent the microphone from making unpleasant low-frequency noises when you blast it with air during plosive sounds. Pop filters can take the form of fitted foam hats or some gauze (you can use hosiery) stretched over a frame (a loop of coathanger wire) a few inches from the microphone.

EQ AND COMPRESSION

Try to leave the EQ as flat as possible. If you are up close to the microphone, the "proximity effect" will make the voice sound bassy, so some low frequency can be cut – say, 100 Hz to 150 Hz. If the voice sounds a bit "essy" on "s", "f" and "sh" sounds, you can use a **de-esser**, but it is best to do that on playback.

> **Jargon Buster**
>
> **A DE-ESSER is a frequency sensitive compressor that listens to the signal and reduces it if the high frequencies get too loud.**

▲ *A de-esser will help reduce the high frequencies, such as on "s" sounds. Be careful that you do not adjust the high frequency and threshold too much as you will give the singer a lisp.*

Recording with compression will make the quiet parts of the music sound louder and the loud parts sound quieter. Try using a ratio of 3:1 with a fast attack time and a medium release time. If you do not have a compressor to record with, try moving away from the microphone during the louder parts. If you cannot compress to disk, you can still compress on playback.

➡ *Special Issues pp. 136–143; Effects and Processors pp. 306–331*

RECORD YOUR BAND LIVE

Some bands play together brilliantly, but sometimes the recording process can inhibit performances. It is very easy to overproduce and engineer the life out of great songs.

This alone is a good reason to experiment with live recordings, and if you are well prepared you can get a lot of great work done quickly and, therefore, cheaply.

RECORDING AT A GIG

Nothing focuses the mind quite like a few hundred people staring up at you looking to enjoy themselves. The adrenalin kicks in and performers find an extra 10 per cent from somewhere within, so that live recordings often capture the unique energy of a band "in the wild", so to speak.

It is possible to make an excellent live, bootleg-style recording with a well-placed pair of condenser microphones and a MiniDisc player, but you will need to be very lucky with the **front of house** (the main power amplification, or PA system) sound that evening. As with any event, prepare for all eventualities.

If possible, you need to get hold of a mixer and a multitrack recorder – preferably digital, and with as much recording space as possible (you do not want to be changing tapes or disk drives mid-gig). You need to record every microphone and line signal coming from the stage; if it is a small gig and the soundman has not miked up the guitar amps, you need to do it yourself. If you can, set up a pair of condensers at the back of the crowd so that you can capture some of the atmosphere, applause and/or heckling!

◄ *Led Zeppelin's live energy pleases their audience.*

ABOUT SPLITS

There are more than enough wires on a live stage, so it is best to have access to the venue's microphone feeds rather than having two setups side by side. This is where preparation is vital. Make sure that you speak to the venue or the PA company in advance – they may already have gear that will make everything easier, or even if they do not, they can probably hire it more cheaply than you can.

Rather than having many long microphone cables between the stage and the desk, which can prove rather hazardous, you should use **stageboxes**. These are units that contain all the microphone inputs, and carry all the signals to the mixer in one long, multi-core cable. The stageboxes are also the best places from which to take splits. It is possible to get **passive split** stageboxes; these split (or parallel) a signal into two or three identical feeds, without using an external

power source. Bigger companies may have active or **buffered splitter** boxes, which comprise racks of 8, 16 or 24 boxes. These externally powered units may have a few more level options and are capable of sending signals over longer distances with little or no loss in signal power.

▲ *Make sure you arrange your wires properly on stage to avoid accidents.*

Feed the split (or parallel) signals into your own mixer, set the input gains, and route the signals to the multitrack via direct outputs without any EQ. The front-of-house desk may have direct outputs you can use – if not, check to see if one of the auxiliary sends doubles as a direct output. You could also try **subgroups**. The main group of a mixer is the left and right output, and subgroups enable you to assign sets of channels to a single pair of faders – all the drum channels to subgroups 1 and 2, all the guitars to 3 and 4, and so on. This means that the whole mix can be done using a few faders rather than all the individual channel faders.

COVER YOURSELF

The sound setup for the gig will be impossible to recreate later on. Organize an early load-in and long soundcheck and play your whole set twice, including the encore numbers, and record it both times. This way, if mistakes are made during the gig, you will be able to patch them up later by copying and pasting.

LIVE RECORDING IN THE HOME STUDIO

Live recordings sound exciting because of the buzz of a band playing together. No one wants to mess up, so people will tend to concentrate more. However, capturing all this at a gig can be quite tricky, and there is only one chance to get it right. A live studio recording can be a good compromise, as it focuses the performers but also gives you the chance to do it again, or to make use of drop-ins when mistakes are made.

The chances are that you will not have a room big enough to set up the whole band and, either way, guitar amps and singers will need to be isolated. Two

things become vital at this point. The first is rehearsal. Because band members may not have visual contact, it is essential that they know the chord changes inside out. The other point for consideration is monitoring; everyone needs a good, clear mix of themselves and the band to work with.

◀ *Nirvana making the best of the space they had available when recording live.*

Pro Tip

Plan the session so that you can spend time with each player and get it right, without the pressure of lots of people waiting for you to hit the record button.

PLAYERS

Bassists, guitarists and keyboard players can be in the same room as the drum kit (without their amps of course) – the bigger the room the better. If they also sing backing vocals, it is probably easier to cheat and add them afterwards. If you are short of microphones, try to get a pair of condensers over the kit and a dynamic microphone on the kick and snare drums. Any additional percussion setups could work well in kitchens or bathrooms, but the reflective sound of these rooms will need to be balanced with the dry sound – experiment with microphone placement.

SINGERS

The vocalist should be in a quiet environment with as little reverberation as possible – for example, a bedroom. If the singer plays acoustic guitar, record both the guitar and the vocal with the best condenser microphone you have. Some singers actually sing better while listening to a quiet mix on the monitors, rather than using headphones. If this is the case, use a dynamic microphone such as the Shure SM57 or 58 quite close to the singer, together with a good pop filter; this will pick up less background spill than a condenser.

GUITAR AMPS

Ideally, you will find a room adjoining the drum room where the guitarists can place the amps. If you have two amps and one room, turn the amps down a little and put them back to back – that should help with separation. If the bassist has a bass amp, it is a good idea for him or her to sit close to it, as he or she may have trouble hearing the bottom end in headphones while a drummer is bashing away.

HEADPHONE BEST PRACTICE

A stereo amp can supply one stereo (left and right) mix, but by wiring two sets of headphones in mono to the left and right outputs, respectively, you end up with two mono mixes from one amplifier, each fed from its own auxiliary send. It is worth hiring a decent monitoring system – if the band members cannot hear themselves, the recordings will have been compromised anyway. Get some adaptors so that the headphones can plug directly into the speaker outputs of the amplifier – this has much more clout. Which adaptors you will need depends on the outputs of your amp, but bare wire or banana clips are the most common.

EXTRA EQUIPMENT YOU WILL NEED

- Headphones, headphone amplifiers and extension leads
- Microphones and long microphone leads
- A guitar channel switcher or pedalboard extension leads
- DI (direct injection) boxes (see p. 190): one for each guitar
- Disk space: a few takes will eat drive space faster than you may think.

➡ *Special Issues pp. 136–143*

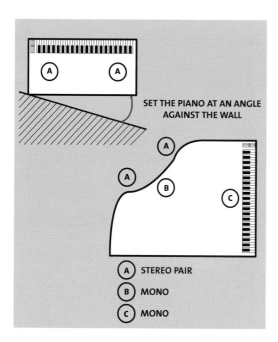

RECORD A PIANO

Although the humble upright piano is generally acknowledged to be an inferior instrument to the grand piano, it is possible to get a well-balanced and atmospheric recording by making a few simple adjustments.

Lift up the lid and remove as much of the casing as possible (including the board below the keyboard), then move the piano so that the soundboard (at the back) faces into the room. If this is not possible, at least pull one side of the piano out so that it is at an angle to the wall; this helps to prevent unwanted resonance.

SET THE PIANO AT AN ANGLE
AGAINST THE WALL

A STEREO PAIR

B MONO

C MONO

▲ *Possible microphone positions for upright and grand pianos.*

MICROPHONE PLACEMENT

When recording a piano, a pair of omni directional condenser microphones will provide the most natural sound. Start by placing the microphones just inside the top of the piano, one facing down towards the bass strings and the other towards the high strings (if you have only one microphone, just cover the high strings). The noise of the pedals can ruin a recording; if you get squeaks or clonks, try placing some newspaper on the carpet below the pedals and apply some olive oil to the wood around the pedals.

MIDDLE AND SIDE

Facing the piano out into the room, and miking the soundboard from 18 inches to two feet away with an **M&S** (middle and side) or **co-incidental pair** of microphones, can also give a good result. M&S is where one switchable pattern condenser is set to omni or cardioid and faces the instrument. Another microphone, set to a figure-of-eight pattern, sits in the identical spot "looking" at the left and right part of the sound. The cardioid microphone is monitored panned centre. The figure-of-eight microphone is paralleled, and the two signals are bought up panned hard left and right. One of these figure-of-eight signals is then put out of phase. The higher in volume the figure-of-eight pair, the wider the stereo image. The term co-incidental pair describes when two identical microphones are used with their capsules in close proximity. An x-y pair will have two cardioid (or figure-of-eight) capsules as close as possible with a 90-degree angle between them, the midpoint of which will face the subject.

A GRAND PIANO

These spectacular instruments can be up to nine feet long, so it is good to get as far as six feet away to achieve the most natural tonal balance. A coincidental stereo pair of microphones looking into the open lid of the piano from the side is a good starting point, but this is such a complex-sounding instrument, capable of so many different nuances, that you may find yourself putting microphones in any number of places to get the sound you want.

If you want to tighten the sound, bring your microphones in closer. Start with your microphones six to eight inches from the hammers and move farther away to soften the sound, or try close (one foot) mics over the high and low strings under the lid. Even a humble PZM taped to the underside of the lid can sound good.

As with all miking, do not be afraid to experiment. Just remember that a close-miked sound will appear even closer and drier in the context of a finished mix, so if in doubt set up an ambient microphone to capture some "air" in case you need it. If you are trying to isolate the piano from surrounding instruments (or vice versa) a pair of dynamic microphones or a PZM under the lowered lid will be the best option.

Finally, always get the piano tuned; preferably once you have it in the right position to record, because moving it could throw it out of tune again.

➡ *Choosing and Using Microphones pp. 118–122*

RECORD A SYNTHESIZER

Synthesizers are possibly the easiest instruments to record. They have a line level output, usually a 1/4-inch jack, which can be plugged straight into your audio interface input, your mixer or your multitrack input, whether analogue or digital.

Jargon Buster

The **DI (DIRECT INJECTION) BOX** converts high-level instrument signals into microphone-level signals, often with level adjusters and earth-lift switches.

Generally, there is more level than you need coming out of a synthesizer, regardless of whether it is digital or analogue. If, however, it is a little on the quiet side, you can use a **DI box** to convert the line signal into a microphone signal. This means that you can take advantage of the microphone inputs on your mixer, which can give a good, chunky sound.

USE THE AIR!

Plugging a synthesizer in directly or using a DI box will give a completely dead sound. In some situations, you may wish to set these sounds in some space; you will need to resort to digital reverb in order to do this. A more natural sound can be achieved by playing the synthesizer through an amp and miking it up with both a close and an ambient microphone. These sounds can then be balanced with the dry DI sounds, helping to create a little more space in your mix.

◀ *Even modern synthesizers like the Roland Juno-G can benefit from miking it through a speaker cabinet to give its sound extra life and presence.*

MIDI AND SOFT SYNTHESIZERS

MIDI gives us the ability to record a live performance exactly as it happens, and then manipulate it at a later date. A MIDI recording can be edited to correct timing or part mistakes. Not only that, it offers you the chance to try different sounds with the same part to see what sounds good, and you can add live filter and FX performances alongside

▲ *You can get the optimal signal from your synthesizer by running it through a DI box such as the one pictured above.*

the original parts. When you are happy with the sound, you can run the synthesizer into an amp and a DI box and capture it safely for posterity.

If your sounds are coming from a soft synthesizer or sampler, you will probably be recording MIDI performances directly into your sequencer anyway. In this instance, you have the choice of routing the output of the soft synthesizer to an output of your audio interface for amping or FX, and then re-recording it back into your audio interface as an audio file – or doing a digital bounce of the part within your sequencer. This is usually achieved by soloing the part in question and stipulating an audio bounce of whichever output the soft synthesizer is routed to. Here you will be able to determine file type and resolution, and how the audio is to be imported back into the session.

Pro Tip

Try running your synthesizers and keyboards through guitar FX pedals, or any experimental gear you think might sound interesting, and then record it like that. Make a note of what you did in case you wish to repeat it at a later date.

➡ *Synthesis pp. 268–287*

RECORD BRASS AND WIND INSTRUMENTS

Here we examine the best ways of capturing the tone of brass and wind instruments, which range from the extremely loud and pervasive to the soft and delicate.

BRASS

A trumpet can make a great deal of noise – up to 130 dB, in fact, which is the equivalent pressure on your ear drum of a pneumatic drill or a loud rock gig! However, there are a few things you can do to ensure that you obtain sweet-sounding recordings. First, try to use a big room with a high ceiling and some soft furnishings. If you have to use a small room, make sure it is as dead as you can make it – bathroom-type reflections will ruin your recording (unless it is an effect you particularly want).

A condenser microphone set to omni, three to four inches off-centre of the bell at a distance of one foot to 18 inches or so (depending on your room acoustics) will give the best results. A dynamic microphone will also work, but you may have to get in closer – in which case keep an ear out for microphone distortion and windy noises.

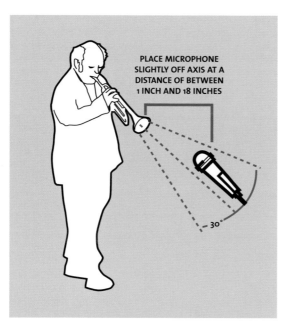

PLACE MICROPHONE SLIGHTLY OFF AXIS AT A DISTANCE OF BETWEEN 1 INCH AND 18 INCHES

30°

▲ *The best position to place the microphone when recording a brass instrument, such as a trumpet.*

HARMONICA (BLUES HARP)

Harmonicas are cupped in the hands, which act like a mouth and allow the reedy sound of the harmonica to be articulated like a wah-wah guitar effect. It is difficult to maintain a constant microphone position, so the player usually holds a dynamic microphone to the back of the harmonica. The Shure "Green Bullet" microphone (520DX) is a favourite among blues players for its gritty tone.

SAXOPHONE

All sorts of saxophones are out there, ranging from deep, curvy baritones to straight sopranos. The B-flat tenor saxophone is probably the most rock'n'roll of the saxophone family. The higher instruments are capable of making sounds at as high as 13 kHz – higher than the human voice – so condenser microphones are still the microphones of choice for capturing all the breathy detail. The microphone should be placed level with the middle of the instrument. For breathier sounds, you can move in closer – but watch out for the clicking sounds of the saxophone keys.

CLARINET AND OBOE

Like saxophones, these are reed instruments, that is, they use reeds to vibrate the column of air within them and produce their sounds. The finger holes change the length of the column and thus the pitch of the note. The most even tone can be obtained by pointing the microphone at the lower finger holes, about one foot away from the instrument.

Pro Tip

When an ideal room is not available, mounting a PZM on a wall can yield good results.

FLUTE

Flutes differ from the other woodwind instruments in that their sound is made by air being blown across a hole. The best balance between the breath and body of the sound can be found by pointing the microphone between the mouthpiece and the player's hand nearest the mouthpiece, at distances of six inches (for a very breathy sound) to six feet (for clearer, solo sounds).

➜ *Special Issues pp. 136–143*

Part One: The Essentials

RECORD A GROUP OF SINGERS

As with most home recording situations, the preferable recording environment for a group of singers is a big room that is not too reflective and that has some furniture to break up the boomy bottom-end response.

When working at home, the living room, lounge or master bedroom is probably your best bet if you want to record the whole group in one go. Remember that it is possible to record parts of the group and add them together later, but this will not sound the same. Always have a printed handout of lyrics for each singer or, even better, a big board at the front, which will prevent paper rustling.

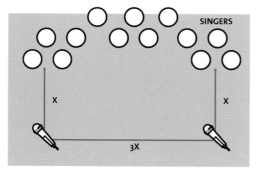

▲ *If you are recording a group of singers, try arranging your microphones and singers like this.*

MICROPHONE PLACEMENT

A stereo pair of condenser microphones set to omni will give the most natural tonal balance. An omni pattern can be unsuitable if you are in an unpleasant acoustic environment, as it will pick up too much of the surroundings. The next-best pattern is cardioid.

Spaced omnis or cardioids should be placed as in the diagram (left). This ratio helps to avoid phase problems between the two microphones. The other two stereo microphone arrays – x-y and MS – are also suited to this kind of recording, and require a central microphone position at a distance of three to eight feet. For a double-size choir, use a stereo microphone array and record the group twice – once on the left of the microphones and once on the right.

HOW DO THEY HEAR THE TRACK?

Monitoring is always tricky for large groups; in order to be in time with the music they will need timing and pitch references. It is best to prepare a track of chord pads and create a very simple rhythm track – perhaps cowbells with a handclap on the two and four – to help them count bars and keep tempo. It is unlikely that you will own enough headphones for every performer, so hire extra sets and a distribution box if necessary. Two people can share one pair by crossing them and using an ear each.

You can also play the backing track to the band on speakers, but try to keep the volume low. If you are going to do this, make sure that the backing track is going to be the same in the final mix – you might not want to hear the cowbell from your guide track banging away in the background of a soulful ballad.

Pro Tip

Ask the singers to empty their pockets and take off their shoes before singing, to eliminate the sounds of jingling coins and keys, and squeaking shoes.

TRICK OF THE TRADE

If you have to use speakers and they have to be loud, use a mono mix of the backing track and wire one of the speakers out of **phase**. (This describes points of a waveform in relation to its complete cycle. Phase problems between two signals can mean loss of volume and incorrect frequency response.) If the speakers are placed equidistant from a single (mono) microphone, most of the backing track should be inaudible on the recording. You cannot make a stereo recording of the choir in this way, but you can record the choir twice and pan the recordings left and right for a stereo effect.

➡ *Special Issues pp. 136–143*

▶ *Your singers may need to hear the backing track during the recording session, so try wiring one of the speakers out of phase so it cannot be heard.*

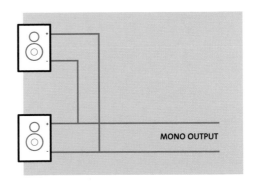

MONO OUTPUT

RECORD A GUITAR

The steel-strung acoustic can be a solo instrument, form the backbone of a band setup or help to provide extra body and rhythm to a mix. It has a warm, low-frequency response in addition to the brightness emanating from the steel strings when played with a plectrum. A condenser microphone set to omni is a good choice for capturing a good tonal balance along with the sound of the room.

Large diaphragm condensers will capture more of the warm, bassy aspect of the sound, while smaller condensers such as the AKG C451 are better at finding the brighter character; for this reason the two are often used simultaneously.

If you are using one microphone, it should be a little above or below the sound hole and slightly off-axis (not pointing directly at the guitar), at a distance of between eight inches and two feet. Experiment to find the right sound for the piece you are working on. A second microphone, usually the smaller condenser, can be positioned near the nut and pointing down the neck towards the centre of the fingerboard. This can help to add brightness and depth to the sound.

This advice applies to 12-string guitars, nylon-strung classical guitars, banjos, mandolins, ukuleles, balalaikas, etc. Any instrument played with the fingertips rather than a plectrum may need closer microphone placement.

◀ *The tone of the acoustic guitar can be captured*
perfectly with carefully positioned microphones.

PLUG IT IN ...

If you are recording an acoustic guitar with a fitted pickup, it will do no harm to record the signal from this as well as from the microphones. It can be added alongside the sound of the microphones, and can also sound great if the microphones are panned to one side and the DI is panned to the other – a good way of making one instrument sound very big.

ELECTRIC GUITARS AND AMPLIFIERS

Getting an electric guitar sound is not difficult, but because it occupies a similar tonal area to the voice it is worth taking special care to make each guitar sound as individual as possible in a mix. That way, each guitar part is doing its bit and the voice can still be heard.

▶ *The Line6 POD, a great amp simulator.*

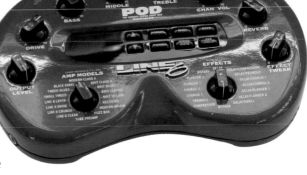

Although large, loud stacks are used in a live situation, they are not necessarily suited to recording in a smaller space. Sometimes a smaller setup or combo can sound as big or even bigger if it is miked up properly. Amp simulator hardware such as the Line6 POD can be a great-sounding and practical option.

WHAT MICROPHONE?

Cardioid dynamic microphones such as the Shure SM57 are usually the first port of call when it comes to miking speaker cabinets. The speakers themselves do not have an extended high-frequency response, so the built-in **presence peak** of most microphones of this type brings out the best in them.

> ## Jargon Buster
>
> **PRESENCE PEAK**
> is an increased output
> between 4 and 8 kHz,
> which adds brightness
> to the sound of
> a microphone.

Part One: The Essentials

WHAT MICROPHONE POSITION?

The microphone should point towards the cone at a distance of two to twelve inches. Very close miking gives you the opportunity to alter the brightness of the sound – the closer the microphone is to the centre of the cone, the brighter it will be. You can experiment by adding a second, identical microphone, with the capsules very close, at between 45 and 90 degrees to the existing microphone. Reversing the phase of the second microphone can be an interesting way of equalizing the sound. It is also worth experimenting with a large diaphragm condenser as well as a cardioid dynamic. This can help to create a richer bottom end, but be careful the condenser does not overload – you may need a pad, or button/switch that turns down the signal. Some microphones and DI boxes have a -20 dB pad option built in.

AMBIENT MIKING

A little space around a guitar sound can work wonders. Some of the classic blues recordings were ambient only, and the character of the room became a huge part of the sound. A single or stereo pair of condenser microphones is ideal for this and can sound great in strange and distant parts of the room. PZMs are also good on walls or wooden floors. If possible, record the close microphone signal and the ambient signals on separate audio tracks so that you can find the right balance in the mix.

RECORD THE DI

Plug the guitar into a DI box and go from the link output of the DI box to the amplifiers. Recording the DI output of the guitar will enable you to re-amp the guitar signal later on, if the sound proves to be wrong. Buffered DI boxes, such as the Alan Smart Deluxe DI system, are designed to help send your guitar signal over long distances, without signal loss, to multiple amplifiers and with multiple DI splits.

◀ *There are lots of tricks you can learn from experts like Jimmy Page, which will affect the sound dramatically.*

Another great advantage of the amplifier's being in another room is that the guitarist can listen to his or her sound on the main monitors in the context of the mix, which makes playing along much more enjoyable. If you are looking for a feedback sound, however, you will need to position the guitar near the amps.

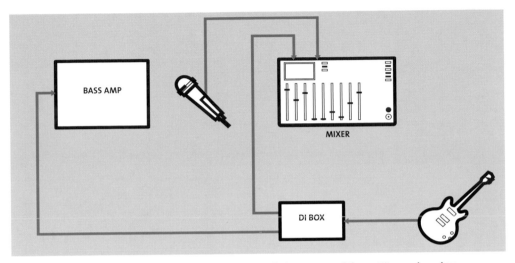

▲ *You can record the DI sound of a bass guitar at the same time as the bass amp sound if you set it up as shown here.*

Bass guitars are usually recorded by miking a cabinet (usually with a dynamic microphone, such as the EV RE20 or AKG D112, or a large diaphragm condenser) and mixing the signal with one from a DI box. It is good to record these on separate tracks.

Amp simulator plug-ins, such as IK Multimedia's AmpliTube or Alien Connections' ReValver, enable you to plug a guitar straight into an audio interface and record the direct signal while monitoring through a virtual guitar amp and FX setup. Latency may be a problem and will vary according to your processor, but this still can be a great-sounding, flexible system.

➡ *Special Issues pp. 136–143*

▲ *The IK Multimedia AmpliTube.*

DJ YOUR OWN MUSIC

The boundaries of traditional DJing and other forms of live music presentation are becoming increasingly blurred; it is not uncommon these days to find decks, live playing and computer editing all happening in and around the booth. An abundance of products and software has been tailor-made for you to do this the way you want.

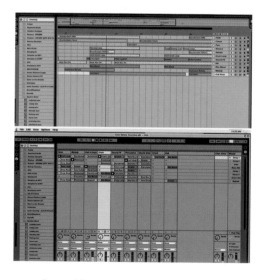

◀ *Here are the two main pages from the Ableton Live performance sequencer program. All editing and effects work can be done "live" while the loops and audio are playing, without affecting the smooth playback of the audio.*

BACK TO BASICS – THE DUBPLATE

If you want to play your tune on a turntable you have to press vinyl, or make a **dubplate**. The word dubplate conjures up images of fat bass speakers seen through the smoky haze of an old reggae sound system; indeed, in 1960s Jamaica, this was a way in which new and exclusive music could be included in a set the day it had been mixed. Access to the hot tunes guaranteed a good reputation for the DJs and systems themselves, as well as promoted the artists and producers and created a pre-release demand for the product.

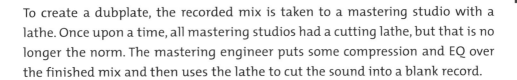

To create a dubplate, the recorded mix is taken to a mastering studio with a lathe. Once upon a time, all mastering studios had a cutting lathe, but that is no longer the norm. The mastering engineer puts some compression and EQ over the finished mix and then uses the lathe to cut the sound into a blank record.

IT IS ALL ABOUT THE GROOVE

The cutting engineer really earns his money here – there is a science to getting the best sound from a record. The wider apart the grooves are, the more bass and volume is available. For example, on a 12-inch record, an eight-minute track would let you have the most volume and bass, and because the grooves are deep and wide the needle will not jump out during back-cueing or scratching.

The cost for pressing a dubplate is well within price band B (see p. 11), but it will wear out as it is only supposed to be the "positive" from which to make the "negative" to press up the actual records. The resulting records are made from harder-wearing vinyl.

CD MIXERS

This is a very straightforward way of getting your music to the outside world. You can burn a CD straight out of your session, and if the venue has a pair of CD decks you can add this to the set; it is as simple as that! CD decks have become more and more popular – carrying around CDs is certainly easier than carrying around heavy boxes. There is a slight compromise on sound, however; vinyl does sound warmer and chunkier, but with the power and EQ available on modern PA systems this need not be an issue.

▶ A CD mixer, such as this Numark Axis-9, is an acceptable – and much more portable – alternative to traditional decks.

THE MP3

Even more portable than CDs are MP3 files – thousands of tunes on a pocket-sized drive. Again, you can export your music as an MP3 straight out of your session, but you are going to need a computer with the right software or an MP3 player to play it to the outside world. Fortunately, a laptop and audio interface will do the job.

THE SOFTWARE

Using a software-based mixer opens up a whole new world of creativity that vinyl does not allow you, with features like:

- Independent pitch/speed control
- Tracks displayed as waveforms, making it easy to navigate
- Automatic tempo detection, meaning less time beat-mixing and more time thinking about the music
- Up to half and double speed time stretching
- Easy looping facilities and locators
- Onboard FX
- Flexible control options
- Track databases, where all your music is stored and easily recalled
- Full automation of mixes, fades and effects
- Mix export – the ability to save a whole set in different file formats.

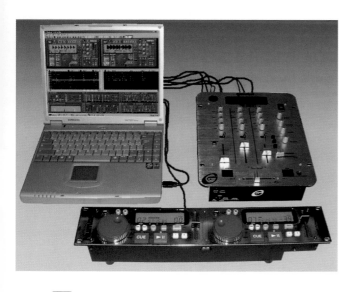

Products to look out for are Traktor, which is a fully comprehensive MP3 mixer that also deals with WAVs, AIFFs and audio CD formats, and MixVibes 5, which has up to 16 simultaneous players available and also comes in different versions – at varying expense – from Pro Ex down to Free.

◀ *This laptop is connected to a DJ mixer and CD-style controllers, enabling MP3 audio files to be mixed like vinyl in a live situation.*

HYBRID AUDIO AND SYNTHESIS SOFTWARE

It is possible to keep your music in its component parts and do the mix on the spot. Propellerhead's Reason is a self-contained MIDI studio incorporating soft synthesizers, samplers, drum machines and effects, as well as a sequencer. Reason offers you a virtual mixer with assignable controllers, so you can decide which sounds to pre-organize and which sounds to play around with over the top.

ABLETON LIVE

This program brings together all the facilities we have looked at and creates a performance-based track and loop organizer, designed to let you do things on the fly without having to worry about file formats, sample rates and bit depths.

The idea is that when you drag and drop loops, FX plug-ins or whole mixes into the performance area, they will seamlessly be converted to the right tempo and there will not be a break in the sound. With a multiple output audio interface you can even set up separate private listening outputs, so you can audition material prior to its inclusion in the mix.

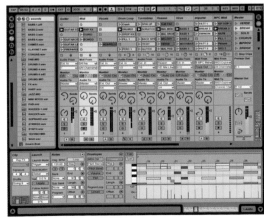

▶ *Ableton Live 6 began life as a loop organizer geared to live performance, but has become an increasingly popular studio tool that rivals some long-established audio applications.*

➡ **Getting Your Music Out There**
pp. 369–371

MAKE A DANCE TRACK

When you make dance music, it is safe to say that you would judge your mission a success if you wandered into a hip club of your choice, heard a superstar DJ dropping your tune at the high point of the night and saw everyone dancing to it.

In order for this to happen, you need to realize that the record you are making is essentially a tool for a DJ. If the tune is going to be played, it has to be unique enough to be recognizable, yet genre specific enough to be included in a set.

◀ *If you want your record played by top DJs like Judge Jules, you need to ask yourself some questions. Who are you aiming your track at? Where do you envision it being played?*

KNOW YOUR GENRE

When you make your tune, it is a good idea to visualize it being played by the DJs you hope will love it. This will keep you focused and inspired. Keep it simple and true to the genre you are working for, and do not experiment to such an extent that the energy or focus of the track is lost.

Whether you are into ambient, drum and bass, UK garage, R&B, gabba, hardcore, house or techno, there will be certain rules to follow and tempos that keep you within the genre. Stay inspired and go clubbing as often as you can to keep up with new sounds and influences. If you are a DJ yourself, you should already know where to look for the new stuff.

WHAT DO I NEED?

- A sequencer to program and record your parts. Logic Audio, Cubase, Digital Performer, and Pro Tools are just a few examples
- A sampler for recycling sounds and playing drums
- A synthesizer for bass lines, lead lines and pads
- Filters and FX for warping things out, and compression for toughening things up
- A pile of CDs and records for source material.

All these things exist as software or hardware products. A well-equipped hardware setup can be more flexible, and analogue hardware can sound more punchy and raw, but some great records have been made entirely in the digital domain.

ESSENTIAL RAW MATERIALS

Apart from the spooky world of ambient DJs, it is fair to say that, generally, the most important elements of a dance record are:

- The groove and drum beat. It has to be tight and solid, and must make you want to dance.
- A bass line that complements the drums and gets you into the groove.
- A vocal hook. This does not have to happen frequently, maybe just at key points in the tune.
- An instrumental hook. This does not have to be an annoying lead line; it can be as subtle as two chords that change in an interesting way, or a sound that enhances the bass line.

EQ AND COMPRESSION

When it comes to the beat, keep it simple and make it loop properly. If it is a programmed beat, check your **quantize** parameters and try some swing settings to help create the right feel. Bass drums have to be strong, but try filtering out some extreme sub-bass frequencies (anything up to 45 Hz) before equalizing low frequencies in. This might help to make it tougher and make the speakers move the air in a punchier way. You could also try routing all of the drum elements to one pair of channels and using some compression followed by equalizing over everything. There are no rules – just play around until it sounds good and try to go easy on the sub-bass.

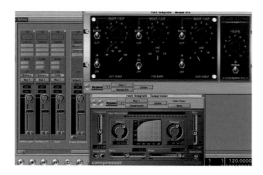

◄ *Route the drum elements of your track to one pair of channels.*

The bass line should be in-your-face, like the bass drum, but this does not have to mean adding loads of bottom end EQ. Try taking out some low frequencies and then adding this to your equalized and compressed drum group. Turn it up and gradually add bottom end back in, making sure that the bass drum does not start to sound weedy. Keep checking your mix against records you like, to help achieve a good sonic match.

There are also some excellent virtual instruments, such as Spectrasonics' Stylus or IK Multimedia's SampleTank, which are self-contained sample libraries and players with their own on-board FX, and are capable of master quality results.

EFFECTS AND FILTERS

Effects such as echo, chorus, phaser and flanger are generally used over the mid-range musical parts of the mix. Flanging will make simple chord pads sound animated and harmonically rich. Delay will add controlled space and rhythm to percussive musical parts, especially if synchronized to tempo. Reverb can create exciting small ambience "tiled room"-type effects to liven up percussive parts, or huge, stadium-sized effects on "anthemic" commercial dance tunes.

Filters are your sound-sculpting tools. To use them, set a sound looping, put a low-pass filter over it, take the frequency down to 0 Hz and gradually open it up. This results in the familiar sound of a repeating loop gradually growing in intensity. Filters can bring energy to plain and simple sounds, especially if you are using automation.

STRUCTURE

Follow these guidelines to create your dance track:

▲ *The effect of a filter on your track can be startling.*

- **Introduction:** Easy to mix, beginning slowly and growing in intensity.
- **Break:** Have a little breakdown, maybe one of your vocal hooks, and then kick in with a hefty version of the beat.
- **Develop:** Keep the bass line trucking along and getting stronger, establish the main hooks and keep building.
- **Big Break:** Break down dramatically, but keep the rhythm simmering by allowing a bare minimum of rhythmic elements to continue pulsing subtly.
- **Build:** Open up filters over the main hook, spin sounds off into reverb soundscapes and start building back to the beat with an extended drumfill ... then stop for a moment and ...
- **Bring It Back:** Do this with a vengeance, using the full groove, bass line and main hook together.
- **End:** Gradually remove the elements in a way that makes it easy for the DJ to get to the next record.

Pro Tip

Set 16-bar loops of your track going and record yourself bringing things in and out and playing with filters and effects. Sometimes, you can chop up these recordings and edit your track together with them.

➡ *Drum Loops and Grooves pp. 99–101; Software: Sequencers pp. 220–233*

COMBINE DRUM SAMPLES AND MIDI

Using off-the-shelf drum sounds can sound unnatural and drum machine-like, especially when the patterns are quantized. Quantizing MIDI events will adjust the position of their start and/or end points.

The start points could be made to land exactly on every crotchet (quarter note), quaver (eighth note) or semi-quaver (16th note) of the bar, putting the events perfectly in time with the selected grid. To make the drums and percussion sound more human, use sampled sounds with a realistic sense of hard and soft playing.

SAMPLERS

Whether you are using the hardware or the software version, the sampler is the tool to use for reproducing sounds of the real world. Software samplers are usually cheaper and are also more convenient, since their libraries of sounds live on your computer and no extra audio or MIDI connections need to be made.

A software sampler such as Native Instruments' Battery is designed for single-hit sounds and has 10 velocity layers for each virtual pad. This amount of expression, plus the basic library of sounds included, makes it possible to create very realistic sounding drum and percussion parts. When creating drum sounds, it is very important for you to understand the way in which a drummer plays his instrument. If you know any drummers, ask them to show you how it is done; programming with this in mind will improve your results no end.

Many sample libraries come in multiple formats and with **groove control**. This means that any of the grooves you like can be loaded up in slices with

▶ You can use Native Instruments Battery to create realistic sounding percussion and drum parts.

corresponding MIDI files, for instant manipulation. The quality of these libraries is constantly improving, making it possible to create natural-sounding drum and percussion parts entirely within a software environment.

LOOPS

The drum loop has been part of pop music for the last 20 years and is a great way to give programmed music a human feel. Using a loop as the backbone of your song and then playing MIDI parts in, leaving them un-quantized, will give you the loosest and most natural-sounding result.

Sometimes, loops can have the perfect sound but not quite the right rhythmic feel. Software like ReCycle! can help with this by analyzing the loop and slicing it up wherever there is a noticeable hit. A MIDI file will also be generated that shows where the original position of each hit was. This information can be taken to different software in different forms for playback.

▶ ReCycle! will slice up your loop, enabling you to use slices of it in different software.

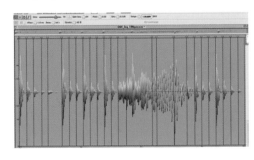

As a Rex file, for example, the slices can be dropped into Reason's Dr.Rex player, or dropped straight into the main arrange page of a Rex-enabled sequencer. Because the loop is sliced and played as individual MIDI sounds, the global tempo of the song can be changed and the loop will change with it. The MIDI positions of each hit can be changed too, which means that the loop can effectively be quantized or rearranged to suit your needs.

➡ *MIDI pp. 252–267*

PROFILES

STEVE LILLYWHITE

Getting his start in the business at the tender age of 17, British-born Steve Lillywhite eventually landed the job of house producer at Island Records, and by the mid-1980s had accumulated scores of major credits including the first three offerings from a young U2 (*Boy*, *October* and *War*). After years of settling for office work (as managing director of Mercury Records in London), in the 1990s Lillywhite began hanging mics once more, capping his studio comeback with a triumphant reunion with U2, which netted him consecutive Grammy awards including 2006's Producer of the Year for *How To Dismantle An Atomic Bomb*.

Lillywhite – who counts iZ Technology's Radar V Classic 48-track system (as well as all things analogue) among his favourite studio tools – is a firm believer in the intangible element that a good producer brings to the session. "What a producer should be able to give to a project is something you can't necessarily define," Lillywhite once told *Billboard* magazine, "you want to notice a production, but in a way have it not be noticed. You want to bring out exactly the best of what an act has to offer, and just that. And for me, with a well-produced record, the first thing you say isn't, 'wow, that's a well-produced record.' You say, 'that's a great record,' and you only discover the production – maybe – after a few listens."

DANIEL LANOIS

Canadian Daniel Lanois got an early start in recording running his own makeshift home studio in Ontario; like his colleague Steve Lillywhite, during the 1980s Lanois, a disciple of Brian Eno, used his sonic know-how to good advantage behind U2, for whom he cut *The Unforgettable Fire* and *The Joshua Tree* (as well as 2000's tour de  force *All That You Can't Leave Behind*). Lanois would spend the 1990s in the company of greats like Bob Dylan, The Neville Brothers and Emmylou Harris, working chiefly out of his stately Kingsway Studio located in New Orleans' French Quarter.

A proponent of Sennheiser mics and Neve pre-amps, Lanois has been known to get the job done using much simpler equipment; on a number of U2 sessions, for instance, Lanois cut Bono's keeper vocal tracks with a Shure Beta 58 hand-held dynamic mic, recorded right in the control room using monitors for playback instead of headphones in order to achieve a stage-like vibe.

JON BRION

Connecticut-bred producer, composer and multi-instrumentalist Jon Brion sprung into the musical mainstream during the 1990s, working with everyone from Jakob Dylan's Wallflowers to songwriter (and ex-girlfriend) Aimee Mann, for whom he produced, arranged and co-wrote 1996's stunning *I'm With Stupid*. While writing film scores (*I ♥ Huckabees*, *The Break-Up*) and working with additional clients like Tom Petty and Dave Navarro, Brion found the time to install an Ampex tape machine and various other pieces of gear into his Los Angeles home studio (where he laid the foundation for his lone solo outing, *Meaningless*). In 2006 Brion found an unlikely ally in hip-hopper Kanye

West, who enlisted Brion – a man with nary a rap track to his name – as co-producer and creative muse for West's *Late Registration* album. So successful was their collaboration that Brion was back in the control room for West's follow-up project, *Graduation*.

Brion, a stickler for organic sounds who'd rather plug in to an old amp than plug in to a plug-in, remains an ardent disciple of classical recording tools and techniques. "The thing about tube mikes is that if you play quietly, they do the work for you," says Brion. "They make everything sound larger than life."

LIAM WATSON

Back in the early 1990s when everyone was tossing out old tapes in favor of new ADATs, Liam Watson aspired to make records like his mentors from the 1960s, and came to the conclusion that simply aping the sounds on modern equipment wouldn't cut it. Instead, he went out and found an affordable eight-track tape machine, some inexpensive microphones and a few other gadgets, and before long was cutting records in the London facility he'd dubbed Toerag Studios. Over the years Watson would acquire new pieces of old gear bit by bit, including a Studer 1-inch 8-track recorder and a 1956 EMI REDD 17 console originally used at Abbey Road studios, along with a steady stream of clients. On the job, Watson is even known to don a white smock reminiscent of the old EMI engineer's attire. But it's not all about looks: in 2003, the thoroughly un-modern White Stripes entered Toerag and emerged 10 days later with *Elephant*, an album that

continues to influence the world's minimalist minions and gain analogue converts. Today, Watson – whose credit list also includes names like R&B ace James Hunter and garage rockers The Kills – still believes that eight tracks is more than enough for anyone.

BRIAN ENO

Beginning his music career as the odd-looking keyboard player in glam art-rockers Roxy Music, Eno showed his taste for experimentation early on, and 30 years later his name is synonymous with avant-garde production techniques. He has worked

extensively with David Bowie and U2 and has a reputation for keeping an overview of the whole creative process.

One of Eno's claims to fame is that he is one of the few people to master the art of programming Yamaha's DX7 FM synthesizer. Now he uses Native Instruments' FM7 software synthesizer instead. Although acknowledging the opportunities offered by computers, Eno remains wary of making music that is too digitally sanitized and lacking in expression: "I tend to quantize things like everyone, it makes them sound better ... initially. In the long run it makes them sound more boring, I have come to realize."

His "Oblique Strategies" cards contain many suggestions and comments and can be consulted like the I-Ching at times of musical confusion or when new ideas are needed.

DAVID BOWIE

Few artists have maintained the long career and credibility of the "Chameleon of Pop", David Bowie. His experimentation with pop, together with his cultural knowledge and love of art, have given us some of music's most enduring images.

Bowie teamed with guitarist Mick Ronson before making *Hunky Dory* for RCA in 1972. Its commercial, glam-rock sound was inspired by wild times in New York with the likes of Andy Warhol and Lou Reed, for whom Bowie would later produce the seminal *Transformer*. *The Rise And Fall Of Ziggy Stardust And The Spiders From Mars*, *Aladdin Sane*, *Diamond Dogs*, *Low* and *Scary Monsters* were all to follow, and before the first phase of his career had ended he had firmly established himself at the forefront of technological experimentation.

Bowie had also made a good friend in collaborator Brian Eno, with whom he worked on the album *Low*, a brilliant example of bending technology to create organic sounds. The distinctive soundscapes were made by layering lines from an EMS AKS "briefcase" analogue synthesizer. Bowie's die-hard fans would probably say that the earlier albums, made on analogue tape, sound warmer and more lifelike than the more recent digital recordings. Judge for yourself.

PETER GABRIEL

In the late 1970s the British progressive rock band Genesis, was led by the often flamboyantly dressed front man, Peter Gabriel. As he developed his groundbreaking video-driven solo career, Peter and his team created elaborate recording setups at the legendary Real World studios in the south of England. Gabriel's production technique often involves dozens of different artists working in different places at different times. Gabriel's crew, particularly his right-hand man Richard Chappel, pioneered procedures for archiving musical data and distributing it to collaborators.

Real World houses state-of-the-art gear such as Sony's Oxford digital console. The music begins with Gabriel at his keyboard, often a Kurzweil K2600, with his microphone, usually a Sony C800 valve microphone or a humble Shure SM58 dynamic. The material will often get crunched with old guitar stomp boxes and then recorded into Logic Audio, before ending up in Pro Tools or on analogue tape.

GARY NUMAN

Gary Numan burst on to the British pop scene in the late 1970s with the semi-industrial, super-synthesizer sound of "Are 'Friends' Electric?". The songs used synthesizers instead of guitars to play big, fat riffs, and sounded as if they were created by huge analogue synthesizer patches, even though the man himself is not a huge analogue fan: "I use whatever I think sounds best. I like digital; I think they've helped create the most amazing sound and textures. People should care less about the type of synthesis they use and worry more about the quality of sound they're getting out of whatever equipment they're using."

The heaviness of Numan's riffs has inspired bands like Nine Inch Nails, Foo Fighters and Marilyn Manson to adapt and recycle his material, and samples of his work have anchored tracks by Sugababes and Basement Jaxx.

Numan's early albums *Replicas* and *Tubeway Army* were all recorded on 16-track analogue tape machines, and Numan remains convinced that technology in its own right does not make creating music any easier: "You can still end up with as many parts played on a four-track system as you can on one with a hundred and twenty-eight. It's the level of control over them which is different."

NITIN SAWHNEY

With multiple albums and in hot demand for soundtrack composition duties, classically trained musician Nitin Sawhney is reaping the rewards of putting on fantastic live shows over the years for festivalgoers around the world.

Initially compelled to use only live ingredients for his music, Nitin was soon drawn into the world of music technology when he realized that it was simply too expensive and impractical to use the drummers and orchestras that he heard in his head. Now he relies, at least during the early stages of his work, on the ESX24 soft sampler and the sound library he has built up over the years.

His initial naivety has given way to a wholehearted embracing of current music technology. "I thought you could record something on one tape deck ... stick a mike in front of the speakers, add another instrument on top ... I just couldn't work out why it sounded so awful ... Over the years I've realized just how important mic placement really is." He uses an Akai MPC4000 and Apple Logic Pro's EXS24 sampler, as well as Propellerhead ReCycle! for creating group quantize templates.

WILLIAM ORBIT

William Orbit had been at the cutting edge of the ambient underground for years before crashing into the mainstream with the huge-selling *Ray of Light* album, which he wrote and produced with Madonna. His early pieces were highly influential on today's electronic artists and he has remixed anybody who is anyone, with a distinctive sound that owes a lot to his collection of vintage analogue synthesizers.

His two oldest keyboards are the Korg MS20, a two-oscillator and two-filter, semi-modular mono synthesizer with an upright control surface, and a Roland Juno-106, a classic analogue polyphonic synthesizer with a legendary warm and versatile sound. Orbit also uses the Yamaha DX7, Roland JD800 and JP8000, and Novation Bass Station.

Of sequencing, Orbit says: "Often I won't quantize at all. I do believe that you can make something un-listenable by quantizing too much."

Orbit is a great inspiration to those with no formal music training: "I don't consider myself a keyboardist at all," he says. "I'm a two-fingered virtuoso. Wax pencils play a large part in my keyboard playing, and I use them to label what I'm doing – what samples are assigned to what key..."

DR DRE

From South Central Los Angeles, California, the rap group N.W.A., featured Dr Dre, Ice Cube and Eazy E. The group brought the reality of gang culture to the rest of the world with all the subtlety of a bullet in the head. Dre is now recognized as one of the most influential producers in the industry, taking the genre through the glitz and glamour, through "gangsta" and almost back to its socially relevant, culturally expressive roots.

Dre is a diehard analogue fan who has preferred SSL (Solid State Logic) mixing consoles and Studer two-inch tape machines along with the Sony C800G microphone, Neve 1073 preamp and dbx160SL compressor for vocals. For backing tracks Dre has used the Korg Triton and Akai MPC3000 sampler, Clavia Nord Lead and a Korg MS2000 synths, and vintage keyboards from Rhodes, Wurlitzer, Moog and Roland.

In the studio, Dre is a perfectionist: "I direct well. I'm a person that will spend three hours working on one line of a song to get it correct." Collaborations with artists such as Eminem keep Dre right at the forefront of rap production, and a list of stars including Snoop Dogg and Warren G. owe much to his magic touch.

DANNY ELFMAN

One of the most outstanding television theme songs ever is the one for the show that brings us that most dysfunctional of all families: The Simpsons. Rather than concoct a "comedy" arrangement, Danny Elfman composed a piece that had more in common with a theatrical overture, which, when paired with the animation, seemed to capture the thrills, spills and drama of daily life in an ordinary family.

In the 1980s, vocalist-guitarist Elfman fronted the band Oingo Boingo and recorded his first film soundtrack. It was also during the 1980s that Elfman met director Tim Burton and started writing the scores for his films; *Beetlejuice* and *The Nightmare Before Christmas* are both fine Elfman soundtracks, as is *Batman*, for which he won a Grammy.

The staple pieces of gear in the Elfman rig are E-mu samplers and Macintosh computers running Mark of the Unicorn's Digital Performer sequencing software. He has two duplicate Pro Tools systems, one at home and one on the move. This is because much of the "demo" percussion and synthesizer parts by Elfman himself will end up on the final soundtrack.

INTRODUCTION
PART TWO

One of the prime movers in the democratization of music production is the fact that there is something out there for everyone looking to create their own tunes. Whether you are a seasoned expert or a dabbler simply looking to put together a quick soundtrack for your latest home video, countless solutions are on offer for every level of ability.

So far in the *Illustrated Home Recording Handbook* we have looked at the basics of music technology. In Part Two: Resources, References and Technical Stuff, we go deeper into the principles and technologies introduced in Part One. From hereon in you will find a wealth of in-depth guides to the most important elements of your home studio: recording software and hardware, synthesizers, samplers, effects, and concepts such as MIDI and music notation.

Perhaps the most important decision to be faced when setting up a home studio today is whether to centre operations around a computer running a range of music software or a standalone hard-disk recorder.

With the staggering power of today's Macs and PCs, it might seem like madness to invest in anything as seemingly limited as a proprietary hardware recording system, but for many musicians, the simplicity of operation and immediacy offered by such machines is tempting. No matter how stable Windows and Mac OS may be, computers inevitably require a certain level of constant system maintenance – a problem you won't have with a dedicated hardware recorder or personal digital studio.

It cannot be denied that you will get a lot more bang for your buck with a Mac or PC, but since the idea here is simply to make music, if you do find yourself drawn to the stability and low-maintenance approach of a hardware-based system, do not think you are making a bad decision. It is indeed a computerized world, but the only thing that matters is that your personal music-making process is exactly the way you want it to be.

Once you have digested all the information presented over the following pages, we suggest you keep this book close at hand in the studio for future reference and periodic "mental refreshment". We are about to hit you with a lot of information – more than anyone could be expected to memorize in one go – so think of the *Illustrated Home Recording Handbook* as a manual for your whole studio and refer to it often.

CONTENTS

SOFTWARE
NOTATION SOFTWARE

In this section we take a look at various applications that help you to print out your musical ideas in score form. A wide range of products and prices is available, from the simple (and free!) right up to the professional – with matching price tag.

Producing a score with a computer takes time; you can learn to enter notes moderately quickly with a mouse and computer keyboard or play them in with a **MIDI** keyboard, but it takes time to correct and format the results and to add slurs, dynamics and so on. Once your score is complete, however, it looks great, and printing individual parts from it is considerably quicker than copying by hand.

FREE AND LOW COST

Finale produces a range of applications – NotePad is a freely downloadable, simple scorewriter – and Magix produces another entry-level application, Notation 2, which is virtually the score editor from the much higher-priced and thoroughly professional Logic, minus the sequencer.

NOTATION FLUENCY

Using any of these packages requires fluency with notation. In other words, if you cannot already write out your score with pen and paper, then none of these applications is going to help you much. If music notation does not make sense to you, it is unlikely that your scorewriter's output will make sense to a reading musician.

▲ A band arrangement being produced on Logic's score editor.

INTEGRATED WITH SEQUENCERS

Don't forget that most of the major sequencers have score editors; Cubase SL's is relatively limited but Cubase SX and Sonar (Windows) and Logic and Digital Performer (Mac) all sport fairly comprehensive score editors, which can print out scores of a dozen or more staves with a degree of control over formatting. They can also transpose and extract parts, as well as add slurs, accents, coda signs and other devices.

These are ideal for composers and arrangers who need a clear printout – parts for their own band, perhaps – but who are not too fussy about the precise details of the layout. Other lower cost applications include Magic Score (www.musicaleditor.com) (Windows), VirtuosoWorks Protégé (both platforms), and a little father up the scale, MOTU FreeStyle (Mac), and MakeMusic Allegro (both platforms).

DEDICATED PROFESSIONAL APPLICATIONS

Here the main contenders are Sibelius and MakeMusic Finale. They come with a hefty price tag, although educational discounts may be available to students and teachers. While they will play back your scores, these are not sequencers, so do not consider them if that is what you really need. They are essentially graphics programs, with a high degree of

▲ Finale will help you present your score in a highly professional-looking way.

flexibility when it comes to the presentation of your music on paper.

Predominantly these programs would suit composers of classical music or film music that uses a large orchestra – situations where all the details of interpretation must be on the paper. They are often the applications of choice for engravers who prepare immaculate scores for commercial or serious publication.

▲ Finale has many features that allow you to include a high level of detail in your score.

GUITAR TAB

Those who are more fluent with guitar tab than staves are not neglected either; Logic, Sonar and Cubase SX all have tab editors. Sibelius G7 and eMedia Guitar are dedicated guitar tab applications With advanced features. Shareware tab generators are also available.

➡ **How to Read Music pp. 364–368;** **Internet Sites pp. 376–378**

SOFTWARE SEQUENCERS

REASON

Propellerhead Software's Reason is a software studio as opposed to a traditional sequencer such as Cubase, SONAR and Logic. It is essentially a self-contained musical environment in the form of a virtual rack well stocked with mixers, synthesizers, samplers and effects – an emulation of the sort of hardware collection most producers aspired to before software synthesizers came along.

Reason contains its own sequencer, which makes all the equipment work together, though it will not record audio or control external pieces of hardware via MIDI, nor can you add **VST** or **DirectX** plug-ins. Reason

▲ *The ReDrum module, NN-XT sampler and part of the sequencer window.*

3.0 introduced the Combinator, a software device that allows you to build elaborate chains of Reason units and save as them as patches. A new sound bank added huge quantities of instruments, sounds, and patches to Reason's substantial library. MClass is a new mastering suite with four separate pro level mastering units.

INSTRUMENTS AND EFFECTS

A choice of high-quality Reason-only instruments and effects may be installed into the rack:

- **Subtractor:** An emulation of a very flexible analogue synthesizer.
- **Malström:** A synthesizer that uses inbuilt samples, though the results are definitely synth-like.
- **NN-19:** A straightforward sampler.
- **NN-XT:** More complex, but both are capable of playing multiple stereo samples; only NN-XT can layer samples.
- **ReDrum:** A sample-based 10-channel drum machine.
- **Dr.Rex:** A loop player.

In addition to this, a host of proprietary audio effects can be utilized (**reverb**, **delay**, **compression**, etc.), ranging from basic to extremely sophisticated.

You can load up as many instances of each device as your computer can handle.

If you need 15 stereo samplers running through four different reverbs, you can have them, provided your computer's CPU is up to the job. Reason's onscreen rack can be flipped round to reveal virtual cables connecting inputs to outputs and so on. By dragging and dropping virtual jack plugs on the various connection points, you can create massively complex signal routings with ease. You can enter notes into Reason's sequencer either by playing your MIDI keyboard or by clicking them in with the mouse.

GETTING TO GRIPS WITH IT

Many people find that fluency with Reason comes fairly easily and a new tune is soon up and running. If you want to make a purely instrumental piece, it can all be done with Reason.

On the other hand, Reason can be used for sketching out a basic arrangement for a song, which can later be refined and added to. This can be done in two ways: first, it is very easy to export audio files from Reason, either as short phrases or whole tracks, which can then be imported into the sequencer of your choice in order to add vocals, guitars, etc. Then again, Reason is a ReWire-capable application, which means that it can be easily synchronized to other pieces of ReWire-enabled software, such as all three sequencers mentioned above.

An advantage of the exporting audio

method is that replaying several audio tracks places a light load on your computer compared with running two major applications side by side.

▲ *The Mixer, two effects units and a Subtractor synthesizer.*

An advantage of ReWire is that Reason's output has not been fixed (by rendering it as audio), so you retain more flexibility, for example, to vary the tempo in the host sequencer.

➡ *What Is a Sequencer? pp. 44–47; What Is a Software Studio? pp. 52–55*

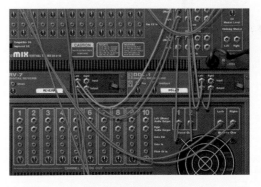

▲ *Some of the "cabling" possibilities behind the rack.*

Part Two: Reference

CUBASE SL/SX

Steinberg's Cubase has long been one of the most popular sequencers. Like Reason, it is cross-platform and boasts a large base of PC and Mac users.

In addition to the entry-level Cubase LE, the program comes in more expensive and powerful versions: : Cubase SL and Cubase SX. All three versions are available in various bundled packages with hardware (sometimes from other manufacturers), or with different combinations of features or plug-ins.

Cubase is a MIDI and audio sequencer and has the same general range of functionality as the other major DAW applications. In other words, it provides the user with the means to record, edit, play back and mix both MIDI tracks and audio recordings. Cubase 4 added four

new software synths with over 1000 sounds, including sounds from the Motif synth by Yamaha, which bought Steinberg in 2005. Cubase 4 also added 34 new VST 3 plug-ins (surround capable with drag and drop support).

The main display, the Project window, still harks back to the days of multitrack tape recording; each recorded phrase, MIDI or audio, is represented as a strip running from left to right, one above the other like tracks on a tape or parts in a score. These elements may easily be moved around, looped, duplicated, transposed, deleted, reinstated and generally tinkered with.

▲ *A score in Cubase.*

Steinberg was the original developer of the **VST** (Virtual Studio Technology, see p. 248) standard so, as you might expect, it is fully implemented in their products. This means that a variety of plug-in effects may be applied to your audio recordings, either as you record them or as you mixdown.

▲ *Cubase's Project window.*

As VST is an open standard, many other companies can supply plug-in effects at a variety of prices from totally free to the very expensive. Cubase also comes with many other essential effects, including delay, chorus/flanging, and compression. There are also several useful MIDI plug-ins, such as an arpeggiator.

Cubase also comes with many other essential effects, including delay, **chorus/flanging**, and compression. There are also several useful MIDI plug-ins, such as an arpeggiator.

THE EXTRAS

The VST standard also allows for the inclusion of software instruments as well as effects, played via MIDI but residing inside the host program – Cubase in this case. Cubase 4 added the VST3 instruments HALion One (sample playback), Prologue (virtual analog synth), Spector (a spectrum-filter synth) and Mystic (modeling and comb-filter synth). Cubase includes a drum editor for creating basic rhythms and works extremely well with VST-based rhythm applications like Steinberg's groove Agent 3.

These instruments can easily be replaced or supplemented as your taste and pocket dictate. All effects available to your audio tracks may also be used to enhance the sounds of VST instruments.

BE PATIENT

Learning to use any major piece of software with fluency takes time and patience. Those who have used one of the major sequencers for years may be tempted to forget all the earlier puzzlements and frustrations, so that when they look at a rival application, it appears unfriendly and counter-intuitive and they will probably advise you that "their" product is better and easier to learn.

The truth is that all the major sequencers (and quite a few minor ones) can do much the same job. Most are available in demo versions, so you can try them out and make up your own mind which one suits you best before you buy.

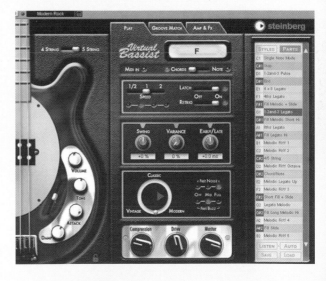

▲ *Steinberg's Virtual Bassist VST instrument.*

LOGIC PRO

Apple's Logic Pro, in its various guises, has been synonymous with professional sequencing since it was first developed by eMagic. Logic is a modern, powerful and fully featured MIDI and Audio production package.

Logic has an almost unlimited amount of flexibility and power, which has also led to its being thought of as overly complicated. Despite the initial learning curve, thousands of music producers use Logic to record artists from Ron Isley to Rammstein, and for composing everything from classical movie scores to the Eminem albums.

Logic Pro 7 offered new features like distributed audio processing, network operation, and compatibility with AppleLoops. The program included three new instruments: Sculpture (a modeling

▲ *Logic Pro 7 offers powerful and flexible tools for music production.*

synth); Ultrabeat (a modern drum machine); EFM1 (an FM-style synth). There were also nine new effects plug-ins, including Guitar Amp Pro, Linear and Match EQs, and Pitch Correction. Apple also listed more than 100 other new enhancements.

The basic features of Logic are familiar to users of most sequencing packages. You can record both audio and MIDI data, edit them, mix them together and print a file of the output. Logic Platinum offers up to 192 tracks of 24-bit/192-kHz sample rate audio tracks, and a virtually unlimited number of MIDI tracks. Logic also has a special kind of track, the Audio Instrument track, designed especially for software synthesizers In Logic, an Audio Instrument is a software synthesizer that outputs audio based on MIDI data that you perform or program.

In addition, Logic is compatible with Audio Units. An Audio Unit is Apple Computer's native plug-in format for OS X audio effects and synthesizers. Any effect or synthesizer available as an Audio Unit can be directly integrated into Logic.

QUALITY EDITING

Logic includes a professional-quality sample editor for the precise editing of audio data, and a number of different editors for editing MIDI data. Depending on your needs and preferences, you can edit your MIDI graphically in the Matrix editor, as text in the Event List, as musical notation in the Score Editor, or in the unique Hyper Editor. Finally, you can also graphically split, copy, move, edit and rearrange all your audio and MIDI material in the aptly named Arrange window.

OTHER FUNCTIONS

This is not all. Logic includes a number of unique functions, editors and features that you cannot find in any other package. First of all, perhaps the most flexible feature of Logic is its Environment window (see the picture to the right). In the Environment, you can literally build entire virtual studios filled with representations of hardware instruments and MIDI effects that you could not dream of with other applications.

The Hyper Editor in Logic is a unique drum editor/MIDI event editor that allows you to step program and edit everything from drum and synthesizer patterns to pitch bends and MIDI Controller events. Logic's Project Manager does far more than manage only Logic projects – but it serves as a multimedia database for all the media on all of your hard drives and even over a network.

Logic features many other powerful functions, such as Freeze Tracks, amazingly powerful and flexible screenset and key command integration, MIDI learn

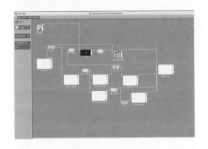

▲ *No other application offers anything like Logic's Environment, in which you can cable objects together to create your own instruments, effects, editors, mixers – you name it!*

functionality for Logic's powerful Automation, control-surface integration and much more.

If you are a Mac user, Logic is definitely worth a serious look. In Logic's Environment you are presented with icons representing MIDI functions, processes and instruments. You can cable them together to design your own unique effects, transformations and instruments.

➡ *VST Plug-ins pp. 234–238;*
Audio Units Plug-ins pp. 244–245

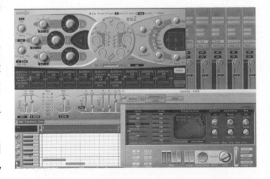

▲ *In addition to its powerful audio and MIDI features, Logic Pro includes some of the best software instruments available.*

SONAR

When computer music was in its infancy, only a small number of software sequencers was available. With its unwieldy and unfriendly DOS operating system, the PC was seen as a sort of "businessmen-only" affair.

Twelve Tone Systems changed that with a MIDI sequencer entitled Cakewalk. Cakewalk was so successful that the company took the name for itself. By the twenty-first century, the application itself morphed into Sonar, the predominant Windows-only digital audio application.

Needless to say, it was extremely successful. Cakewalk existed through many generations, and through many advances in both computing power and what the customers expected to see in a sequencer. When disk-based audio hit the scene, so did the company's Pro Audio packages.

PROFESSIONAL APPROACH

In 2007 Sonar had reached version 6 and boasted all the features of comparably priced DAW applications, including recently added features like the first 64-bit audio engine, advanced automation enhancements, clip-

editing improvements and full integration of VST plug-ins – finally Sonar no longer needed an external VST to DX adapter (see p. 248 for more on the VST plug-in format).Sonar includes everything you might expect from a professional software recording and sequencing environment. Disk-based audio recording, notation and virtual effects, and instrument plug-ins are all available to the user. Cakewalk has made a few innovative choices in Sonar, including the ability to create and use editable audio and MIDI loops – some are included in the package. This makes arranging tunes easy and enjoyable.

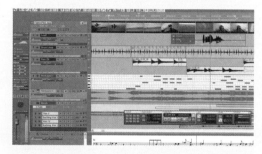

▲ *In SONAR, most of the action takes place on this single page.*

Cakewalk stuck with the PC platform to take complete advantage of Windows. The company maintained a rigid adherence to the DirectX standard (which it was instrumental in implementing), and the use of **WDM** (Windows-driven model) drivers for low-latency audio performance. The latter allowed Sonar users to monitor their input devices in real time. Recent versions of Sonar allowed the use of **ASIO** (audio streaming input output) drivers, as well as VST instruments by using a VST wrapper, which simply makes Sonar VST use plug-ins as if they were DirectX ones. Now VST is supported directly.

THE PLUG-INS

Sonar has included plug-ins that may be worth as much as the asking price of Sonar itself. Previous versions have seen flagship products such as Applied Acoustics Systems' Tassman modular synthesizer and Sonic Timeworks' superb mastering equalizer and compressor included. Later, SpeedSoft's popular Vsampler was included, as well as professional-quality effects from Lexicon and Ultrafunk. Sonar 6 includes Roland's GrooveSynth and the TTS-1 GM 2 General MIDI synth. For effects you get Cakewalk's Sonitus:fx Suite, a bundle of standard effects, and Lexicon's Pantheon reverb, a great font of studio-standard reverb effects.

GOOD FOR BEGINNERS AND PROS

With such a stellar set of tools, it is no wonder that Sonar has risen in popularity. With the ability to integrate hardware and software gear, as well as

its flexible handling of audio recording and editing, Sonar represents an excellent choice. Add to that the fact that like Cubase it comes in a variety of guises (including the Sonar Home Studio incarnations), at just about every conceivable price point, and it is easy to see why Sonar has become the DAW of choice for so many beginners and professionals alike.

➡ *Hardware: Mac Or PC? pp. 332–333*

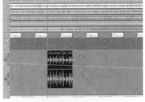

▶ *To create a Groove Clip using SONAR, select the audio file you wish to use, and trim it to the correct size.*

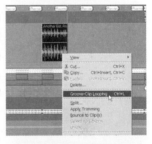

▶ *Next, right-click on the selected audio clip, and select Groove Clip Looping from the menu, or use the key command Ctrl+L.*

▶ *The fact that it is now a Groove Clip is indicated by its rounded corners. It can easily be dragged to the desired length, and will lock to the project's tempo without altering pitch.*

PRO TOOLS

Digidesign's Pro Tools has occupied the top spot in the sequencer market for many years, but until recently its fearsome price tag meant it remained the sole domain of the professional user. The release of Pro Tools LE and the integration of budget hardware from Digidesign and M-Audio (which Digidesign purchased) changed this, and now there is a Pro Tools solution to suit all pockets.

Originally, Pro Tools was designed for use in post-production suites or by people working with sound as a medium. This was in contrast to the other main sequencer programs, which have always had their feet firmly planted on the music-making side of the fence. So, from the outset, Pro

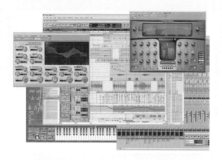

▲ *Pro Tools has evolved from a high-end pro-studio investment dependent upon expensive custom hardware to a standard application available to all home studio owners in three different versions and supporting a wide range of compatible audio interfaces.*

Tools was different from its rivals. First and foremost, its **TDM** (time division multiplexing) technology allowed it to record and play back multiple tracks of audio simultaneously, a trick that took other sequencers a few more years to pull off. Pro Tools' secret was the **DSP** (digital signal processor) hardware that was an integral part of the system; by including computer- expansion boards loaded with DSP chips, a Pro Tools system was, in essence, a music computer mounted inside a desktop computer – and with a multiple-computer price tag to match!

HOST-BASED PROCESSING

Eventually, Digidesign bowed to the inevitable and produced a version of Pro Tools – Pro Tools LE – which uses host-based processing (digital-signal processing that relies on the main computer's CPU for calculations rather than external hardware) to cater to the home and semi-pro user, while continuing to increase the power of DSP-based Pro Tools TDM systems. The LE systems also require a hardware component, but this is little more than an audio interface and does not perform any of the actual processing duties.

In 2007 Pro Tools LE had reached version 7 and added features of newer software rivals while strengthening some of its traditional weaknesses. Pro

Tools now featured instrument tracks, real-time MIDI processing capabilities, support for multi-processor computers, improvements to the RTAS environment (see p. 240), streamlined and better-organized menus, and support for more hardware interfaces and peripherals.

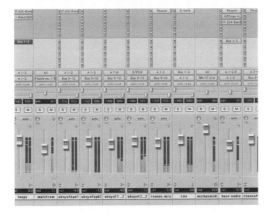

▲ *Pro Tools' Mix window.*

SIMPLE APPROACH

One of Pro Tools' biggest selling points is the simple elegance of its software interface (shared by both TDM and LE versions). Practically every operation within Pro Tools is carried out on one of two screens. The Mix window takes care of all the mixing duties within the session, while the Edit window allows you to work with the audio and MIDI parts, as well with as any mix and effect automation data that has been created.

Like other sequencer packages, Pro Tools can use plug-in effects and instruments to further enhance its capabilities. LE systems can use Audiosuite and **RTAS** (real time audio suite) plug-ins, and DSP-based systems also work with TDM and **HTDM** plug-ins, (HTDM is the latest plug-in format for use with modern Pro Tools TDM systems).

A RANGE TO SUIT ALL BUDGETS

In 2007 Pro Tools LE systems ranged from the basic (say, built around Digidesign's M-Box 3 or M-Audio's Fast Track USB audio interfaces) to Pro Tools HD systems costing tens of thousands of pounds or dollars. In between are full-featured systems that use Pro Tools LE with Digidesign or M-Audio FireWire audio interfaces, interface/control surfaces, and even musical keyboard interfaces. In other words, a Pro Tools for every budget on both Windows and Mac platforms – something inconceivable a few years ago.

➡ *RTAS Plug-ins pp. 240–241; TDM Plug-ins pp. 242–243*

▲ *Pro Tools' Edit window.*

DIGITAL PERFORMER

Like Steinberg's Cubase, Digital Performer began life as a MIDI sequencer with no audio-recording capabilities. Known simply as Performer, it was created by the US company Mark of the Unicorn (MOTU) and became the most widely used Macintosh sequencer in pro recording studios.

▲ *Digital Performer provides an almost unlimited number of features for projects ranging from basic songwriting through to advanced film scoring.*

Adding audio recording features in the 1990s, the renamed Digital Performer maintained its lead among Mac-only audio programs in pro studios, although it faced stiff competition for entry-level users from Cubase and the newly Mac-only Logic Audio, as well as Pro Tools' expanded line of products.

HOST BASED

Digital Performer is a host-based sequencer that can take advantage of Apple's dual processor systems and supports 24-bit/192-kHz audio. MOTU markets a line of external hardware products designed to operate seamlessly but not exclusively with the program, including advanced FireWire and USB audio/MIDI interfaces. Digital Performer also supports other audio hardware

schemes, including TDM (Pro Tools), Direct I/O, ASIO, and the Mac's native (pre-OS X) Sound ManagerMac OS X's Audio Units format.

FAMILIAR APPROACH

Digital Performer (DP) offers the same working options found in the other major audio software packages. A Tracks window displays recorded tracks stacked vertically and creates wave forms on the fly as you record. You can view your MIDI and audio tracks in a single, unified Mixer window. The Soundbites window organizes and manages recorded and imported sound files.

Among other tools, you can configure up to 20 effects inserts per audio channel and 32 stereo busses; and you can automate just about anything, including

▲ *Digital Performer 5 introduced six new instrument plug-ins, including BassLine, PolySynth and NanoSampler.*

effects parameters. The package comes with dozens of real-time DSP effects, including 2-, 4- and 8-band EQ, tube-simulation and distortion effects, three reverbs, two noise gates, two compressors, a synthesizer-style multi-mode filter, and echo and delay effects.

All these effects, as well as scores of others from third-party vendors such as Waves, are coded for the MOTU Audio System (MAS), but many also appear as Audio Units plug-ins. For sample editing, Digital Performer includes a built-in wave-form editor, which provides a pencil tool that allows you to remove clicks, and a loop tool for auto editing of cross-fades. You can make drum loops conform to tempo, add vocal harmony or change the gender of tracks.

In 2006 DP added six new virtual instruments, including: Bass Line, an analog-style bass synth; Nanosampler, a new sample player; and the Model 12 drum module.

MULTIPLE CAPABILITIES

This does not begin to scratch the surface of Digital Performer's capabilities, which also include sample-accurate audio editing, MIDI time stamping, QuickTime movie support for scoring, notation editing, tracks that can be individually zoomed, a choice of four surround panner plug-ins, and on and on.

If Digital Performer has a major flaw, it is that it packs on feature after feature (like some word processors) and always requires a top-shelf computer configuration to handle it smoothly. A feature announced for 2004 is a Beat Detection Engine, which promises to bring ReCycle!-style loop analysis and division to all audio tracks via artificial intelligence code.

An almost unlimited feature set and supporting hardware, as well as a giant base of well-known musicians and producers who have stuck by the program, have ensured Digital Performer's success. To many Mac users who need MIDI as well as audio recording (or who just do not want to learn another complex program), Digital Performer is still the best in town.

➡ *MAS Plug-ins pp. 246–247*

ABLETON LIVE

The Berlin-based Ableton's Live software began as a simple audio manipulation tool for coming up with loops and ideas that could then be transferred to a DAW like Pro Tools or Cubase. As the name implies, it soon became a staple of live performance for electronic musicians worldwide. In recent years the rapid introduction of new versions that increasingly add all the functions of digital sequencer software have turned Live into a full-fledged, competitive DAW.

LOOP-CENTRIC

Live can fulfill all the functions of a Logic, or Pro Tools: audio and MIDI can be recorded, effects applied and bussed, and mixdowns rendered. With Live 6 the application began to take advantage of the multi-core and multi-processing computing power of the new laptops and towers, as well as adding video capabilities for scoring to picture.

What sets Live apart from other DAWs is its live performance applications. You can work in its Arrangement view just like the editing section of any sequencer, but its unique Session view allows you to trigger audio and MIDI "clips" at will, creating

▲ *Ableton Live 6 takes advantage of more powerful computers by adding new features such as video support for scoring to picture.*

arrangements on the fly to record or perform them. One of Live's main specialties is the ability to audition loops played at the project tempo from the software browser, then drag and drop them into either the Session or Arrangement view. There, through Live's proprietary "warp" function, they will play at the project tempo, and can be easily modified to lock into a groove with other loops, as well as with recorded audio or MIDI material. Entire projects can be sped up or slowed down 10 or 20 bpm with minimal artifacts. This makes the software a favourite of DJs, who can easily beat-match their tunes using this powerful function.

REAL TIME

Another thing that makes Live different, and ripe for performance applications, is that all operations can be initiated in real time – you never have to stop playback to record, modify loops, add VST or AU plug-ins, or add and record soft-synths. Users claim that this also works to their advantage by enhancing the creative workflow. Bands, too, are able to augment their sound with triggered Live loops, adjusting the tempo to the players – not vice-versa. They can also extend or shorten solo backing tracks in real time as inspiration strikes (or fails).

EFFECTS INCLUDED

Though Live can host a huge variety of third-party plug-ins, it comes with enough high-quality effects to allow a complete project to be realized using only its own – and therefore stable – plugs. These include an Auto Filter; Filter, Grain, Ping Pong and Simple Delays; Saturator, and Dynamic Tube distortion devices; Chorus, Flanger and Phaser; Reverb; manglers like Erosion, Redux (bit reduction), Vinyl Distortion, Beat Repeat, and Resonators; as well as various compressors and eqs. Live also comes with MIDI plug-ins that generate, chords, arpeggios, random play and other effects, as well as a sampler and drum sampler.

▲ Live can host third-party plug-ins such as Prosoniq's Orange Vocoder for special effects.

CONTROL ISSUES

Almost every function and parameter in Live is MIDI controllable from loop triggering to drum sample tuning. A wealth of controllers is available from companies like M-Audio and Edirol. Live 6 introduced effect and instrument racks that allow advanced MIDI control of multiple parameters on multiple effects or soft synths. Live can also be ReWired into other DAWs like Logic or Sonar, as well as allowing programs like Reason and DrumCore to be ReWired into it.

▲ Almost every function and parameter in Live from loop triggering to drum sample tuning is controllable by MIDI using controllers from companies like M-Audio and Edirol.

EASY OPERATION

Ableton Live has been widely adopted by a host of DJs, electronic and experimental performers in a relatively short time. They appreciate that for all the depth of its feature set, it is still intuitive to operate and extremely flexible, easily adapted to an artist's personal working methods.

➡ *DJ Your Own Music pp. 200–203;*
MIDI pp. 252–267

PLUG-INS

VST

When the first generation of software plug-ins hit the scene, they brought with them a plethora of incompatible formats that forced the would-be user into a platform stranglehold. Some were included in host DAWs and some were available as optional add-ons for one particular sequencer or another, but they were almost never compatible with the competition's host.

Even if they were compatible with more than a single host, they were certainly not platform independent, and drove yet another wedge between the Windows and Mac users. Some even required expensive hardware DSP cards to work. Such issues served to keep the costs high and did little to foster the kind of third-party involvement we see today. Many of those that were there at the beginning still thrive. Israel-based Waves is a good case in point.

VST IS RELEASED

However, the entire musical universe changed when Steinberg unleashed its Virtual Studio Technology (VST) format in 1996. This was a cross-platform, native plug-in system designed to run in Steinberg's own flagship sequencer, Cubase. For the first time ever, it did not matter whether your computer of choice was a Mac or a PC. What is more, no extra hardware was required to gain access to the plug-ins and, more importantly, Steinberg made the code accessible to any developer who wanted to use it, free of charge.

▲ *With Steinberg's VST, you can use virtual effects and instruments from within your host sequencer.*

This radical move resulted in a tidal wave of plug-ins being made available to users of Cubase VST, and ensured its position as "top dog" in the sequencer wars. Furthermore, many budding developers created and released their plug-ins for free. A quick online search reveals a bustling network of VST developers and users.

WIDELY AVAILABLE

It is easy to take for granted the availability of VST plug-ins in today's scene, but when VST first came to the marketplace, the cost of decent effects processing plug-ins was prohibitive, and few people besides the savvy studio professional had access to them. When you add to this the fact that hardware effects devices cost hundreds, if not thousands, of pounds or dollars, the importance of inexpensive or free VST plug-ins for the home recording market becomes self evident.

▲ VST support is now integrated into Cakewalk SONAR 6 and no longer requires an external VST to DX adapter.

VST 2

After such a coup, Steinberg followed with VST 2. Three years after giving the world access to world-class effects processing in a native format, Steinberg released a new version of Cubase, this time with the diminutive Neon plug-in sitting in the VST folder. This signalled yet another huge advance in software music production. There had been software synthesizers before, but they were always stand-alone devices with unwieldy interfaces and slow performance. Integrating such a device

into your sequencer was nearly impossible, while playing one in real-time was even harder. With its super-fast ASIO drivers alongside, VST 2 instruments could not only be played from within Cubase, but would respond with virtually no latency whatsoever. And, as with VST effects, VST instruments (or VSTis) began to come fast and furious, beginning with Steinberg's LM-4 sample-based drum machine plug-in.

VST 3

In 2007 Steinberg rolled out VST3 in Cubase 4. Backward compatible with VST2 plug-ins and instruments, the new platform offered improved performance designed to save processor cycles, multiple dynamic I/Os so that plug-ins automatically reconfigure themselves for different output assignments (for example, from stereo to 5.1), and new routing possibilities such as multiple MIDI inputs at the same time.

▲ Synthesizers are not the only things to take the form of VST instruments. Classic instruments have been reborn as plug-ins as well. LinPlug's daOrgan does a great Hammond B3 imitation.

VST PLUG-INS: EFFECTS AND INSTRUMENTS

Using a VST plug-in could not be simpler. To access a virtual instrument plug-in when using Cubase, you have to simply call up the virtual instrument rack, click on it to assign your plug-in to the slot, and assign a MIDI channel to it. You can record your performance, automate it and even bounce it to audio.

To use an effects plug-in, you can call up the desired plug-in as either an insert or send effect, and the same sort of automation and rendering can be applied as with instruments. One of the greatest benefits of working in this fashion is that, unlike some hardware units, no additional digital-to-analogue conversions are taking place, and consequently no noise is added to the signal.

▲ *LinPlug's Sophistry Ambient Synthesizer is a VST instrument that is based on the company's CronoX3 synth.*

Something you should be aware of is that some of the effects and instrument plug-ins can put a strain on your computer's resources, particularly since they are run alongside your **host program**. Reverberation plug-ins and multiband compressors are particularly heavy CPU consumers, as are many complicated synthesizer plug-ins. As modern computers become faster and faster, developers are designing more sophisticated and processor-hungry plug-ins to take advantage of these increased speeds.

POWERED PROCESSOR

This has been addressed in part by a new breed of **powered processor**. These are often PCI cards that pack a host of DSP power, allocated solely to running the included effects plug-ins. Models such as the UAD-1 from Universal Audio include a host of dedicated plug-ins, ranging from guitar amplifier simulators to high-quality reverb. These effects are inextricably tied to the card and will not work without it but, as such, put no strain whatsoever on your computer.

Because of this, the developers do not need to cut so many performance corners to keep the CPU usage down. The results are effects that are often of a much higher standard than their native equivalents. TC Electronic's PowerCore includes built-in

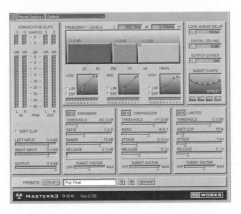

▲ With a dedicated DSP card, such as TC Electronic's PowerCore, you can run advanced plug-ins such as their MasterX3 that demand too much power for most CPUs.

synthesizers and/or samplers alongside the signal processors. The TC PowerCore is available in various versions, with or without plug-ins, and as a PCI card or tabletop or rack-mounted FireWire device.

▲ The PowerCore allows smooth operation of complex third-party and TC plug-ins like the TC Thirty, an emulation of Vox's 1961-vintage AC 30 guitar amplifier.

ACCESSIBLE TO ALL

Still, even without such DSP accelerators, it is now quite possible to create entire

professional-quality productions solely within your computer, complete with synthesis, sampling and signal processing. The impact this has had on both consumer-level and professional music production cannot be overstated.

In the past, musicians might have been restricted to one or two synthesizers and effects devices to create their tunes. Today, they can avail themselves of a wide range of instruments and processors at a mere fraction of the cost. Many people who might otherwise never have been able to afford to experience creating and recording their own tunes are beginning to discover music via this new accessibility.

➡ *Cubase SL/SX pp. 222–223;*

Effects and Processors pp. 306–331

▲ MicroTonic, from Sonic Charge, combines analogue-style drum synthesis and a built-in pattern sequencer for old-school rhythm programming.

DirectX Plug-ins: Effects and Instruments

Steinberg's VST technology may rule the roost when it comes to cross-platform plug-ins, but there are a number of other open standards as well. In the world of Windows-based PCs, the Microsoft DirectX format was almost as widely accepted as VST, at least for effects.

Built on the DirectShow standard, DirectX offers a free and open format with which developers can create and trade plug-ins. As with VST plug-ins, DirectX plug-ins come in a wide variety; these include all the usual reverbs, delays, equalizers, etc. that you might need to perform any audio task at hand.

ADAPTABLE FORMAT

Many Windows-based sequencers and DAWs make use of the DirectX standard alongside VST support, and decent audio editors invariably support the format. Virtually any major commercial plug-in will come in both VST and DirectX guises, but even if they do not have a VST wrapper, such as Cakewalk's VST Adapter

or tonewise's DirectiXer, you can gain access to them from within a DirectX-only environment.

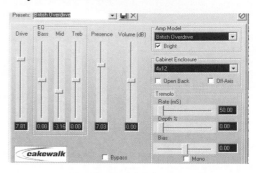

▲ *Always strong supporters of the DirectX format, Cakewalk has a number of DirectX plug-ins in its product range, including Amp Sim, a guitar amplifier simulator.*

INSTALLER REQUIRED

DirectX effects differ from their VST counterparts in that they require an installer to get them into your system, and they alter your registry in the process. This has alienated some users, who prefer VST's foolproof method of simply copying a .DLL file to your plug-in folder. Once written to your registry, some DirectX plug-ins can occasionally be difficult to remove, while others will continue to pop up in your effects plug-ins menu even after they have been uninstalled. To remove them requires a special application made specifically for this purpose. Fortunately, many such applications are free.

With the introduction of Sonar 2, Cakewalk also launched a new type of

DirectX plug-in in the format of the DirectX instrument, or DXi. Cakewalk's adherence to a completely open standard once prevented the company from directly supporting VST technology (which, after all, was owned by a competitor), but Cakewalk's user base was demanding access to the wonderful world of software synthesis and sampling. DXi was a little slow to take off, due partly to the fact that VST 2 seemed to offer a little more flexibility (and because it was there first, thereby gaining more support), but with DXi 2, the advantage vanished.

▲ *Synapse supports DirectX and other formats with its Orion Platinum, a complete virtual studio software application that includes multitrack audio recording, a mixing desk with sub busses and effect returns, as well as powerful sequencers, generators and effects.*

DIRECTX INSTRUMENTS

There are far fewer DirectX instruments than there are VST instruments, although a few of the bigger manufacturers support both (oddly enough, Steinberg's own sampler plug-in HALion comes in a DXi version). Very early on, a British company called FXpansion introduced a popular DirectX-VST wrapper, and this may have slowed developers from tackling DirectX versions of their VST plug-ins.

Cakewalk eventually bought this application when it decided to openly support the VST standard during the development of its Project5 software studio.

Although decidedly fewer DirectX-only plug-ins are on the market, there are some, and just as there are wrappers for running a VST plug-in when using a DirectX host, there are devices that allow you to run DirectX effects in a VST-only host. Vincent Burel Audio's free FFX4 is a good example of such an application.

➡ **SONAR pp. 226–227**

▲ *Though most of the major names support DirectX, some sequencers choose to focus instead on VST plug-ins. Using something like FFX4, you can run DX plug-ins in such hosts.*

RTAS Plug-ins: Effects and Instruments

▲ *PSPaudioware.com's Nitro is a killer filter available in a wide range of plug-in formats, including RTAS.*

Once the domain of high-cost, world-class professional studio owners, Pro Tools was dragged down to earth by the introduction of Pro Tools LE.

This version of the high-flying industry standard boasted many of the same features as its expensive sibling, but without the requirement of costly DSP-based hardware. Pro Tools LE was initially designed to work in a completely native environment, albeit one that began life inextricably linked to the proprietary Audiomedia III card.

Pro Tools' creator, Digidesign, reacted to the modern threat of native DAWs with a string of excellent audio interfaces that by 2007 included the M-Box 2 Family, the 003 family, and the M-Powered family, each with Pro Tools LE in tow. Digidesign was fully aware of the allure associated with the Pro Tools brand and rightly gambled that the home studio user might feel inclined to partake of Pro Tools LE's promise of compatibility with the professional powerhouse. Not to mention the fact that a few of those home users were bound to want to upgrade to the multi-thousand pound version at a later date.

INTRODUCING RTAS

The only problem with this approach was that the DSP hardware required to run the TDM plug-ins that were part of Pro Tools' claim to fame would not be available to the Pro Tools LE user. But Digidesign was hesitant to buy into VST, the only cross-platform plug-in standard at the time. So, in a field overcrowded with plug-in formats, the company offered up another in the form of **RTAS** (Real Time Audio Suite).

This was essentially an upgraded version of the previously available offline plug-in format called simply Audio Suite. This time, however, it was souped-up and ready for real-time prime time. Limited to effects processing, RTAS allowed for direct monitoring and real-time responsiveness.

CROSS-PLATFORM STANDARD

RTAS has many advantages to offer the end user, not least of which is compatibility with the full Pro Tools system, should the user wish to take his or her work to a TDM-equipped professional studio. There is now total parity with recent versions of Pro Tools LE, and RTAS plug-ins are automatically replaced by the TDM equivalents when moved to the full Pro Tools system.

▲ *Another high-quality plug-in from PSP is this emulation of the venerable Lexicon delay unit.*

AVAILABLE PLUG-INS

Support for the RTAS format on PCs has been nowhere near as universal as support for VST, or even for DirectX formats, but as most major plug-in developers have RTAS versions available –Pro Tools users (full version or M-Powered) with PCs have access to the same high-quality plug-ins that Mac users have enjoyed for years with Pro Tools LE.

This list includes the modern classics from Antares, Native Instruments, IK Multimedia, Spectrasonics, and many more. There are even a few freebies to be found, although nowhere near as many

as proliferate on the VST landscape. Still, you get the most commonly used for free whenever you get into any Pro Tools system.

➡ *Pro Tools pp. 228–229*

▲ *Native Instruments' Vokator is available as an RTAS plug-in, and takes vocoding into strange, new territories.*

▲ *RTAS fans can get an emulation of the classic Yamaha CS80 from Arturia. It sounds great and weighs about 90 kg less than the real thing.*

TDM PLUG-INS: EFFECTS AND INSTRUMENTS

TDM (time division multiplexing), created by Digidesign, is very highly regarded in the industry. What makes TDM so special? Security – TDM plug-ins are stable, very stable. With the Pro Tools system and the TDM format, you always know what you are going to get and you can rest assured that there will be no embarrassing surprises in the middle of a costly session.

This is because of the TDM hardware required to make use of the plug-ins. The hardware, created by Digidesign solely for use with its Pro Tools HD system, can run scores of them, all without so much as nudging the host computer's CPU.

IT COMES AT A COST

There is a lot of power under that hood, but it comes at a price. A very high price, as a matter of fact – to gain access to the world of TDM, you must buy into Digidesign's Pro Tools HD standard, and that can cost ... well, you know what they say: "If you have to ask...." Needless to say, Pro Tools users are an exclusive lot and, as such, they have

access to many wonderful plug-in effects and instruments that are simply not available to others. These include the exquisite Virus Indigo TDM, a mirror image of its renowned hardware-synth sibling in both sight and sound quality, as well as Line 6's Amp Farm, an excellent package of Line 6's guitar and amp models in plug-in form. TDM users can also make use of the spot-on recreations of vintage hardware offered by the (very!) independent developer Bomb Factory.

These emulations of classic compressors and effects devices have become almost as legendary as the hardware they emulate. Again, the Pro Tools aficionado must pay the price to gain access to such rarefied processing.

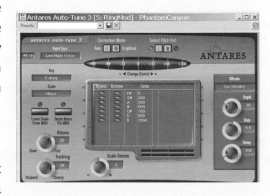

▲ *TDM plug-in Antares' Auto-Tune has been heard on countless hit records since it was first released.*

PRO QUALITY

Almost across the board, TDM plug-ins are more costly than their VST or RTAS counterparts. Still, TDM users can bask in the glory of knowing that they have a system of unbeatable stability and, since they are using the professional recording industry's weapon of choice, compatibility with virtually any world-class facility worth its salt.

If cost were an issue, the Pro Tools user would be, well, a Cubase or SONAR user instead. This is not to say that Pro Tools offers any advantages over those programs, with the exception of stability and compatibility, but someone who remains unfazed by the tens of thousands required to get into Pro Tools probably is not going to quibble over a few hundred here or there when purchasing plug-ins.

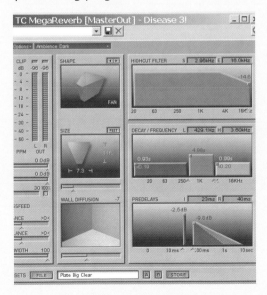

▲ *TC Electronics is widely respected for its high-end processing, and many of the company's products are available in TDM format.*

▲ *A Pro Tools TDM System, though expensive, gives you access to plug-ins, like these emulations of SSL console processors from Waves, that are only available in their original forms in professional recording studios.*

DIFFERENT TO OTHER PLUG-INS?

On the face of it, TDM plug-ins are not used so very differently from your run-of-the-mill VST instrument or effects device. Pro Tools sports all the expected mixer sends and returns, and has the proper MIDI functions in place to drive your software synthesizers.

You may find that automation is a little more advanced at mixdown than you would expect from your bargain-basement department-store sequencer, but the overall territory will not feel at all alien to you the first time out.

Pro Tools is not pretty to look at, but its functionality and performance are second to none – as you would expect from such an unapologetically exclusive system.

➡ *Pro Tools pp. 228–229*

AUDIO UNITS PLUG-INS: EFFECTS AND INSTRUMENTS

Apple introduced its proprietary Audio Units (AU) format with the introduction of the OS X operating system, which included a new audio framework, Core Audio.

The code's seamless integration with the Mac's Unix-based operating system made it easy for developers to create compatible plug-ins in the new format. And when Apple began bundling the basic audio program GarageBand, a fully capable music application (with Audio Unit plug-ins), with each new Mac, the large new base of customers with audio programs ensured the format's acceptance, and ultimately, success. Today

almost all major developers of audio plug-ins include AU compatibility with their products.

HIGH PERFORMANCE

Core Audio provides a complete foundation for writing robust audio plug-ins, because it lives at the OS level rather than the applications level. Just about any music program running on a Mac can host an Audio Unit plug-in. Audio Unit plug-ins work seamlessly with GarageBand, Logic Express, Logic Pro, Final Cut Express, Final Cut Pro, Soundtrack Pro, MOTU Digital Performer, BIAS Peak and many others.

Since Apple maintains the Audio Unit framework, it plays well with everything else in the operating system, now and in the future. In addition, Apple continues to evolve and extend Core Audio features. With the release of Tiger, for example, Apple released two new audio units of its own, AUNetSend and AUNetReceive. (These new units let you distribute sound processing or sound generation over a network – a useful capability in a recording studio with a lot of Macs.)

Core Audio provided a breakthrough in throughput latency (the time it takes for audio to enter your Mac, travel through the system to your application and then

◄ *Native Instruments' Kontakt is a much-lauded sampler plug-in. In addition to many other formats, it supports Audio Units.*

pass back out to your monitors) Core Audio also allowed multiple applications to share the same device, without causing additional latency. So you could have, say, Logic Pro and Reason active at the same time sending output to the same interface. You could also have multiple audio interfaces active at the same time.

▲ *Always one step ahead, VirSyn offers its products in Audio Units format, including its additive synthesizer, Cube.*

PLUGGED IN

Making a high-performance audio engine part of the OS made a system-level plug-in architecture a logical fit. Although Audio Units (AU) added to the alphabet soup of plug-in formats, developers rushed to turn out AU

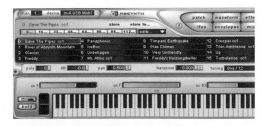

versions of their plug-ins because of the increased efficiency and savings in CPU load, not to mention that large numbers of musicians working on Macs.

Apple includes several AU plug-ins in Mac OS X, including one that adjusts timing without affecting pitch, a Velocity Engine-optimized (on PowerMacs) reverb and one for streaming audio over a network. Apple also provides a software instrument that supports both the DownLoadable Sounds (DLS) and SoundFont formats for high-quality, low-latency sample playback.

THE NEW STANDARD

Where there was once doubt about the need for a new plug-in format on the Mac, the advantages of Core Audio made Audio Units plug-ins inevitable. Although the MAS format (for the popular Digital Performer DAW application) continues to thrive, some companies have stopped creating MAS versions of their software because of DP's compatibility with Audio Units. Apple's Logic Pro accepts both VST and AU plug-ins.

➡ *Logic Pro pp. 224–225*

◀ *It became legendary in its original Mac incarnation, so it is not surprising that Mac users demanded that Absynth be made Audio Units-compatible.*

MAS Plug-ins: Effects and Instruments

All digital audio sequencers work by simultaneously writing and reading enormous amounts of sound-generating data to and from disk drives. Because personal computers were not originally designed for this task, recording software developers had to create their own mini programs to efficiently handle disk Input and Output (I/O) for the host application.

In the early days of Macintosh audio, for example, Digidesign had to create **DAE** (Digidesign Audio Engine) so that Pro Tools could communicate effectively and reliably with its external hardware.

When Mark of the Unicorn (MOTU) decided to give audio recording and editing features to its flagship MIDI sequencer, Performer, the company devised the **MAS** (MOTU Audio System), which, as a host-based audio engine, would have to handle effects processing and interfacing with other software as well as disk I/O.

As Digital Performer became one of the most popular host-based Mac audio

programs in pro studios, plug-in developers and software synthesizer creators realized that their software needed to be compatible with MAS.

WIDE CHOICE OF PLUG-INS

MAS plug-ins, like their RTAS counterparts, only work with their associated application, Digital Performer (DP), but that certainly does not make them limited in number or variety. Dozens of real-time, automatable 32-bit plug-ins, including reverb, dynamics processors and EQ, are included with the DP package.

Some of these plugs, like PreAmp-1, which provides acoustic modelling of vacuum-tube pre-amp circuitry; and the MasterWorks collection of dynamics processors, which include versatile and

▲ The MasterWorks multiband compressor is one of several high-quality MAS plug-ins that ship with Mark of the Unicorn's Digital Performer.

rich-sounding compressor, limiter and gate plug-ins, can stand toe-to-toe with the most respected and expensive third-party plug-ins available.

In MAS, effects can be used as an insert on a single channel, or accessed via a send/receive bus. The number of effects you can apply at any one time depends only on the speed of your computer, and DP imposes no built-in limit – the faster your Mac, the more effects you can use at one time.

WIDE RANGE OF SUPPORT

DP supports mono, stereo and surround tracks, and MAS allows for effects with mono, stereo or surround inputs and outputs. This enables the plug-in to do things like intelligent mono-to-stereo or surround effects, or to process power-hungry surround-input-to-surround-output configurations efficiently.

AVAILABLE PLUG-INS

Traditionally MOTU has had dozens of developer partners creating scores of plug-ins and virtual instruments, not counting those in widely used and highly respected bundles from companies like Waves and TC Electronic.

With the acceptance of OS X and its Core Audio and Audio Units features, along with MOTUs emphasis on hardware products that work with

Windows Vista as Well as Macs, some see the days of MAS plug-ins as numbered. However, DP's continued popularity means that owners of large collections of MAS plug-ins – such as MOTU's own MachFive sampling system; Absynth, B4, Battery and FM7 from Native Instruments; and IK Multimedia's SampleTank – will still be able to use them with DP in the foreseeable future.

Some featured MAS plug-ins in mid 2007 included iZotope's Ozone 3 set of mastering processors, Arturia's ARP2600 V emulation, Wave Arts' Power Suite bundle and SpinAudio's RoomVerb M2.

➡ *Digital Performer pp. 230–231*

▲ *Mark of the Unicorn's MachFive sampler is one of many software instruments, such as those from Native Instruments and Propellerhead Software, that are compatible with MAS.*

MORE ON SAMPLES

This chapter assumes that you have absorbed the earlier section on samples and delves a little deeper into some of the details.

SAMPLING LEVELS

Like some dates in ancient history, digital sound levels are counted backwards, with zero as the loudest permissible level. This may puzzle the uninitiated but there is good reason for it, which has to do with **distortion**. Distortion is often applied by guitarists and other instrumentalists to their sound for expressive purposes. Here we are talking about analogue distortion, such as that created by a fuzz box, which makes its characteristic sound by overdriving the input amplifier stage. The results range from warm and mellow to jangly heavy metal but they are all useful in some musical style.

Digital distortion, on the other hand – when the sound recorded is too loud

◀ *The master section of Cubase's mixer. Levels up to zero are fine; anything louder than that will light up the clipping warning lights at the top.*

to be represented by the ones and zeroes the computer uses – sounds pretty awful; it comprises clicks and blips for brief overloads, and continuous crackling for sustained excursions above zero. The optimum level at which the sound is presented at its loudest without **clipping** is referred to as **zero dB** (0 dB). In digital recording, anything above zero will create distortion. Recordings close to but not over zero are favoured, an optimum range being, perhaps, -6 to zero. A trial run before you start any serious recording will give you an idea of the range of levels your sound source is outputting.

BIT DEPTH AND SAMPLING FREQUENCY

There is a good reason for recording samples as close to zero dB as possible. The strength of sound at any moment is recorded as a series of numbers. The maximum size is determined by the number of bits allocated to each number; the more bits, the more faithful to the original sound the sample will be. **Bit depth** determines how many steps there can be between maximum volume and silence, so if sounds are recorded at a low level using only half the available bits, half the possible dynamic range is wasted. CDs are produced at 16-bit depth although modern **sound cards** can work with 24 or 32 bits.

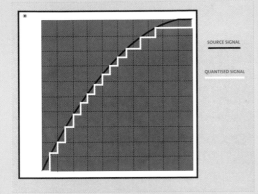

SOURCE SIGNAL

QUANTISED SIGNAL

▲ *Here the curve of a sound wave is digitized, turning it into a series of discrete levels that closely match the original sound.*

SAMPLING RATES

Another crucial factor for digital fidelity is the number of times per second the sound is sampled. CD sound is sampled just over 44,000 times per second at 44.1 kHz. Again, modern sound cards and audio interfaces can handle sampling rates of 48 kHz, 96 kHz or even higher. Sound engineers and musicians with canine-keen ears claim to be able to hear an improvement (on studio-quality monitors), but most people will not be able to tell the difference.

More samples per second and higher bit depths are good for fidelity but require more disk space; a 32-bit sample takes up twice as much room as a 16-bit version of the same sound.

The Nyquist Theory states that a sound must be sampled at least twice its highest frequency to be reproduced faithfully. Young humans can hear up to around 20,000 cycles per second (Hz), hence the CD rate of 44 kHz.

LAYERED SAMPLES

Some samplers will allow the programmer to **layer** sounds, that is, to allocate more than one sample to the same key, thus playing more than one sample simultaneously.

A simple example might be two recordings of a drum; in one the drum is struck softly, in the other, loudly. There is not just a difference in volume; the harder drum hit will sound different in sound quality and pitch from the softer one, as a real drum would depending on whether it was struck hard or softly.

The softer sample can be set to play at a modest level however hard the note is struck, while the louder one has a velocity-sensitive setting, so that it will not be heard unless the key is struck more firmly. Thus, as you play a series of notes from softest to loudest, the soft drum sample will gradually be replaced by the loud one, approximating the response of a real drum.

A variation on this is to have a range of drum hits, e.g., four at a range of volumes allocated to the same key, with each sample only sounding within a particular MIDI velocity range. For example, the softest might play only up to a MIDI velocity value of 32, while the second takes over between 33 and 64, the next loudest between 65 and 96, and the loudest hit up to the maximum of 127.

Of course, layering is not solely concerned with simulating reality; it serves equally well to create new timbres by blending diverse samples, such as a percussive hit with a sustained sound.

SUSTAIN LOOPS

These are different from the rhythmic loops previously discussed. A **sustain loop** is a portion of a sample marked out to be repeated while a key is held down. The advantage of this is that a relatively short sample can be sustained indefinitely.

Finding good looping points is a highly skilled art and the details of it are beyond the scope of this introductory book. However, the essence of the technique is that the sound at the beginning and end of the loop must be closely matched, otherwise an abrupt change in the sound (a **glitch**) will spoil the loop. Your software sampler will probably allow you to switch the looping function on or off.

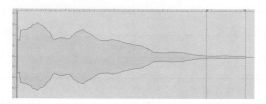

▲ *The portion of the sample between the lines will be repeated indefinitely until the note is finished.*

Commercial samples may already be looped, but to do the job yourself you will need some help in the form of a good audio editor with looping tools, such as Bias Peak, Steinberg WaveLab, Sony Sound Forge, or a DAW with similar capabilities.

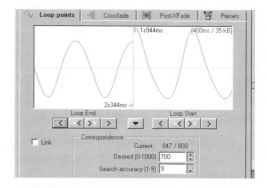

▲ *WaveLab's loop editor lets you visualize the moment of looping back. The loop points may be adjusted by as little as a single sample at a time. The left half of the display shows the end of the loop, while the beginning is on the right so that you can check on how smoothly the sample will loop – not at all in this case.*

AMPLITUDE ENVELOPES

An **amplitude envelope** is the rise and fall of the volume of sound during the course of a note. Percussive envelopes start quickly, with a very short "attack" time. As well as most percussion instruments, piano- and guitar-type sounds would be included here. Sounds with a slower attack begin more gently – string and synthesizer pads, for example. Some sounds, such as a plucked string, will naturally decay to silence, while other sounds, for example, an organ chord, may be sustained indefinitely.

All samplers will have at least an amplitude envelope and perhaps an envelope for the filter as well. The most common envelope type is **ADSR** with controls to adjust the attack, initial decay, sustain phase and release of the note. The sampler may be able to impose an amplitude envelope on a sample, but be aware that each sample will also have its own inherent envelope. If the sampled sound has a slow attack, then shortening the sampler's own attack time will have no effect at all. On the other hand, a slow attack may be imposed on a sample that begins abruptly.

To speed up an attack that is too slow, the sample may need to be edited. Some samplers may allow you to start playing the sample from any point, enabling you to omit the slow buildup of volume.

If the sample dies away, raising the sustain control on the sampler's envelope shaper will also be futile. You will have to find suitable looping points so the note can be sustained beyond its natural length.

▲ *A sustained sound with a slow attack.*

FILTER ENVELOPES

Filter envelopes usually have the same parameters as the amplitude envelope –

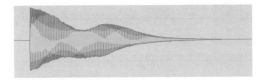

▲ *A decaying sound with a fast attack.*

attack, decay and the like – but applied to the filter's **cutoff frequency** rather than the sound's volume. This may possibly have an effect on the overall volume of the sound, but principally it will change the harmonic content of the sample, cutting off some frequencies or boosting others, subtly or radically changing the **timbre**, or sound colour, of the note.

This can be relevant to shaping naturalistic sounds, as some instruments vary in timbre during the length of a note, but may equally be a creative tool in sculpting new sounds. Depending on the sampler involved, it may be possible to link amplitude, filter envelopes, or both, to velocity to make keyboard input potentially more expressive.

As with amplitude envelopes, when applying a filter envelope to a sample you must take into account the sample's own envelope and not expect, for example, a long lingering fade at the end of the filter envelope (otherwise known as a long release time) to have any effect if the sample is a short one.

➡ *Samples pp. 88–103; Synthesis pp. 268–287*

Part Two: Reference

MIDI
ADVANCED MIDI

MIDI has graced all kinds of music-making gear, from synthesizers to effects processors, for more than 20 years. Despite its relative antiquity, MIDI remains an essential weapon within the sound engineer's arsenal. To take full advantage of its flexibility, you must first understand how it works.

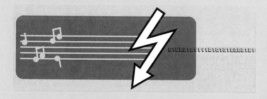

▲ *MIDI turns your music into a stream of ones and zeros.*

FIRST PRINCIPLES

Although the acronym MIDI (Musical Instrument Digital Interface) refers to the computer-based electronics that first gave musical instruments a way to communicate with each other, most people also use the term to refer to the *language* of MIDI: a way of communicating the performance required to reproduce a piece of music. When you record MIDI data, you're recording information about the notes you played and when you played them. It is not a recording of the actual music you were hearing, just as a paper piano roll on a player piano is not music, but rather tells the piano what notes to play. Because of this, it is possible to record a MIDI part using one sound and then play it back with an entirely different one. MIDI's biggest advantage is that it is possible to edit intricately and adjust the performance that was recorded: removing bum notes, changing the pitch of others and adjusting the timing of a part so that it matches the tempo of your song. MIDI can also be used to control and automate parameters within a lot of studio equipment, from mixing desks to effects units. This data can also be edited from within a modern sequencer.

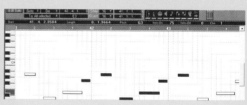

▲ *MIDI allows you to edit and adjust the notes you have recorded.*

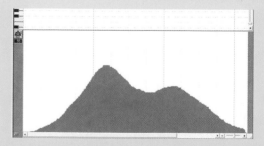

▲ *Continuous controller information allows you to adjust synthesizer parameters in real-time.*

MIDI CHANNELS

Every cable that you use to connect one MIDI device to another carries a total of 16 channels of MIDI data. The concept of a MIDI channel is very easy to understand, by using an example of a typical setup, comprising a controller keyboard that has been connected via MIDI to a sound module.

The keyboard can be set to transmit its MIDI data on any one of the 16 MIDI channels; the sound module can likewise receive data from any one of these channels. For the sound module to make a sound at all, however, it must be set to receive the same MIDI channel on which the keyboard is transmitting.

MULTIPLE CHANNELS

Some devices, particularly computers, may have more than one set of MIDI ports available. In this instance, each port typically carries its own independent set of 16 MIDI channels. A computer that has, for example, two sets of MIDI ports has a total of 32 individual MIDI channels available to it (that is, 2 x 16 MIDI channels).

Although it can become a bit more confusing, the same rules apply when working with a sequencer. Some

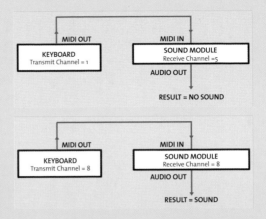

▲ *The receiving device must be set to the same MIDI channel as the transmitting device. Here the top diagram shows an incorrect setup; the diagram below is correct.*

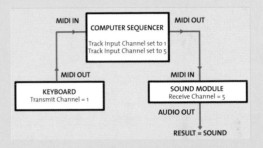

▲ *A sequencer's track settings can re-route MIDI data from one channel to another.*

sequencers will use any incoming MIDI data as the recording source for a track, while others require you to specifically select the appropriate port and channel that your transmitting device is using on a track-by-track basis.

Whichever method is used, all sequencers allow you to allocate a MIDI port and channel to which the track's MIDI output is sent.

LINKING UP MIDI DEVICES

There are three types of MIDI connector: out, in and thru. All MIDI-enabled devices will sport at least one of these connectors, although not all MIDI equipment will have, or indeed need, all three (for example, a controller keyboard only outputs MIDI data, so it needs no in or thru port).

OUT

A device's MIDI out port transmits **MIDI messages** being generated by the device. With a keyboard, this will mainly be note and controller data addressed to a single **MIDI channel**, whereas a sequencer will normally send far more data than this to the MIDI out port, and address it to multiple MIDI channels.

The MIDI out port of one device is normally connected to the MIDI in port of another device.

▲ *There are three different types of MIDI connector: in, out and thru.*

IN

The MIDI in port receives incoming MIDI messages. The device will respond to any messages addressed to MIDI channel(s) it is set to receive on. In this situation, the device sending the MIDI messages is the **master** and the receiving device is the **slave**.

THRU

The MIDI thru port re-transmits a copy of the MIDI data arriving at a device's MIDI in port, and allows you to connect multiple slave devices to a single master. This is done by "daisy-chaining" the MIDI thru port of one slave device to the MIDI in port of the next slave in the chain.

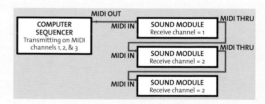

▲ *The MIDI thru port allows you to connect a number of slave devices to a single master device.*

Look out, though; each slave device daisy-chained in this way introduces a small delay in the MIDI signal passing through it, and once you have more than six or so devices, the cumulative effect of this delay can become a major problem, causing sounds to be heard long after the triggering MIDI data has told their sources to play them.

MULTITIMBRAL MODULES

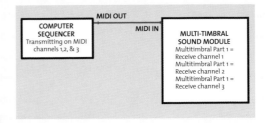

Some synthesizers, samplers and sound modules are only able to produce a single instrument sound at a time, meaning they can only be used to reproduce a single musical line or part.

▲ *A multitimbral sound module can assign different sounds to different MIDI channels.*

Other sound modules, however, are able simultaneously to produce multiple independent instrument sounds. Modules capable of doing this are called **multitimbral**.

▲ *IK Multimedia's SampleTank is a multitimbral plug-in instrument.*

Multitimbral sound modules are most useful in a MIDI sequencing environment, as you can assign each multitimbral instrument ("part") within the sound module to respond to a different MIDI channel, thereby reducing the number of sound modules needed to produce sufficient instruments for an entire song. Another use is to assign different multitimbral parts to the same MIDI channel; this allows you to layer different sounds together yet still play them from a single keyboard or sequencer track.

MIDI MODES

MIDI Modes, then, are a way of identifying to a MIDI system the type of unit contained within that system: multitimbral or not; **polyphonic** or **monophonic**. There was a time when this could make a difference in the way a device needed to be addressed by MIDI, but the increasing standardization of modern MIDI devices means that this requirement has been ironed out of the MIDI specification, so try not to lose any sleep over it.

Chords, as you will have deduced, can only be played on polyphonic instruments, while monophonic instruments are only really suitable for basslines, lead lines, pads and the occasional string – parts that only require one note to be played at a time.

ANATOMY OF A NOTE

There are two main families of MIDI message: system messages and channel messages.

SYSTEM AND CHANNEL MESSAGES

System messages are used for communicating global information: synchronization, master tuning, song position, the parameters associated with a synthesizer patch, etc.

▲ *Cubase's List Edit page shows a list of all the MIDI messages associated with a part.*

Channel messages differ in that they are addressed to individual MIDI channels, and they comprise the bulk of the MIDI data that you will create and work with during a MIDI recording session. Note that controller, pitch-bend and program/bank change messages all fall under the channel message umbrella.

A MIDI message is made up of a number of **bytes** (eight bits), and always takes the form of a **status byte** followed by one or more **data bytes**. The status byte declares the type of message to which the following data bytes relate. To demonstrate this, let us use a typical example of playing a keyboard that is connected to a sound module.

When you play a key on the keyboard a **note-on** status byte is generated and addressed to the MIDI channel that the keyboard is set to transmit on. This note-on byte is followed by a pair of data bytes, the first representing the note played and the second the velocity (or hardness) with which the note was played. When the note is released, a **note-off** message is generated, and again the status byte is followed by a pair of data bytes that represent the note released and release velocity. Most systems actually use a note-on message with a velocity value of zero to represent a note-off message, but unless you are using early MIDI-enabled hardware this variation will never be apparent.

CONTINUOUS CONTROLLERS

The continuous controller (CC) message is a type of channel message and is used to control all sorts of different settings and parameters.

A total of 128 independent controllers is available. Some of these have standardized uses: CC 7 is used for sending volume-change messages and CC 10 to make pan adjustments. Even though there are pre-defined CC numbers, the results can vary from synthesizer to synthesizer.

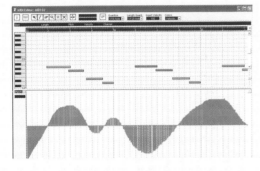

▲ CC data can be edited in much the same way as note data.

For example, turning your keyboard's **modulation wheel** will always produce a modulation CC message and send it to any connected slave devices. If the slave was creating a piano sound then it may interpret the modulation message as a **vibrato** (that is, pitch modulation) effect, whereas an electric-guitar sound may translate it into a **tremolo** (that is, volume modulation) effect. It is important to understand this relationship between the master device producing and transmitting the MIDI CC data and the slave device that is receiving it. The master device simply creates the message; what is done with that message is determined by the receiving device and how it has been set up.

Let us say that as you hold a note down, you add a bit of vibrato with the modulation wheel. This generates a modulation CC message. The CC status byte is followed by a pair of data bytes, but the change of status means the data bytes now represent the controller number (in this case CC 1) and the amount of modulation applied, respectively.

PARAMETERS

In the context of MIDI devices and sequencing, a parameter is generally thought of as any value or setting that can be adjusted by the user.

One of MIDI's biggest benefits is its ability to access and adjust many of the parameters within your MIDI devices. This does not just have to be synthesizers and sound modules – many modern digital effects units and plug-ins can be controlled in this way.

Basic parameters, such as a synthesizer's attack time or an effects unit's **wet/dry balance**, are normally controlled using MIDI CC messages. In the **general MIDI** specification, many of these settings have been assigned their own standardized CC numbers. Some parameters cannot be controlled in this way, but these can often still be

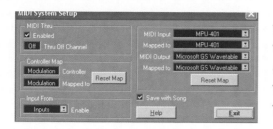

▲ Sequencers are full of parameters as well.

controlled via MIDI using **system exclusive** (SysEx) messages.

SysEx is a special type of non-standardized MIDI message. Unlike other MIDI messages that have a rigidly defined function (for example, a note-on is always a note-on), SysEx messages can be used to control any parameter that a manu-facturer sees fit, and it is the manufacturer that defines the SysEx data structure for its devices. Each MIDI manufacturer has a unique ID number, and every model of MIDI device it produces is also given a unique ID number. These numbers are combined in the transmitted data so that a message intended for, say, a Korg Z1 will have no effect on any other make or model of MIDI device.

PROGRAMS AND BANKS

Most synthesizers, sound modules and the like store the parameters that are used to create a given sound in programs, variously known as patches, timbres, performances and so on. MIDI allows you to call up any of the programs on your devices using MIDI program change messages.

These messages are channel specific, so you can direct them to specific slave devices in your MIDI setup. **Program change** messages only have a value range of one to 128, but modern synthesizers contain far more programs than this, which is where the **bank change** message comes in, a bank being a collection of programs.

BANK CHANGE MESSAGES

A bank change message is made up of two CC messages (CC 0 and CC 32), which describe the **most significant byte** (MSB) and **least significant byte** (LSB) of the bank change number; in other words, **coarse** and **fine** values that are combined to determine the bank change number. Both the MSB and LSB have a value range of one to 128, which gives a total of 16,384 (128 x 128) available bank change numbers.

PROGRAM CHANGE MESSAGES

A bank change message should always be followed by a program change message, otherwise it will be ignored by any attached slaves. Many manufacturers arrange things so that only the MSB or LSB is required to

▲ *Most plug-in instruments can also have their programs selected via MIDI.*

change banks on their devices, although you should still assign a value of zero to the other half of the MSB/LSB pair. Consult the manufacturer's literature to determine which bank is assigned to which bank change number.

AFTERTOUCH

Aftertouch is the effect produced by pressing harder on a key you are playing on a keyboard. The end result of aftertouch depends entirely upon the way in which the receiving device is set up to respond to it, but it is commonly used for vibrato, tremolo and volume-swell effects. There are two types of aftertouch message: polyphonic aftertouch and channel aftertouch.

POLYPHONIC AFTERTOUCH

These are both note and MIDI channel specific. In other words, each key you are playing, and therefore each note that is sounding, can have its own independent amount of aftertouch applied. Although polyphonic aftertouch has been part of the MIDI specification since it was first devised, the reality is that it is very rarely used by manufacturers due to the complexity, and therefore cost, of implementing it. A few high-priced controller keyboards produce polyphonic aftertouch messages, but far fewer instruments can actually do anything with it!

CHANNEL AFTERTOUCH

This is a far easier system to implement and is therefore used by most keyboards and sound modules. As the name suggests, channel aftertouch is transmitted on a specific MIDI channel, but it does not distinguish which note the aftertouch is being applied to and so all the notes being played on that MIDI channel will be affected.

One problem with aftertouch messages is the ease with which you can inadvertently produce copious quantities of them. This is a particular problem when working with a sequencer, where the cumulative effect of multiple tracks containing extraneous aftertouch messages can lead to timing problems.

MIDI
SYNCHRONIZATION

Up until now, we have been mainly discussing MIDI messages that are generated as a result of some sort of user interaction (pressing a key, jiggling a knob – that sort of thing). However, there is a family of MIDI messages, known as system real time, that can be used by MIDI devices that work to some kind of time or tempo grid (for example, sequencers, drum machines and arpeggiators) to allow them to synchronize (sync) their timing with other similar devices.

PLAYING IN TIME

Making a drum machine play in time with a sequencer containing all the other parts of the song is a common example. When setting up MIDI sync, one device is nominated as the master or source device, and any other time- and tempo-based devices are set up as slaves to the master.

The master device sends out a steady, regular stream of MIDI messages and the slave device(s) syncs its own timing and tempo to the incoming messages. The messages themselves can be made up of one of two kinds of MIDI sync

▲ Cubase's synchronization settings screen.

messages: **MIDI clock** and **MIDI time code**; these function in significantly different ways.

MIDI CLOCK

This is the simplest form of MIDI sync, and is intrinsically tied to the tempo you are working at. This is because clock signals are sent out at a rate of 24 **pulses per quarter note** (PPQN – a measure of the number of MIDI messages that are sent by a sequencer or other time-and-tempo based MIDI device, during each quarter-note or crotchet), so adjusting the tempo, and therefore the length, of a quarter-note, alters the rate at which the master device emits the clock message.

Some sequencers actually subdivide each clock pulse into a further 20 sub-pulses, giving a total of 480 PPQN, thereby increasing the accuracy of the sync signal. This is done in such a way as to ensure that a slave device that works only with the standard 24 PPQN will not be confused.

TICK TOCK

As its name suggests, the MIDI clock message itself is analogous to the ticking of a clock. Every time a slave device receives a clock message it knows that 1/24 or 1/48 of a quarter note has elapsed. The slave device then matches its own internal clock signal to the incoming clock and perfect synchronization is achieved.

DRAWBACKS

There are, however, more than a few drawbacks to using MIDI clock for synchronizing your MIDI devices. First and foremost, a MIDI clock message does not contain any song position information, which means that while master and slave may be playing together in perfect time, they could actually be playing different parts of the song.

For example, you may be using a sequencer as your master and have a drum machine set up as slave to the sequencer's master clock signal. Your sequencer's song position is set to the beginning of your song, but you had previously been editing a few patterns on your drum machine, and so its song position is, say, 10 bars into the song. When you hit play on the sequencer the drum machine will dutifully follow suit and start playing in time with the incoming MIDI clock signal – but it is playing 10 bars ahead of the sequencer!

This shortcoming of MIDI clock signals can have another unwanted side-effect: it is not impossible for MIDI messages to get lost or corrupted during transmission from the master and decoding by the slave, particularly if a lot of other MIDI data is being sent down the same cable.

If this happens to a MIDI clock message, the slave device will think there has been a momentary change of tempo and, all of a sudden, master and slave are no longer playing in time with each other. Because of these problems, a lot of devices utilize additional **song position pointer messages**: the master will send one of these at regular intervals (although less frequently than MIDI Clock messages), and any connected slave devices will use them to update their current song positions, thereby making sure everything stays properly synchronized.

TIME CODE

The other form of MIDI sync signal is called MIDI time code (MTC). This is radically different from MIDI clock and is based upon a standard of marking and counting time called **SMPTE** (pronounced "simp-tee"). It was developed by the Society of Motion Picture and Television Engineers for synchronizing audio to film. SMPTE breaks down time into the usual hours, minutes and seconds, but it then

Part Two: Reference

subdivides the seconds into **frames**, with the number of frames per second (FPS) varying depending upon the application. SMPTE times are written as: H:M:S:F.

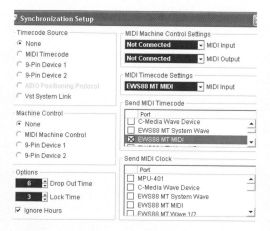

▲ *Computer-based sequencers can deal with both kinds of MIDI sync.*

MTC sends out a MIDI message when a frame of time passes, and the message contains the time at which it was sent in H:M:S:F format. It is common to use a 25-frames-per-second time code for MIDI syncing, but this is not imperative, as long as both master and slave(s) are working at the same frame rate.

In contrast to MIDI clock, which is tied to tempo, MTC is an absolute time reference and contains no information concerning the tempo that the master device is running at. However, it does ensure that both master and slave are locked to the same absolute time

reference point, and as long as both are set to the same tempo then perfect sync will be achieved.

USING A COMBO

It is common for devices, in particular sequencers, to use a combination of MIDI Clock and MTC. The MIDI clock messages provide the tempo information, while the MTC messages ensure all devices are locked to the same absolute time reference. But keep in mind that not all time- and tempo-based MIDI devices will recognize MTC messages. Indeed, to devices such as delay effects units and arpeggiators, such information is irrelevant.

SYNCING TO TAPE

So far we have only been talking about syncing MIDI equipment, but what if you want to synchronize a MIDI sequencer with a separate audio multitrack recorder? If the recorder does not have MIDI functionality, an extra piece of hardware – a **SMPTE generator** – is required to work as the bridge between the MIDI and audio equipment.

The first thing to do is to "stripe the tape", an operation that involves recording a SMPTE track onto the multi-track recorder, typically to the highest-numbered track. This SMPTE track is then fed directly back to the

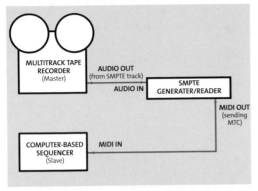

▲ *A SMPTE generator can act as a bridge between an analogue recorder and a digital sequencer.*

SMPTE generator so that, when the tape is played, the SMPTE generator can monitor and decode the SMPTE information, thereby determining the exact time position of the tape. The SMPTE generator then converts the SMPTE into MTC, to which you can then slave your MIDI devices.

MIDI DRUMS

Many sound modules and synthesizers, particularly multitimbral devices, feature a special mode, bank or program for creating drum sounds (from here on we will refer to this as a drum program).

Unlike other programs, where the same sound is laid out across the whole keyboard, a **drum program** has a different drum or percussion sound assigned to each key on the keyboard.

While being able to play drum sounds from your keyboard can be handy, drum programs really come into their own when being played by a sequencer.

DRUM EDITOR

Many sequencers have a dedicated drum-edit screen, where individual drum sounds are listed against a time grid, and by placing hits into the grid you can create drum patterns for your songs. This programming approach to creating drum parts is not for everyone, as many prefer the human feel that is imparted by actually playing the drum part from a keyboard.

However, it is not easy to play an entire complex drum pattern with a standard keyboard, so a good technique is to record the bare bones of the pattern – for example, the hi-hat or kick and snare parts – and then build up the pattern using successive overdubs.

DRUM MACHINE

Another way of getting drum sounds and patterns into your recordings is to use a drum machine. You can use this simply as a dedicated drum-sound module in place of a drum program on a multitimbral sound module or similar, or you can slave it to your sequencer using MIDI clock and/or MIDI time code.

GENERAL MIDI

In the early days of MIDI there was very little standardization of how a given device would react to a MIDI message.

This lack of standardization meant that a **standard MIDI file** (a standardized file-type for storing MIDI data) was anything but standard. If you played it back through a device other than the one(s) it was composed with, the notes would come out right but would invariably be using the wrong synthesizer programs and drum maps – piano part on a drum kit, anyone?!

GENERAL MIDI IS DEFINED

In an effort to bring some semblance of order to this controlled chaos, the **MIDI Manufacturers Association** (MMA) and the **Japan MIDI Standards Committee** (JMSC) defined the **General MIDI System Level 1**, otherwise known as General MIDI or, simply, GM. The MMA and JMSC jointly govern the MIDI specification and oversee its ongoing development. The organizations are made up of a lot of the main players in the music-technology world, such as Yamaha, Roland and E-MU.

GM did not add any new features or capabilities to the original MIDI specification; rather, it defined the way in which certain aspects of the original specification would be implemented in instruments carrying the GM logo.

▲ *The General MIDI logo only appears on devices that fully comply with the standard.*

The sound set and program numbers were standardized so that, for example, Program Change 1 always calls up an acoustic piano sound, Program Change 34 a fingered bass etc. MIDI drum maps were also standardized. Some CC numbers had their uses set in stone too – CC 64 for the sustain pedal, CC 1 for the modulation wheel, and so on.

GS AND XG

Roland quickly followed the release of the GM standard by releasing its own General Standard (GS) specification. This improved on GM in many areas, including the number and variation of

▲ *Devices that are compatible with Yamaha's Extended General MIDI format bear the XG logo.*

▲ *GM standardizes which drum sounds are mapped to which notes on a keyboard.*

and **General MIDI System Level 2** (GM2) was born. This new standard has given GM the sound palette and level of control expected from a modern instrument. GM2 has also managed to close the gap between GM and the proprietary GS and XG standards and, thanks to its inflated sound set, GM2 has far more credibility as a usable standard for anything other than karaoke backing tracks than the original GM ever had.

MIDI TODAY

The MIDI protocol has continued to grow and expand and in the twenty-first century is barely recognizable as the little message system designed to connect two synths with a 5-pin plug. The Standard MIDI File format now encompasses lyrics. MIDI messages have been extended to control recording equipment and stage lighting. MIDI messages are now used inside computers and cell phones to generate music, and transported over any number of professional and consumer interfaces (USB, FireWire, etc.) to a wide variety of MIDI-equipped devices. There are different message groups for different applications, All popular computer platforms can play MIDI files (*.mid) and there are thousands of web sites offering files for sale or even for free. Anyone can make a MIDI file using commercial (or free) software that is readily available.

sound presets and drum kits, standardized MIDI controllers and even some standardization of SysEx messages. Yamaha then issued its own eXtended General MIDI (XG) standard, which offered two million sound preset slots, access to the all synthesizer parameters and a large number of high-quality from reverb to speaker simulation. Better still, the XG standard included an input connector, allowing you to process other signals through the synthesizer's circuitry, meaning you can record external sounds using the inbuilt filter, reverb or other effects. As proprietary standards, GS and XG are usually only fully supported by Roland and Yamaha, yet both versions were fully compatible with the basic GM standard.

GM2

In 1999 the MMA and JMSC brought the rapidly aging GM standard up to date,

GM Voices and Drum Maps

General MIDI defines the characteristics of 128 synthesizer sounds, and groups them by instrument type. The groups are piano, chromatic percussion, organ, guitar, bass, strings, ensemble, brass, reed, pipe, synth lead, synth pad, synth effects, ethnic, percussive and sound effects.

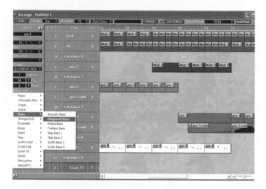

▲ GM groups its voices by instrument type.

These groups are further divided into specific instruments, and any GM-qualified synthesizer will have an identical set of instruments.

DEFINING SOUND

However, differences in synthesis technique, hardware quality and so on mean that the actual *sound* of, say, a GM piano can vary greatly from one GM synthesizer to another – what remains consistent is the basic character of the sound. This is all fine with emulations of acoustic instruments that have a defined sound for the synthesizer programmers to aim for, but things are different when it comes to the synthesizer and special effects categories – after all, what *should* a "goblins" synthesizer FX sound like?!

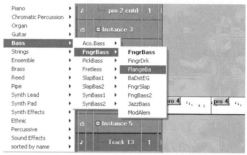

▲ Yamaha's XG format adds an extra layer of sound variations.

The same situation exists with GM drum maps. Although drum-note assignments are standardized so that, for example, MIDI note 38 (D2) is always an "acoustic snare", there is still a lot of room for differences from device to device. Because of this, GM is little more than a convenient means of ensuring that a MIDI composition will sound similar on any system it is played on.

If, however, you want your MIDI compositions to sound distinct, then you would be better off dipping into your synthesizer's non-GM soundset (if it has one), or creating your own sounds tailored specifically to the song you are creating.

MIDI AND SEQUENCING

Without doubt the biggest advantage of the MIDI standard occurs when it comes to sequencing. Because MIDI captures a musical performance rather than the sound that results from that performance, and the performance itself is represented by nothing more than a series of numbers, it is possible to change those numbers to edit and adjust the details of the performance.

Of course, to be able to work with this string of numbers in any sensible way, they need to be arranged and laid out in a meaningful and usable manner; this is what a sequencer does.

Sequencers can be hardware units, but these days it is far more common to use a computer-based sequencing software package such as Steinberg Cubase.

The most basic function of a sequencer is to record and play back MIDI data, but this is only the tip of the iceberg.

Modern software packages have made huge advances in ways of displaying MIDI data in a graphical environment, so that editing and tweaking your MIDI data becomes an intuitive and simple process.

Indeed, so powerful is the MIDI sequencer as a musical tool that it has had a big impact on practically every genre of music: from classical, where composers can hear realizations of their musical musings without having to go to the expense of hiring an entire orchestra; to pop, where the MIDI sequencer has had such a profound effect that without it the modern music scene would be entirely different – which would not be a bad thing in some people's eyes!

▲ *Was Pete Waterman's (of Stock, Aitken and Waterman, the 1980s manufactured-pop producers) fame really the fault of MIDI?*

➡ *What Is MIDI? pp. 28–31; What Is a Synthesizer, pp. 32–35; What Are Samplers? pp. 40–43; What Is a Sequencer? pp. 44–47; What Is a Controller? pp. 56–59; What Is an Effect? pp. 68–79; Samples pp. 88–103; Plug-Ins pp. 104–109*

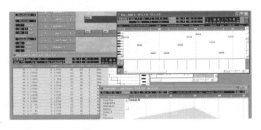

▲ *Computer-based sequencers can display your MIDI data in a number of different ways.*

SYNTHESIS
WHAT IS A SYNTH?

Although they have been commercially available for almost 40 years, nothing conjures up a feeling of a "high-tech" musical instrument quite like a synthesizer. From the moment the public first became aware of the synthesizer, thanks to Wendy Carlos's groundbreaking *Switched on Bach* album over three decades ago, the instrument has captivated and enthralled both musicians and audiences alike.

CHANGE AND PROGRESS

Through changes and upheavals in both technology and fashion, the **synthesizer** has held sway as the technological torchbearer. From the days when they were mammoth devices, festooned with myriad knobs and patch cables, through the early digital era that ushered in the stark and cryptic front panels, and now back again to the knobs- and slider-laden beasties, the synthesizer has weathered the trends of the day.

Ever since Keith Emerson's histrionic performances forever freed the keyboardist from the confining role of sitting behind what was, to all intents and purposes, a piece of furniture,

synthesists have been forced by fad into one stereotype or another. However, in the past couple of decades, due to the effects of dance and industrial music, synthesizers have once again become "cool". With the advent of software synthesis, the synthesizer may be the most accessible instrument for the impoverished young musician to get his or her hands on. No more begging the parents for a guitar: he or she can now download a free software synthesizer to the family computer's hard drive.

▲ *In the past, huge, knob-encrusted, cable-laden front panels were the sonic playgrounds for synthesists lucky enough to afford them. Synthesizers have made a comeback in both hardware and software varieties, such as this Moog Modular clone from Arturia.*

So what exactly is a synthesizer? In practical terms, it is an instrument (usually, but not always, a keyboard-controlled instrument) that generates synthetic sounds. These are often used to imitate other musical instruments, such as strings, brass, drums and pianos, but they can also create brand-new and never-before-heard audio anomalies. The methods by which these goals are achieved are quite diverse. There are many and varied forms of synthesis on the market, but by far the most popular form is known as **subtractive synthesis**.

THE ROLE OF THE SYNTHESIST

Playing a synthesizer and being a synthesist are two different things. Many synthesizer players are relegated to "orchestration duties" by their fellow bandmates, and spend the gigs dialling up preset sounds to fulfil some musical need or another. Others, however, prefer to synthesize sounds from the ground up. This is a challenging and rewarding endeavour and can guarantee that you have a unique voice at the end of the day.

However, contrary to popular belief, being a good synthesist is not an easy task. If you are under the illusion that a synthesizer does all the hard work for you, then you will be disappointed. Becoming a skilled synthesizer player demands a mastery of both the technology and the technique. Unlike, for example, a trumpet player, the sound made by your synthesizer is not written in stone. You must create it, or depend on others to create it for you. Not only that, you will need to develop your playing or programming skills to make good use of that sound.

▲ GMedia is responsible for some of the best software recreations of classic synthesizers, such as this Arp Odyssey emulation.

HARDWARE OR SOFTWARE?

Whether you choose a hardware or software synthesizer will depend upon your needs. Each has advantages, although the line between them has become less clear. You may want to make use of both. Fortunately, the techniques and knowledge demanded of you will be useful in both the soft and hard varieties. A software analogue emulation does not sound exactly like its hardware namesake, mainly because the real analogues never sounded the same. One Minimoog would sound significantly different from another Minimoog, never mind the discrepancies between diverse models from diverse manufacturers.

One myth should be dispelled straight away: hardware synthesizers do not sound inherently better than their software counterparts. Some hardware synthesizers sound great, while others sound lacklustre, and the same can be said of software synthesizers. At the

Part Two: Reference

▲ *It seems impossible to imagine that a synthesizer as powerful as LinPlug's FreeAlpha can be yours for the price of – well – nothing.*

same time, software and hardware can both suffer from cost cutting or feature bloat, with the same result.

Of course, there is no such discrepancy between two of the same instances of software synthesizer, but the number of soft synthesizers available is legion and many are free. The same cannot usually be said of the hardware versions. The following pages will help you get up to speed with the fine art of synthesis. It is assumed that you have a synthesizer available to you. If not, then try one of the downloadable freeware synthesizers.

The FreeAlpha from LinPlug is a great example and, being a cross-platform plug-in, it should fit right in with whatever working method you prefer. You may need to get hold of a VST wrapper to use it in your host of choice if it does not support VSTis. This synthesizer, or any decently fitted out hardware or software synthesizer, will serve the purpose of following along with many of the discussions in the text.

THE NATURE OF SOUND

Before diving into the deep end of synthesis, it is necessary to understand something about the nature of sound.

Sound comprises vibrations in the air that are picked up by your ears before being translated by your brain into recognizable signals. Even the simplest of sounds is made up of a massive number of these sound waves, all interacting, combining and changing over time.

No doubt you have seen the complex wave forms appearing in the display of your audio editor or hard disk recorder as you record them. These are a graphical representation of the thousands upon thousands of sound waves happening simultaneously to form the audio signal you have recorded.

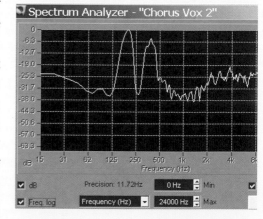

▲ *A fully featured DAW may include analytical tools for examining your wave forms. Here is a bit of extraneous noise as seen in Nuendo's Spectrum Analyzer tool.*

Illustrated Home Recording Handbook
Illustrated Home Recording Handbook

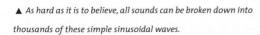

▲ As hard as it is to believe, all sounds can be broken down into thousands of these simple sinusoidal waves.

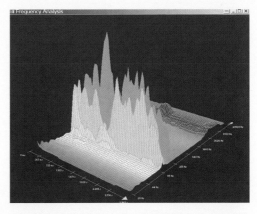

▲ Ever wondered what your voice looks like? Here is a vocal as seen through WaveLab's analysis tools. One axis represents time, while the other represents frequency.

UNDERSTANDING SOUND WAVES

Take some time to study the wave form display offered by your software of choice as you work, and the secrets of sound itself will soon be revealed.

As you are aware, different notes of a musical sound vary in pitch, or more accurately, they vary in **frequency**. You may have heard this term more times than you can count, but have you ever given it any real thought?

You might know what an A below middle C sounds like, and you may even know that it has a frequency of 220 Hertz, but do you know what that means? **Hertz** (Hz) is a term used to describe how many times per second something cycles. If you look closely at a display of a simple sound wave with a pitch of A below middle C, you will see that it repeats itself (or completes its cycle) 220 times per second.

The best wave to use for this example is a **sinusoidal** (or **sine**) **wave**. These are the simplest of all waves, and the tone is absolutely pure. Any analogue synthesizer will be able to produce a sine wave. Theoretically, any sound can be broken down to its constituent sine waves. The dominant wave will be the "fundamental" or recognizable pitch. Any additional sine waves will be the "partials" and, therefore, less prominent in terms of your perception of that sound. Waves bearing an integral mathematical relationship to the fundamental are considered **harmonics**, while those without such a relationship will be **inharmonic** waves, and more dissonant. The harmonic and inharmonic content of a given sound is called its timbre. This describes the overall shape and colour of the tone. The overall harmonic content is also known as the sound's **spectrum**.

SUBTRACTIVE ANALOGUE SYNTHESIS

Of all the synthesis types available, far and away the most common (and some would insist the most useful) is the method known as subtractive synthesis. The idea behind subtractive synthesis is that you start out with a complex, harmonically rich waveform and then chip away at it with filters and envelopes.

Although most people are quick to identify subtractive synthesis with the sound of analogue synthesizers, both old and new, it is also the basis around which most samplers and sample-playback synthesizers are built. That identity with the vintage wood and metal monstrosities runs deeply, and learning the techniques involved with analogue synthesis is still the best way to get your head around any other subtractive device.

It is for this reason that our attentions will initially fall squarely on the venerable analogue (or virtual analogue) synthesizer. It will not take too long for you to see the relevance of subtractive synthesis to virtually every corner of music and recording.

An understanding of subtractive synthesizers will give you a better understanding of both audio editing and effects processing, not to mention the very fabric of the sound that surrounds you in your everyday existence. For our part, we will begin at the very start of the analogue synthesis signal path, and walk you through to the very end. In so doing, we will explain the practical use of each link in the chain along the way, from oscillator to output.

OSCILLATORS

The very first step in any synthesizer's signal path is the oscillator.

Any given synthesizer will have any number of **oscillators**, although two or three could be considered the norm. This is the feature that generates the initial sound, which is shaped and moulded by the rest of the synthesis functions. An oscillator's job is to produce an audible wave form. It might be as simple as a sine wave, or, in the case of a sampler, which uses samples as oscillators, as complex as a sampled choir. In a subtractive synthesizer, the more complex the wave form, the more the filters will have to work with.

A simple sine wave, for example, will not offer much in the way of frequency shaping. As we have seen, a sine wave consists of only the fundamental frequency, with no additional partials. There will not be much to subtract without subtracting the sound itself. A sampled waveform, on the other hand, might be harmonically rich. Somewhere in between lies the traditional fodder of the analogue oscillator.

The typical analogue oscillator will generally allow you to choose between a number of basic wave forms, including the aforementioned sine wave, a **square wave**, a **pulse wave** or a **sawtooth wave**. Each of these wave forms has a different harmonic content and serves as a good starting point for subtractive synthesis. You might want to listen to the waveforms available in your particular synthesizer, with all the filtering and effects turned off.

THE DIFFERENT WAVEFORMS

You will find that the sine wave is fairly dull and seemingly quieter than the others, while a square wave is more akin to a woodwind sound (and would, therefore, make a good starting point for one). You will hear a raspier tone from a sawtooth wave because it is very well fitted out with both odd- and even-numbered harmonics. This makes it a great choice for brass or string sounds.

▲ *A common wave shape present in many analogue oscillators, the pulse wave can be the basis for sounds with a woodwind-like quality.*

All these wave forms derive their names from the shape of the wave on an oscilloscope (or in your wave editor). A square wave, for example, looks symmetrical and boxy. Some synthesizers have a **noise generator** among their oscillators; more often than not this involves **white noise**, which is created when most or all frequencies (or partials) are heard simultaneously.

This cacophony of harmonic and inharmonic frequencies is often perceived as a whooshing or wind noise. Other forms of noise might have some frequencies filtered out (such as **red noise**). Noise is usually unpitched. It is also present in many natural sounds: the breath of the player when a flute is blown, or the attack of a pick on a guitar string.

MORE THAN ONE OSCILLATOR?

The chances are that your synthesizer will have more than a single oscillator. Most synthesizers have signal paths that have evolved from Dr Robert Moog's classic Minimoog synthesizer. This was one of the very first performance-oriented synthesizers ever put into mass production, and its signal path comprised three oscillators (one acting optionally as a **low frequency oscillator**, or LFO) fed through a resonant filter and then an amplifier (but not before being shaped by both a volume and a filter envelope). This simple but powerful configuration is capable of sustaining a synthesist's interest indefinitely, without ever producing the same sound twice.

▲ *Looking very much like a Nord Lead, Discovery from DiscoDSP provides two oscillators that can be synchronized.*

If your synthesizer does indeed sport more than a single oscillator, you will find that even more harmonically rich wave forms can be handed to the filter section by combining two or more of these oscillators together. If you are looking for a particularly "fat" sound, you can detune them a little from one another. The resultant chorus of frequencies will be far thicker than using both of them locked firmly together. Of course, this might prove in itself to be an interesting sound, and it is for this reason that many synthesizers have oscillators that can be lashed together via a sync button. This forces them to produce the same frequencies, and can be useful for a nasal and obtrusive lead sound.

If you have not guessed it by now, the trick is to use the oscillators and their available functions to create a wave form with the necessary harmonic content before moving on to the next section of the synthesizer. Myriad methods have been devised by manufacturers and developers to add interest to their oscillators' outputs. One of the more common in recent years is some form of **wave shaper**. If you own Native Instruments' popular Absynth or RGC Audio's superb z3ta+, then you may have already tried this for yourself. These software synthesizers allow you to draw or "reshape" the oscillator's output via a graphical tool. This can provide some seriously complex tones. In the days of the modular behemoths, wave-shaper modules were quite common, although they worked a little differently, relying on harmonic distortion methods to alter the waveforms.

ANTI-ALIASING

Aliasing is a phenomenon that occurs when the digital converters in a modern synthesizer are forced to interpret frequencies beyond their range. The result is a high-pitched whine from those frequencies being misrepresented. Anti-aliasing oscillators do not suffer from this problem.

FILTERS

Second only to the oscillator, the filter is the single most important element in subtractive synthesis. You can have the finest anti-aliasing oscillators on the planet, but they will mean nothing unless your filter is up to scratch.

The qualities and merits of various makes and models of filter is as hotly discussed and debated among synthesizer aficionados as microphones are among engineers, and it has been so for decades. The rallying cries of "24 dB versus 12 dB" and "2 pole versus 4 pole" have been echoing from the day the first Moogs and Arps rolled off of the assembly lines.

TYPES OF FILTER

A filter does precisely (or less-than-precisely, depending on the filter) what the name suggests: it filters out frequencies and harmonics from the signal provided by the oscillator. Even the humble equalizer is a filter of sorts,

assuming you are using it to cut frequencies rather than boost them. Filters come in a wide range of flavours, including the common **low-pass filter** (LPF), which allows all frequencies below a selected cutoff value to pass through. In addition to the low-pass filter, your synthesizer might also have a **high-pass filter**, which allows all the frequencies above the cutoff value to pass through. Or maybe you have a **band-pass filter**, which allows only a narrow band of frequencies to escape unscathed. Conversely, a **notch** or **band-reject filter** will remove only a narrow band of frequencies. Any synthesizer that sports more than one of these is said to have a **multimode filter**.

You might also see a switch for selecting between 12-dB and 24-dB filter types, or perhaps you have only one of the two on your instrument. This refers to how sharply the filter clamps down on the undesired frequencies.

▲ *Filters are a crucial element in subtractive synthesis. Any subtractive synthesizer you have will feature some sort of filter, and there are even standalone filter plug-ins such as PSP Audioware's Nitro.*

A filter with a cutoff slope of 24 dB is much less forgiving than one with a 12-dB slope. Most people seem to prefer 24-dB variety, but this may just be a matter of fashion, as many excellent instruments with 12-dB filters are also out there, such as Yamaha's CS series.

CUTOFF FREQUENCY AND RESONANCE

It almost goes without saying that your filter will have controls for both **cutoff frequency** and **resonance** (also called **Q** or **emphasis**). The cutoff frequency does exactly as you suspect: it determines the frequency beyond which no other frequencies shall pass above, below or around, depending on the filter mode.

The resonance is an unusual **gain control** of sorts. It increases the gain of the frequencies immediately surrounding the selected cutoff frequency. The results can be anything between a low rumble (low frequency and high resonance) and a high-pitched squeal (high cutoff and high resonance).

Resonance is often used to produce a squelchy, squawking sound, such as that heard on a multitude of acid house and techno tracks, courtesy of the Roland TB-303 Bassline or its modern emulations. Dynamically controlling the filter via a modulation source can work wonders to add interest to your sounds.

COMB FILTER

One more filter type worth considering is the **comb filter**. This is not actually a filter at all, but a **delay line** with many fast, multiple echoes. A delay line is an effect that delays the signal input and replays it at a later time. When mixed with the original signal, this is heard as an echo. Delay lines usually let you determine how many echoes are present, as well as their volume level. This effect imbues the sound with a rather metallic quality.

ENVELOPES

Without control over how a sound is heard over time, synthesis would be pretty dull, no matter how fascinating the waveform was.

The **envelope generator** of a synthesizer is the primary function for governing how your sound will behave in time once the sound is triggered.

An envelope generator usually has a number of stages, or steps. The most common envelope generators have four of these stages: one each for the attack, decay, sustain and release portions of the sound. When applied to the amplitude, the attack stage determines how long a sound will take to reach its full volume once the envelope is triggered. A long attack is used for sounds that seem to fade in, while a short attack is ideal for punchy basses or percussion.

The decay segment of an **ADSR** (Attack, Decay, Sustain, Release) envelope determines how long the sound will take to go from full volume to its steady state or sustain. That sustain is the level that will be held for the length of time the note is played by the performer, and the release segment determines how long it will take to fade into silence once the key is released.

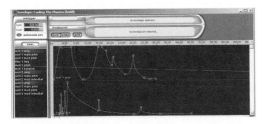

▲ *Native Instruments' legendary Absynth software synthesizer was one of the first to popularize complex, multistage envelopes.*

Your synthesizer may have a separate envelope for controlling the filter amount or any other modulation destination. Many modern software synthesizers have **multistage envelopes** offering 12, 64 or even more stages to play with. Some allow you to loop and sustain the envelope between any stage or group of stages. This can be a powerful tool for creating sounds that evolve over time.

MODULATION

Most synthesizers offer a wealth of opportunities to modulate parameters with a wide selection of modulation sources.

The most common is the LFO, which operates at a very low frequency. So low, in fact, that it is inaudible on its own (although many classic synthesizers have LFOs that can be increased to frequencies well within hearing range). Like their audible counterparts, LFOs are usually equipped with a selection of wave forms from which to choose.

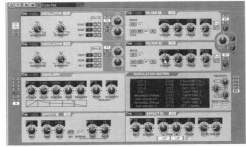

▲ *LinPlug's Albino combines a powerful semi-modular synthesizer with the sound-design prowess of top sound designer Rob Papen.*

When applied to a modulation source, an LFO causes the source to modulate to the shape chosen. This is most often used to create **vibrato** (with the LFO applying a sine wave to the oscillator pitch), or tremolo (a sine wave modulating the amplitude of the sound), but LFOs can be used for a wide range of effects.

The **hearing range** of the human ear can reach from as low as 20 Hz all the way up to 20 kHz. The sample rate of a commercial CD is 44.1 kHz to allow for this (the famous scientist Henry Nyquist's theory dictates that the sampling rate must be twice as high as the highest frequency in the sound being sampled for it to be reproduced faithfully).

OTHER MODULATION SOURCES

These include envelope generators, built-in sequencers and the physical controls of your keyboard, such as aftertouch or velocity. The modulation routings are often handled by a built-in **mod matrix**, allowing you to assign the modulation sources to the destinations and determine the amount of modulation taking place.

Another sort of modulation takes place at the oscillator level, when one oscillator is used to modulate another. This is seen in the form of **frequency modulation** (FM), **amplitude modulation** (AM) and **ring modulation**. The first two are self-explanatory, but ring modulation is what happens when the sum and difference of the frequencies of the two oscillators are present at the output but the original frequencies are not.

SAMPLING

Often dismissed as something wholly separate from subtractive synthesizers, that is exactly how most samplers, in general, should be considered. After all, they come equipped with filters, LFOs, envelopes and all the other sundry functions that we have covered with regard to analogue subtractive synthesis.

The only real difference is that instead of simple wave forms such as sawtooth and sine, the sampler's oscillators are engineered to play back a digital audio recording that has been stored onboard. When the amplitude envelopes are triggered, the selected sample is spat out through the filters and envelopes just like the simpler waves produced by an analogue oscillator.

As a matter of fact, if the samples in question are raw sine, square and sawtooth waves, a digital sampler makes a pretty good replacement for a vintage analogue synthesizer. Many synthesists use their samplers to archive the sounds of their temperamental vintage instruments, thus freeing them from the tyranny of tuning instabilities and all the other quirks for which these archaic voltage-controlled beasts are known.

THE SAMPLED WAVE FORM

Going one step further, with the complex wave shapes generated by a sampler's oscillator, all of the modulation possibilities offered by the techniques of subtractive synthesis become even more interesting. Why not use a sample as the modulator in an FM-based signal path? FM synthesis is using the frequency of one signal to modulate another. The results can range from subtle coloration to wild, clangorous noises.

Traditionally, FM synthesis was done with sine waves, but a sampled wave offers much more variety. The sample-based wave form is perfect fodder for such acrobatics.

There are more common uses for the sampled wave form. The obvious function performed by the sampler is as a replacement for acoustic and electric instruments.

No matter what model of sampler you own, whether hard or soft, a huge selection of pre-rolled third-party sounds is probably available. Need a piano in a hurry? The sampler can save you. The sampler's role in this capacity is what has led to the release of a flurry of products known as **ROMplers**. Essentially, these are sample playback synthesizers that call upon a large selection of multisampled instruments of the most useful sort.

The better models also have some of the subtractive functions we are familiar with for the purpose of further shaping the onboard samples. The usefulness of such instruments cannot be denied, although it must be pointed out that their very nature makes it easy to simply call up the same old samples that are likewise available to every other musician that owns the ROMpler in question.

BEAT SLICERS AND LOOP REARRANGERS

Beat slicers and loop rearrangers, such as ConcreteFX's Dicer VST plug-in, are samplers engineered to work specifically with sampled audio loops, which are loaded in and sliced into neat little segments. This makes it easy to change the tempo of the loop without changing the pitch, and vice versa. It also makes rearranging a beat into something entirely new a walk in the park. The better beat slicers allow you to make alterations in the pitch, pan, direction and frequency content of the individual slices, plus a lot more.

If you work with loops, these instruments are invaluable. A standalone solution might be Propellerhead's legendary ReCycle! software, which allows you to chop the loop and then export the results to the sampler and sequencer of your choice.

FM SYNTHESIS

Subtractive synthesis may have been the only game in town for a good many years, but it has not remained in sole proprietorship of the synthesis mantle and for a very brief time was actually shaken from its lofty perch at the top of the heap.

The threat to subtractive security was handed in by mega-synthesizer manufacturer Yamaha in the early 1980s, in the form of its DX7 synthesizer. This groundbreaking instrument offered unprecedented 16-voice polyphony, a velocity-sensitive keyboard and an entirely new method of sound generation – all for under £1,000 ($2,000).

This was not all that much later than the era when a five-voice polyphonic Prophet 5 would set you back more than twice that amount of cash. Needless to say, even if it had not sounded so good, the DX7 would still have sold like lemonade on a hot summer's day. But, the fact is it did indeed sound good.

Based on FM synthesis, the DX7 was an all-digital machine, without a filter in sight. It was a radical departure from analogue synthesis in both approach and sound. Gone were the thick, warm and simple tones of analogue synthesis. The DX7's stock in trade were crystalline digital tones. There was a sort of "acoustic-ness" about the sounds of the instrument. Looking back, it is easy to dismiss the DX7's sound as thin and cold, but at the time nothing of the sort had ever been heard before. It was magic.

▲ *More than just an exact recreation of the legendary Yamaha DX7, Native Instruments' FM7 is a modern-day, super-evolved FM synthesizer.*

FM AS A SOFTWARE PLUG-IN

Sadly, after a very long and successful run, Yamaha's FM synthesis was overtaken by the onslaught of **PCM** (pulse code modulation) -based instruments that followed it. A form of digital audio encoding, PCM-based synthesizers are simply sample playback instruments. FM became extremely unfashionable as analogue recreation swept in on the gale of retro fever.

However, it did not take too long for software developers to realize the potential of FM synthesis as a fantastic addition to the synthesist's palette, and FM re-emerged like a phoenix from the ashes in the form of software plug-ins. From Native Instruments' FM7, an uncanny and steroid-infused version of the classic Yamaha, sitting at the high end of the price scale (although quite inexpensive compared with its near-namesake), down to the lovely freeware Vivaldi on the opposite extreme, FM is available to anyone who cares to try it out.

FM PATCHES

Though these software incarnations of FM have made creating one's own patches far easier than the puny displays proffered by the DX7, creating FM patches is still not easy. Indeed, it involves some radical rethinking if you are accustomed to the more traditional analogue instruments. As mentioned earlier, FM synthesizers often have no filters onboard. Filters are really not needed to achieve colourful and lively tones. In reality, the sound is created by the frequency modulation and interaction of a handful of ordinary sine waves.

When sine waves are forced to modulate one another, the result is often a tapestry of harmonics and sidebands that can be manipulated with envelopes,

LFOs and other tools familiar to synthesists. Complex attacks are easy with FM, and percussive sounds are its forte. By controlling the frequency and amplitudes of the carrier and modulator sine waves, the synthesist can create sounds of striking beauty and delicacy or, conversely, harsh brutality. And although FM synthesizers get a bad rap for being thin and cold, in the right hands they can be lush and warm.

▲ DiscoDSP's Phantom combines classic four-operator FM synthesis with phase distortion synthesis to produce some stellar digital tones.

▲ A beautiful freebie, Vivaldi can reproduce some stunning FM tones.

ADDITIVE SYNTHESIS

Every few years, the form of synthesis known as additive raises its unique voice above the din made by the subtractive synthesizers that litter the landscape. Yet, for many reasons, additive synthesis has never quite taken hold of the public's imagination.

Maybe it is because additive synthesis is so very time consuming, demanding meticulous attention to detail and taxing the patience of stolid programmers to create even the most modest sounds. Or perhaps it is the fact that it offers no instantaneous gratification. With subtractive synthesis, one can accidentally stumble upon an interesting and inspiring timbre with the random flick of a knob or two. Additive synthesis, on the other hand, requires considerable preplanning to make any sort of headway at all.

PARTIALS

What is so difficult about additive synthesis? Well, the basics of harmonics, inharmonics and partials have already been covered at the start of this section. Additive synthesis uses such things as the very building blocks of sound. An additive synthesizer offers the user an oscillator capable of generating large numbers of sine waves (partials), each with its own pitch and amplitude envelopes. These sine waves are combined to create the desired sound. Theoretically, with enough partials and suitably complex envelopes with which to control their pitch and amplitude, any sound can be created. In practice, there would need to be thousands of partials and envelopes with unlimited break points. Such provisions are impractical for developers to implement, and would wreak havoc on CPUs.

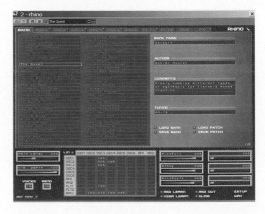

▲ *Big Tick's Rhino combines many forms of synthesis, including additive wave form generation, into one powerful and flexible architecture.*

Fortunately, you can come close to most sounds with dozens of partials; 32, 96, or even 200 or more partials are often available to the modern additive synthesist, although whether the user can be bothered to make use of them still remains to be seen. History has shown additive synthesis to be the purvey of a very patient few who embrace their additive synthesizers and milk every drop of sonic ambrosia from them. Many synthesists might show interest initially, but most eventually return to the predictable offerings of their analogue and sample-playback units.

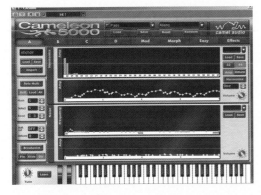

▲ Camel Audio's Cameleon 5000 is one of the small handful of additive software synthesizers. The large and friendly interface makes additive synthesis much less daunting than it once was.

RESYNTHESIS

This indifference might be set to change, however, as more and more software developers begin to offer additive instruments as a remedy the glut of virtual analogue emulations that has saturated the software-synthesizer market. Camel Audio's Cameleon 5000 is an excellent example. This is joined by DiscoDSP's Vertigo and VirSyn's Cube, all

worthy examples of additive synthesis and **resynthesis**.

Resynthesis is a technique by which an additive synthesizer can examine a sample or audio recording, and break it down to its constituent sine waves and their envelopes. The result is theoretically indistinguishable from the original source, but as it is now what amounts essentially to a synthesizer patch, it can be manipulated by all the means available to the additive synthesizer itself.

In reality, the quality of resynthesis varies from synthesizer to synthesizer. Some are very good at it (Symbolic Sound's big-ticket Kyma, for example), while others should best be viewed more as a source of inspiration than as an accurate recreation. Nevertheless, resynthesis goes some distance in relieving some of the tedium associated with programming an additive synthesizer, and it is a welcome arrival on the software scene.

▲ VirSyn's Cube can resynthesize a sample into an additive synthesis patch – great for twisting your timbres!

PHYSICAL MODELLING

When you pluck a string on a guitar or mandolin, or any other stringed instrument, you set into motion an unfathomably complex series of vibrations that are far too chaotic and complicated to reproduce with any sort of subtractive synthesis.

As if that were not enough, if you were to pluck that same string a second time, in seemingly the exact same way, the results would be substantially different from the first time. Such unpredictability is inherent in every acoustic instrument on this, or any other, planet. This makes recreating these instruments via the standard methods of synthesis a no-win situation. At least it did before physical modelling hit the scene.

WHAT IS IT?

Physical modelling is a synthesis technique based on the premise that instruments have a specific behaviour that can be predicted and reproduced mathematically. A physical model consists mainly of **exciters** and **resonators**. An exciter is an event or device that sets into motion whatever it is

about the instrument that causes the air to vibrate. On a guitar, the exciter might be the pluck of the string, while the resonator is the vibrating string itself. The physical modelling synthesizer will use a variety of methods to add the element of unpredictability to the proceedings. It is, on a good physical model, quite impossible to create precisely the same sound twice, just as in real life.

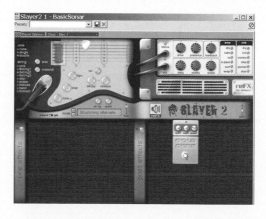

▲ *The famous plucked string model shows up in ReFX's uncannily realistic guitar emulation, Slayer 2.*

MYRIAD SOUNDS

We say it started with a plucked string, because that was the very first popular physical model to come to the attention of the public, in the form of the Karplus-Strong plucked string model. This model, created decades ago, still serves as the basis for a great many modelled string sounds. But plucked strings are not the end of the line. There are also models of bowed strings, reeds, brass,

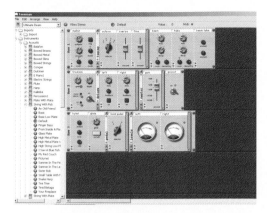

▲ *Realistic acoustic models combined with modular analogue synthesis gives Applied Acoustics Systems' Tassman synthesizer a sound all its own.*

INTERFACE

How you interface with a synthesizer is vital to your success with the instrument. It used to be that you had a control panel with a connected and integrated piano keyboard.

mallets and more in the slight handful of currently available physical modelling synthesizers.

Probably the most widely known is Applied Acoustics Systems' Tassman. This is a **modular software synthesizer** that merges physical models of acoustic sounds with models of vintage analogue synthesis. A modular synthesizer is an instrument without a fixed signal path. Each section is an independent module, and can be connected to any other section in any order. There are filter modules, oscillator modules, envelope modules and more. These modules can be arranged and combined in whatever fashion you like. Do you want to hear a bowed marimba? Tassman will get you there. The results can be downright haunting.

This keyboard might have pitch and modulation wheels, aftertouch and velocity sensitivity and any number of other controllers attached. It might also be festooned with knobs and sliders to control the synthesis parameters directly. Many modern hardware instruments still possess some or all of these features, but obviously a software synthesizer cannot.

▲ *In addition to its excellent sound quality, Arturia's Moog Modular V offers a familiar interface to veteran modular synthesizer fans.*

The software synthesizer's interface is depicted on your computer screen as a graphical representation. Some of them look like hardware emulations, while others might have a look all of their own. The extra space provided by the computer screen is invaluable. Compared with the minuscule LCD screens commonly found on hardware synthesizers, software GUIs provide a wealth of information.

▲ *MIDI learn functions are just part of what makes VirSyn's additive Cube easy and enjoyable to use.*

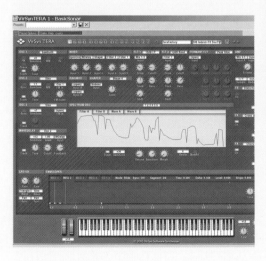

▲ *VirSyn's mighty Tera is fully multitimbral, and even has a dedicated mixing page and sequencer.*

CONTROLLING THE SYNTHESIZER

However, such information is not nearly so valuable if you have no means to control it. Pointing and clicking with a mouse is hardly an inspirational or immediate exercise. Fortunately, control can be obtained via the use of a MIDI keyboard controller, a MIDI knob or fader box, or a hardware MIDI synthesizer. All these can provide the same sort of control and response that one gets from a hardware synthesizer.

▲ *P-Soft's Void combines old-style modular synthesis with drop-down menus for ease of use.*

When using these controller devices with your MIDI sequencer, all the moves and adjustments you make can be recorded in real-time and edited to perfection. This is made even easier if your software synthesizer has a **MIDI learn** function. This handy feature can be used to teach the software synthesizer which of its controls should respond to your hardware controls: select the knob or fader on the synthesizer that you want to control, hit the Learn button, move the knob or fader on the hardware unit and the synthesizer will automatically assign the selected software parameter to that specific hardware control.

ANCILARY SYNTHESIZER FEATURES

POLYPHONY

This the number of voices a synthesizer can play at once. A synthesizer with eight-note polyphony can simultaneously trigger eight notes. Most modern software synthesizers limit the available polyphony only by the amount of CPU on hand.

A monophonic synthesizer can play just a single note at a time. While this may seem like a limitation, it is actually quite desirable when playing certain types of leads and solos. When using a synthesizer in monophonic mode, you might want to make use of any available **portamento** or **glide** function. This is a function that causes one note to "glide" smoothly into the next in terms of pitch, instead of switching abruptly.

MULTITIMBRAL ABILITIES

These are often mistaken for polyphony. A multitimbral synthesizer can play not only more than one note (usually), but more than one distinct sound at a time. Often each sound, or **patch**, is played from a different MIDI channel. Put simply, a patch is a sound created on a synthesizer. The name is derived from the days when sounds were created by literally patching together modules with cables.

Software synthesizers often have the advantage of having built-in patch management and librarian functions, but similar convenience can be had with hardware synthesizers and effects devices, by using a software patch editor and librarian.

These applications give you the same sort of large graphical editing interface offered by software synthesizers, and make editing and creating sounds on a hardware synthesizer almost as easy to manage.

➡ *What Is a Synthesizer? pp. 32–35; Samples pp. 88–103; Software Plug-ins pp. 234–247*

SEQUENCING

SEQUENCING
THE PRINCIPLES

Looking at today's software sequencers, with their advanced digital audio and MIDI recording and editing features, their sample accurate timing and control, and their ability to host both software instruments and effects processors, it is almost unbelievable that their lineage stretches directly back to the clunky wood and metal hardware sequencers of yesterday's modular synthesizers.

In the days when beknobbed monolithic structures ruled the synthesizer landscape, a sequencer did just what its name implied: it sequenced. Not MIDI, not audio, but voltage was the target of the sequencer's chugging, rhythmic pulse. The synthesist programmed the pitches of the notes by adjusting the knobs to the desired intonation. If the synthesist was fortunate, the pitch would not fluctuate. These sequencers also had no ability to store what you programmed.

THE ADVENT OF MIDI
It was not long before the first digital sequencers began to appear. These might let you store a few hundred notes, but they often suffered from cryptic programming schemes. These were snapped up and used by many electronic musicians looking for that second pair of hands, and the synthesizer continued to evolve until MIDI blew the doors wide open on the world of sequencing. By giving instrument manufacturers and software developers a common language, MIDI taught the dinosaurs to speak. And if that was not enough, the personal computer revolution gave them a more powerful brain.

What followed was a continuous stream of software sequencers, each exponentially more powerful than the last. From eight tracks of MIDI, they leapt to 16 and then to 24, and eventually gave users an unlimited number of tracks with which to compose their masterpieces. And not only notes were recorded. All manner of information was game, from volume and pan, to knob movements, to the entire contents of a synthesizer's memory in the form of SysEx data.

SEQUENCERS TODAY
Fast forward to the modern era of desktop recording studios, where the word sequencer means so much more than merely stringing MIDI notes or voltages together. Today's sequencers are marvels of complexity, and sequence not only

MIDI but audio as well, giving the desktop producer access to the very fabric of sound, to be manipulated and mangled in much the same way as MIDI data.

No longer restricted to automating MIDI controllers at mixdown time, contemporary desktop engineers can automate effects processors, equalizers and more. They can even control the pitch and tempos of recorded audio tracks. The mind reels at the possibilities.

WHAT ABOUT THE COST?

For a surprisingly reasonable price, a software sequencer can give you capabilities that world-class professional studios could not have touched a few years ago. All this power does, however, come at a price. By putting so many possibilities and features at your disposal, it goes without saying that the modern software sequencer can be somewhat complex. Even for veteran electronic musicians and engineers, it is easy to be intimidated by the sheer number of things that these programs can do.

Not only does the user need to face the imposing learning curve offered up by the software, but he or she must also learn how to make the most of his or her equipment. This means a crash course in recording, engineering, MIDI, mixing, mastering and more. Just because the software gives us the tools to produce the masterpiece does not mean we can automatically use the tools well.

WHAT A SEQUENCER CAN DO

The power these applications provide gives you freedom as musicians, engineers and producers to experiment and to take artistic chances without watching the clock. For many musicians, particularly those who cut their teeth on rickety four-track cassette portastudios, the challenge may not be so daunting. The experience of doing so much with so little can translate very well to desktop production. Where once you might have been glad to squeeze three or four overdubs out of your recording medium, you can now add as many as you like – but you do not have to. If you know how to work within limitations, you may find that some self-imposed limitations are key to getting your work done in the software studio environment.

To start, simply use your software sequencer for the basic necessities required to get the job done. Record your tracks just as you have always done, but take some time here and there to learn a new function of your software that might be interesting to play with. It will not be too long before you are whizzing around the program like an old pro, and the new things you learn will hopefully inspire you to produce more and better recordings.

SOUND SOURCES

A sequencer is not going to be worth much without something to sequence. Chances are, if you are buying a sequencer, you probably already own some instruments and effects, or are counting on the software plug-ins that come with your host.

A sequencer can be used to sequence everything from a simple monophonic synthesizer to a roomful of hardware effects and instruments. Most modern hardware devices have MIDI connections and capabilities. The sequencer can be used to perform all manner of convenient tasks with regard to your hardware. You can do simple things, such as tell an effects device which preset it should be using, or you can do very sophisticated things, such as bulk dumps of the internal memories of every device in your studio.

THE BASICS

To begin with, the primary function of the sequencer will probably be to record your performances, whether they are synthesizer arrangements recorded as MIDI data or acoustic performances captured as digital audio.

Though our hardware history might have taught us otherwise, in today's software music environment there are great advantages to understanding that all recordings and sound sources, whether MIDI, audio, or plug-in software devices, can be manipulated in very similar ways. Pitch and time are no longer written in stone. Everything is malleable.

PLAN AHEAD

What are you intending to record? Does your sequencer package contain any built-in synthesizers, drum machines, samplers or effects? Is it capable of hosting third-party plug-ins, and do you know where to find them? Or do you already have some hardware synthesizers or samplers at your disposal? Maybe you will only be recording your voice and an acoustic guitar. Do the available sound sources and effects fulfil your needs? Can you complete the arrangements you envision with what you have, or with what is included with your sequencer?

No matter how you answer these questions, you will be recording and arranging your compositions as either MIDI or audio files.

THE POWER OF MIDI

When recording MIDI devices such as external gear or plug-ins, the recordings are not stored as audio files but as MIDI data. This data can be easily manipulated and changed without any negative effect on the music itself, since it is only sending out a stream of commands that tell the device how to behave.

For instance, if you record an intricate bass line as an audio file, and then later decide that you want to transpose it to another key, you may be out of luck. Modern sequencers can work wonders with time stretching and pitch shifting, but you will still probably have undesirable effects in the audio if you transpose an audio clip by anything more than a few half-steps. Besides that, with an audio recording of your bass line, you would be setting that performance and that sound in stone.

If you decide that there are too many notes, you can do nothing short of re-recording the passage. And, even then, you may not get exactly the same sound again. With MIDI, it is all infinitely controllable. You can change, remove, add or copy any or all of the recorded performance in any way. Erasing notes, drawing in new ones or moving around those you have recorded is as simple as a mouse click.

If, at the time of mixdown, you decide that your snare drum is too obtrusive, you can simply replace it with another without having to recreate the performance itself. This is incredibly

powerful, and it is easy to see why MIDI took both home and pro studios by storm when it was ratified.

DO IT WITH AUDIO

What really makes today's sequencers seem so miraculous is that many of the things you can do with MIDI can also be done with audio. In the past, if you wanted to edit a recorded passage, you were literally required to cut and splice the tape, or re-record.

Today, you can cut, paste, copy and move audio just as you can in a word processor. To anyone who has never worked this way, it is a real revelation. You can do as many takes as your computer can handle (and that is an awful lot), and cut, copy and splice them together to form the perfect take. While some may argue that this technique is responsible for the overly glossy production of today's pop music, one can hardly complain about the convenience and power.

It is worth noting that audio files do make more demands on your computer's resources than MIDI files. More memory is needed, as well as more speed, and faster and bigger hard drives are required to make the most of these tools. Even so, today's average desktop computer has more than enough under the hood to accommodate even the most intensive recording sessions.

THE INTERFACE

When looking at a cross-section of the various sequencers on the market, it is easy to come to the false conclusion that they all are essentially the same.

A cursory glance at Cakewalk's SONAR or Steinberg's Cubase reveals certain similarities. Most have a central page for arranging your tracks, both MIDI and audio, and many sport a mixer that is painstakingly modelled on a real console. You will probably find the sorts of familiar things that musicians have demanded over the years, such as piano rolls and event lists.

Other sequencers, however, do not adhere to this familiar idiom, including Mackie's Tracktion which deviates from the hardware paradigm. Still, it has a piano roll and an arrange page of sorts, so it's not completely in foreign territory.

TRY THEM OUT

Which sequencer you choose will (or should) depend primarily on how comfortable you are with the interface. Demo versions of many can be found at the various companies' web sites, and we really must encourage you to try them out before plonking down your hard-earned cash. After all, the sequencer is going to be your closest studio companion, and it would be a shame if you had to constantly struggle against a mismatch.

One sequencer may be utterly off-putting to you, while another may be inviting and inspiring. Your composition and recording process should be fun, not an eternal battle against clunky and overwhelming features that are hard to grasp and harder still to find.

▲ *SAWStudio is revered by audio engineers, who feel at home with its no-nonsense interface.*

THE ARRANGE PAGE

It might be called a Track View, a Project window, or something similar in your particular sequencer, but regardless of the manufacturer's nomenclature, there will be a main arrange page.

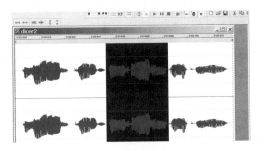

▲ *Many sequencers have extensive audio editing functions built in. However, you may still find a dedicated editor to be of value. Seamless Looper, from Zero-X, has many functions not found in built-in editors.*

Usually depicted as a large and colourful grid with the MIDI and audio tracks arranged vertically from top to bottom, and the bars and beats of the song laid out horizontally from left to right, the arrange page is where you will be spending most of your time.

▲ *Most of the action in a sequencer may take place on the arrange page, with a combination of right clicking and tool bars.*

Audio and MIDI clips are represented by colourful bars that stretch horizontally along the time line, and you usually have a toolbar full of useful commands for cutting, copying, pasting

and other sorts of editing functions that will be used to arrange your tracks.

If you wish, for example, to take a vocal recording you made in the first chorus and copy and paste it into the third chorus, this will be done on the arrange page, hence the name.

ADDITIONAL FUNCTIONS

In addition to these functions, the arrange page may be where you set up a track's audio inputs and outputs, as well as its record, mute, play and solo status.

There will be some function for adding MIDI or audio tracks, as well as some way to gain easy access to the most useful mixing tools, such as volume, effects inserts and pan controls.

Some of the more independently minded developers might have all of their sequencer's mixing functions available only on the arrange page.

PROJECT SETTINGS

Before you begin recording, you will need to determine all of the appropriate settings for the project at hand. You may have to set up the input and output busses of your audio and MIDI interfaces, as well as things such as your preferred bit-depth and sample rate. CDs are recorded at a depth of 16 bits, and a sampling rate of 44.1 kHz.

Even the least-expensive home recording equipment is now capable of up to 24-bit, 96-kHz quality. This will be most noticeable when recording acoustic instruments with crystalline high frequencies, but can also be instrumental in achieving transparency in your final mixes. If you do record and mix at higher rates, you will need to convert down at the mastering stage if you plan to put your music on an audio CD.

PLAN THE BASICS

If you plan to make use of any surround-sound functions, this is the time to tell the sequencer exactly what your speaker setup will be, so that those options will become available to you during recording and mixdown. You will also need to select the appropriate audio drivers for your sound card. Will you be using ASIO, WDM or DirectX? This is the time to determine such things. Oddly, some sequencers need to be told to keep the audio "always on", otherwise, you will only hear a sound while the sequencer is playing or recording. This is particularly annoying when trying to audition software synthesizers.

TIME AND TEMPO

Other project settings that will be needed at the outset are tempo and time signature. Many sequencers default to 120 bpm, and a time signature of 4/4 (also called **common time**). Obviously, not every recording you make will fall into this narrow category, so you might be looking for your sequencer's **tempo track**. Often, the tempo track is represented as a grid in which tempos can be entered numerically, or by pointing and clicking. It is possible to create an accelerando or other dynamic changes to the song's tempo here. Many sequencers do not support multiple time signatures or tempos, although this can be achieved by changing the settings right in the main window or transport bar.

▲ *Considerably more functional than its hardware namesake, Nuendo's transport bar is the control centre for common functions.*

FILE MANAGEMENT

You may also have some sort of file management system. This will include instructions as to where the sequencer should look for and store audio files once they are recorded. It is a good rule of thumb to keep these on a second, separate hard drive, so that all of the drive's bandwidth can be allocated to your sequencer's audio streaming functions.

Some sequencers need to be told where the song should be stored at the outset. Cubase and Nuendo users, for example, are expected to create a folder for the project, and all audio recorded for that project will be kept in another folder inside that project's folder. This makes backing up a song and all its audio files a snap. Cakewalk's SONAR, on the other hand, does not require the user to do this. If you do not wish to be bothered with creating a logical folder hierarchy yourself, it will attempt to automatically keep track of all of the audio files used for a project .

VST PLUG-INS

If your sequencer hosts VST plug-ins, you may also need to tell it where to look for them. Some sequencers will only allow you to keep the VST .dll files in a specific folder. This makes it a little more difficult if you have more than one VST host you like to use. When you first launch the sequencer, it will scan for all the plug-ins in that folder, and make them available for use.

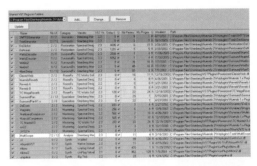

▲ Most VST hosts have some method of setting up file paths and preferences.

▲ One handy feature of software recorders is the ability to automate many of their mixing functions. Here, a volume envelope is being edited in Cakewalk's SONAR.

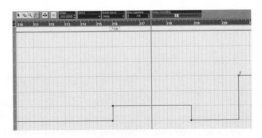

▲ Some advanced sequencers allow you to set up complicated tempo and time-signature maps.

WORKING WITH AUDIO

There are as many ways to work with audio in sequencers as there are sequencers themselves. Generally speaking, the most common audio functions needed are the ones that involve recording continuous tracks, such as when adding a guitar track to a MIDI arrangement.

These sorts of tasks are handled in much the same way as they would be in a tape-based studio. You record your takes, cut and paste the best bits together, then add and mix them down with the rest of the material.

TOOLS TO HELP YOU

In even the most modest sequencers, there are plenty of helpful tools to aid you in capturing the best possible recording. Most of them offer some variation on a "cycle" recording mode. With this activated, loop start and end points are positioned, and the sequencer will continuously cycle between them, so that you can rehearse your performance or record multiple takes.

Some sequencers will automatically create a new track every time the cycle is begun, so that you need not worry about erasing a previous take. This is a wonderful feature if you work alone, as it prevents endless trips between your vocal booth and your computer.

Another very useful function is a **click track**, or **metronome**. Most sequencers have them, but some, such as SONAR, require you to rely on a tiny PC speaker or a MIDI device to hear them. An audio click track, such as the one provided by Cubase, is a welcome feature.

EDITING OPTIONS

Once you have your audio recorded, as mentioned earlier, plenty of editing options are available. In addition to the real-time plug-in effects you might be adding when recording and mixing down, there are often offline effects and processing that will directly alter the audio you have recorded – sometimes irrevocably – depending on the sequencer.

Effects such as these are useful for, say, **normalizing** your track (bringing its loudest peak up to zero dB, which has no effect on its relative dynamics), reversing it, changing the gain, or adjusting its pitch or tempo. You should be cautious about normalizing an audio clip, or increasing its level in any way. Leave yourself some **headroom** (the difference between the highest level present in any signal and the level at which distortion takes place – zero dB in digital audio) so that you can add equalization, resonant filters and more. You do not want to end up with nasty distortion at mixdown time.

FADING

You will probably find some destructive version of fade-in and fade-out commands, although there may be a better way to create such things in the arrange page itself. Many sequencers allow you to click on "handles" that appear on the audio clip, and drag the fades to the desired points. You can generally choose from a variety of fade curves, or even create your own. These can make the fades seem slower or faster, depending on which is selected.

THE MIX ENVELOPE

A much more sophisticated approach to the fade-in and fade-out and gain functions appears in some sequencers as a **mix envelope**. This feature is directly tied into the mixer's automation, but is handled on the arrangement page.

A mix envelope can be used to click, draw and drag the mix function – such as volume or pan – into any position you desire. You can add envelope **nodes** for creating very complex shapes. It is quite easy when using such a tool to create

extremely dynamic mixes that would be impossible to achieve with a hardware mixer and a single pair of hands.

Any envelope position will be reflected in the fader positions of your software mixer (or your hardware mixer, if you are fortunate enough to have one with motorized faders). Do not be fooled into thinking that volume and pan are the only things that these envelopes are useful for. You can also use them to control effects send levels, or to even out the parameters of a plug-in or hardware device.

REAL-TIME MIX AUTOMATION

Speaking of automation, any sequencer worthy of the name will have some ability to record and play back any real-time mixing you perform with the included mixer, or with a hardware controller device. Some of them allow for direct, two-way communication between specific hardware controllers and the sequencer itself.

There is generally some sort of device list that tells the sequencer which controller you are using, while some controllers have presets onboard for a variety of sequencers and software synthesizers. Such equipment makes anyone coming from the hardware studio feel much more at home, and can make mixing a great deal more intuitive and enjoyable.

SLICERS

Some sequencers have built-in beat slicers to achieve beat and tempo matching of audio loops, while others may allow you to import ACID or REX files for this purpose. ACID support is available inside many of Cakewalk's products, while Cubase and Nuendo allow for the use of REX files. ACID files are pre-sliced to work within Sony's ACID application (although Cakewalk calls them Groove Clips). SONAR users can create and save their own. REX files are created using Propellerhead's ReCycle! tool, and comprise both a sliced loop and a MIDI file for playback that contains the exact positions of the slices in the loop. This is most useful for matching a new beat to an existing one. In addition to allowing for REX file input, Cubase and Nuendo also have a built-in "hit point" system for matching the tempos of disparate audio loops.

▲ *Propellerhead's ReCycle! slices loops into REX files, which can be imported into Cubase. These REX files will lock to the project's tempo without altering their pitch.*

RECORDING AND EDITING MIDI

In many ways, recording and editing MIDI are usually handled in a similar fashion on any given sequencer, though some things will vary a little from sequencer to sequencer. Many of these involve how MIDI data is presented, entered and edited.

MIDI sequencing has been around almost as long as people have been marrying desktop computers and keyboards; therefore a sort of standard way has evolved in which certain functions are presented. If a sequencer developer veers too far from this accepted path, he or she is likely to be met with considerable criticism.

USING PLUG-INS

However, there is still room to grow and evolve, even this late in the MIDI sequencing game, and some companies offer up the occasional innovation. A good case in point is Jorgen Aase's popular energyXT plug-in. This is a software VST instrument and effects plug-in that has the ability to host other VST plug-ins, as well as drive external MIDI gear. It offers up a range of creative MIDI arpeggiators, sequencers and routing possibilities, and verges on being an entire sequencer in itself. Such a tool is a welcome addition to anyone using a sequencer with less-than-wonderful MIDI capabilities.

Another fairly recent innovation is the **MFX** (MIDI FX) plug-in standard. This is a standard for creating and implementing useful MIDI tools that can be plugged into the host sequencer. Both Cakewalk's and Steinberg's sequencers support MFX plug-ins. A handful of companies is also producing the plug-ins themselves, most notably MusicLab, whose line of MFX applications includes such things as guitar strum simulators, drum pattern sequencers and more.

QUANTIZING

When recording MIDI tracks in a sequencer, the options are legion. The traditional route is arming a track and hitting the Record button to track a real-time performance. Of course, this implies that you have decent keyboard chops. Or does it? MIDI sequencers commonly have a variety of **quantize** functions.

Quantizing your track will nudge any wayward notes into place so that they snap to a selected note grid. You can quantize to whole notes, 16th notes, and many other divisions. You can often set your sequencer up so that it quantizes what you play as it is recorded.

A very interesting variation on the theme is **groove quantizing**, which takes a live performance stored as a groove file, and applies its timing to the recorded material. This can give a static performance some real life.

Swing is a similar, if a little more primitive, function of groove quantizing. Swing (also called **shuffle**) moves the notes that fall between the beats in the bar left or right by a certain specified amount, and is an obligatory function for anyone making dance music.

The available track parameters for a MIDI track usually differ a little from those used for audio. You still have controls for volume level and pan, but you will probably also have controls that determine which MIDI channel the data is sent to, along with the preset that should be played. Many sequencers will default such settings to General MIDI standards.

▲ MIDI plug-ins such as Nuendo's Arpache can be inserted into the signal path just as you would insert audio effects plug-ins.

OTHER MIDI EDITING TOOLS

THE PIANO ROLL

It can be assumed that your sequencer will have some sort of **grid editor**, or piano roll. This takes the form of a grid divided into musical values with note pitch represented on the vertical axis according to the piano keyboard on the left-hand side, and time and note values represented on the horizontal axis. Horizontally, the grid is divided into bars and beats according to the current quantization value and time signature. You will invariably have a brace of editing tools for drawing, cutting, copying and changing the values of notes in the grid. You may even have a snap function for ensuring that any notes you add or move about will always adhere to a certain note value – quavers or semiquavers, for example.

In addition to entering and editing MIDI notes, your sequencer's piano roll will have some method by which MIDI controller values may be drawn in or edited. These values represent MIDI CC (control change).

There is a standard list of which controllers belong where (volume on MIDI CC 7, pan on CC 10, and so on), but many are unassigned and may be used

for anything at all. None of these are written in stone, and you may find yourself changing them about as needed. Using your sequencer's ability to edit these controller values is very similar to the mix envelopes we discussed earlier, and can work wonders in adding some motion and life to your MIDI recordings.

DRUM GRID

Closely related to the piano roll, the **drum grid** is an editing window specifically designed for entering and altering drum parts. This is a variation on the piano roll, but with drum kit mappings in the vertical column instead of note pitches. More often than not, drum machines and drum synthesizers will adhere to a standard key mapping scheme designated in the General MIDI standard: kick drum on C 1, snare on D 1 and so forth. However, there is usually some method for creating and saving custom drum maps if you prefer to do so on your drum module.

STEP ENTRY

Besides the ability to enter notes via a pencil tool or in real-time, both the piano roll and the drum grid will have some sort of arrangement for the **step entry** of notes. Using step entry methods, you can play your notes in from the keyboard in step time rather than real-time – press the key for a hi-hat sound, a hi-hat hit will be entered and the current entry position will advance one step and wait for you to enter another note. This means that you can tap in a rhythm after the fact, and have all the notes you step entered fall perfectly into place within your rhythm.

For really detailed editing, you can use your program's event list. A MIDI event is any recordable MIDI command. Notes, velocities, program changes and MIDI CC parameters are all MIDI events.

The event list will be a numerical spread-sheet-like representation of any or all MIDI data for the track. This will include functions such as Note-On and Off commands, note length, velocity level and so forth. Event lists are not for the faint hearted, or for the neophyte MIDI musician, and some people choose to ignore them altogether.

SCORE EDITOR

Yet another place where one might enter and edit MIDI performance data is the **score editor**. This is set up like the traditional musical notation staff, and notes are drawn in using common musical notation symbols. This is crucial for those musicians with a conservative or formal musical background, and is excellent for documenting, printing and preserving paper copies of your compositions.

PRINT OUT YOUR MUSIC

It is somewhat disheartening to see how many musicians depend on techno-logical storage devices such as CDs or removable drives to document their music. After all, the devices by which such media may be played back will not be around forever, so how can future generations enjoy your work? You do not even need to know how to write music to print a paper copy of your compositions.

The sequencer will be glad to do the hard work for you. It should be noted that the results of the printed notation offered by the lion's share of sequencer software is not what would be called publishable in academic circles. That requires a dedicated notation program such as Sibelius. However, the score editor will serve you well as a tool for documenting and trading your charts with other musicians. Many score editors also provide guitar tablature as well as traditional notation.

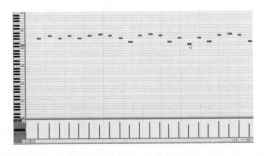

▲ *The classic piano roll is a common feature of most MIDI sequencers. It is an easy and intuitive way to enter or edit notes.*

USING THE MIXER IN YOUR SEQUENCER

While a few sequencers are out there without any sort of mixer at all (Mackie's Tracktion, for one), most software DAWs have some variation on a mixer modelled on – but infinitely more powerful than – a hardware mixing console. The designs include the typical mixer's channels strips arranged just as they would be seen on their hardware counterparts. In other words, fader and pan controls at the bottom, with EQ, effects sends and possibly gain controls above them.

A **channel strip** is a single mixer channel for controlling one track or input. It contains the volume fader, pan pot and any other controls available to one track or input on a mixer, and is sometimes sold individually as a hardware rack unit.

Unlike a hardware mixer, which has a finite number of channels, the software mixer can expand, adding channels as you add tracks to your compositions. Some will also add channels for every

available virtual instrument output. Some software mixers have built-in equalizers, while others expect you to use plug-ins for this purpose (and usually have them included). You might find a built-in dynamics processor such as a compressor or limiter as well. This is an awful lot of information to represent on the screen for each channel, so many mixers are collapsible, meaning that you can hide various components, leaving only what you need to use at the time.

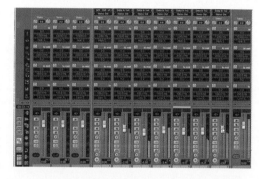

▲ *Considerably better outfitted than most hardware mixers, Nuendo's mixer provides all of the necessary functions right where you need them.*

Software mixers often have very flexible routing designs, allowing you to group channels to be controlled and routed together, and you can usually access whatever extra outputs and inputs your audio interface allows for, as well as virtual auxiliary busses. In more advanced sequencers, you can also have separate channels on the mixer for effects sends and returns for the ultimate in flexibility.

Most software sequencers these days combine both MIDI and audio channels in the same mixer, while some force you to tackle audio and MIDI mixing on separate screens. MIDI and audio channels will have different parameters available in their respective mixer channels.

▲ Many SONAR users never bother to open up its mixer window, as all mixing can easily be done on the arrange page.

One of the best things about software mixers is their automation capabilities. You can record any adjustments you make to any or all channels in real-time, and they will be faithfully recited back the next time the sequence is played. It is common for such automation to be displayed on the arrange page as the same sort of automation envelopes discussed earlier in this section.

Once they are, you can point and click with your mouse to fine-tune them or make any necessary alterations. Just try that with a dusty old Tapco mixer and see how far you get!

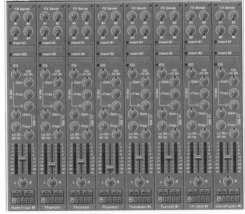

▲ One reason for Orion's popularity among software studio users is that its mixer so resembles the familiar hardware mixer.

Needless to say, it might not take very long for you to grow weary of executing complicated mixes by pointing and clicking with your mouse. This has been the primary motive behind many hardware controllers (control surfaces) that have been designed to offer the tactile experience of a mixing console, but without all of the inputs and outputs. These devices are designed to work specifically with software mixers Mackie's Mackie Control, and M-Audio's iControl are examples.

You can also use a MIDI-equipped digital mixer such as the Yamaha O1V96V2 for this purpose. For mixing, it is best if the device has motorized faders so that what you see on the screen is reflected in the hardware mixer's settings.

OTHER THINGS TO CONSIDER

Although you may have everything you could ever possibly need all within the confines of your software sequencer, there will inevitably be times when you will find it necessary to establish communication between your sequencer and the outside world.

COMMUNICATING WITH THE OUTSIDE WORLD

You may have a hardware synthesizer or effects device that depends on a MIDI clock to synchronize a particular feature. If your synthesizer has an arpeggiator onboard, you might want to lock it to the sequencer's tempo; likewise for any digital delays in your hardware multi-effects device.

These particular functions can be served by MIDI clock or MIDI time code (MTC), which, in all likelihood, can be generated by your sequencer and shuttled through any or all MIDI ports. It is a beautiful sound when all your hardware and software marches along to the beat of the same drum, as it were.

MIDI clock and time code are just two of many synchronization tools offered by the modern software sequencer. You may also have at your disposal the ability to read and write SMPTE. An acronym for the Society of Motion Picture and Television Engineers, which came up with it, SMPTE is an accepted standard form of time code used by professional studios and movie and television production houses to lock sound to picture. If you intend to do any scoring of film or video at all, SMPTE will be a necessity.

▲ *If you intend to do any professional scoring for films, you will need a DAW with support for SMPTE time-code.*

Other common synchronization standards are **MIDI Machine Code** (MMC), which was devised to lock tape decks, modular digital multitrack recorders and such together; and **frequency shift keying** (FSK), which is used to sync up older digital and control voltage gear.

Illustrated Home Recording Handbook

Rarely used today, FSK was once one of the only ways to get a sequencer or drum machine to sync up to a multitrack recorder. We spent far too many years trying to force a Tascam Portastudio and Chroma Polaris to get along with one another via the "miracle" of FSK.

THE FINAL FILE

When you have recorded something, and wish to preserve it or share it with the world, you will need to consider the issue of file formats. Most sequencers do not save the audio with the project file, but instead save pointers to the audio stored on the hard drive used by the project. This means that if you wish to transfer the song from one computer to another, you will need to ensure that the audio goes with it.

Cakewalk's bundle file format performs this task, but users of other sequencers may need to copy all the audio individually with the project. If you used any outboard gear, be sure to back up those presets in the same place. If you used only MIDI instruments, then a **Standard MIDI file** (SMF) will do the job.

Recently, a new standard file format has appeared, the **open media format** (OMF). This allows projects recorded on one sequencer to be opened in another. Keep in mind that if you make heavy use of external hardware or plug-ins, they will need to be available to the destination sequencer for any file exchange.

REMEMBER TO BACK UP

When you back up your material, it is not a bad idea to ensure that a copy of the backup is stored off premises. A safety deposit box is a good choice.

➡ *Notation Software pp. 218–219;*
Plug-ins pp. 234–247; MIDI pp. 252–267

▲ *OMF files allow you to transfer your recordings from one DAW to another. They are an excellent choice for taking your tracks to a professional studio for mixing.*

▲ *A number of options are available for synchronizing your external MIDI gear to your DAW.*

Part Two: Reference

BEFORE YOU START

Audio effects and processors are a mainstay of the recording world – indeed, you would be hard pressed to find a recording made in the last 50 years that has not benefited from some sort of sonic tweaking by such a device.

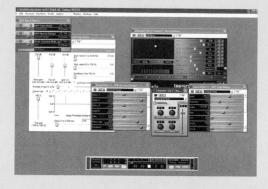

▲ *Software condenses all the controls into a single screen – but you are still going to need to know what they all mean!*

Sometimes the results of effects and processors can be very subtle, so that you would hardly even notice that they were there, while at other times they can be used to wrench and mangle your audio parts beyond all recognition – it really all depends on what you are trying to achieve and, to some degree, the type of music you are producing.

▲ *With so many controls to choose from you had better have an idea of what you want and how to get there before you start.*

The difference between an effect and a processor is a subtle one, and many people would not draw a distinction between the two. An effect adds a new component to the sound – for example, the sound of a reverberant space – whereas a processor changes the entire audio signal, as a compressor does. That said, we are not going to tiptoe around these two distinctions in this chapter and will largely be using the two words interchangeably.

When using effects and processors, you can get a little overwhelmed by the number of cryptically named parameters and options that need to be set, and randomly waggling at the knobs will rarely produce the desired results. It is, therefore, far better to understand what the controls actually do before deciding how to adjust them ... so read on!

DYNAMICS PROCESSORS

This is a catch all term covering many common studio processors and effects such as compressors, limiters, gates and expanders. These are called dynamics processors because they adjust the dynamic content of the sound being worked on – in other words, the volume difference between the quietest and loudest parts of a signal.

Although this might sound like quite a mundane and boring effect, used properly **dynamics processors** can greatly enhance the quality of your mixes and songs. A lot of sequencers sport a dynamics processor on every channel, while others require you to apply a dynamics plug-in to a channel.

But no matter how you get it there, a dynamics processor should be applied as an insert effect so that the entire signal is passed through it.

The controls available on a dynamics processor do not exactly have the most intuitive names, and the results of dynamics processing can be very subtle when not using high settings. It is therefore very important to have at least a vague understanding of how dynamics processing actually works in order to get the right results. To help us illustrate this point, we will be using graphs where a processor's input signal level is plotted against the output signal level that results from processing. We will be using these graphs a number of times over the next few pages, but to get us started the graph below shows what would result if no dynamics processing was being applied; as the input signal level increases, the output level increases by the same amount.

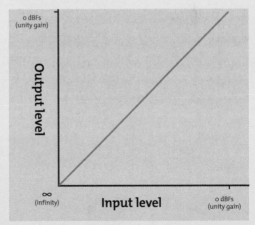

▲ *No dynamics processing applied.*

◄ *Many sequencers have a dynamics processor on every channel.*

COMPRESSORS

Compressors are the most common type of dynamics processor and are useful at all stages of the recording process.

At the tracking stage the most basic use of a **compressor** is to function as an automatic volume control, reducing the fluctuations in level that are common when recording live instruments (caused by, for example, a singer moving around slightly, or an open chord on an acoustic guitar tending to be louder than a fretted one). When it comes to mixing your song, a compressor can be used to increase the volume level of a part or even to make

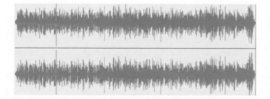

▲ *Notice the large peak in this wave form – this limits the maximum gain that can be applied to the part.*

▲ *A compressor has removed the peak, allowing more gain to be applied – you can see that the part is louder.*

your whole mix sound significantly louder and punchier. Paradoxically, this ability to increase the perceived volume level of a sound is actually achieved by reducing the volume level of the peaks in that sound. In a digital recording system there is a maximum signal level that can be recorded before **clipping** occurs (where a signal is too high to be represented digitally, thereby causing distortion). This is referred to as zero decibels full scale (0 dBFS).

It is the peak volume level of a signal that determines how much gain can be applied before this 0 dBFS point is exceeded. Unfortunately, our ears are not very sensitive to the short, loud **transients** (such as drum beats) that create signal peaks, and it is actually the average signal level that our ears use to give us the impression of loudness (or lack thereof).

Reducing the level of a signal's peaks allows you to apply more gain to the signal as a whole without causing clipping, and this in turn results in a higher average signal level, making it sound subjectively louder.

THRESHOLDS AND RATIOS

The two main controls associated with a compressor are **threshold** and **ratio**. Threshold is the level above which the incoming signal must pass before compression is applied, while the ratio

Illustrated Home Recording Handbook
Illustrated Home Recording Handbook

determines how much the output level is reduced by; in other words, how much compression is applied. To clarify this, look at the graph below left. The compressor's threshold has been set to -15 dB and the ratio set to 3:1.

This means that until the input signal level exceeds -15 dB (that is, 15 dB below 0 dBFS), no compression will occur, and every 1-dB increase in input level will result in a 1-dB increase in output level. However, when the input signal level exceeds -15 dB, compression is applied, and now the input signal level has to increase by 3 dB for the output level to increase by 1 dB. Once the input signal falls back below the threshold, the original 1:1 uncompressed ratio is restored.

The threshold and ratio controls work in conjunction to determine the amount of compression that is being applied to a signal. Let us say that you reduced the threshold to -30 dB and left the ratio at 3:1 as in the graph below right. This would mean that the input signal would be more likely to exceed the threshold and trigger the compressor, resulting in more compression being applied to the signal. The relatively gentle ratio of 3:1 will ensure, however, that the compression effect remains subtle and unobtrusive.

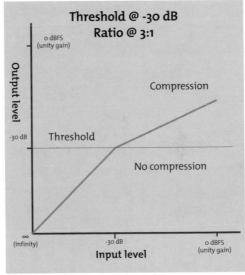

▲ The threshold is set to -30 dB and the ratio set to 3:1.

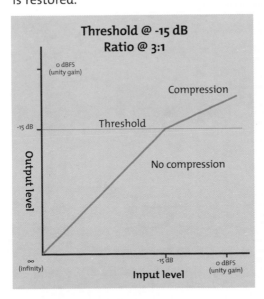

▲ The threshold is set to -15 dB and the ratio set to 3:1.

Conversely, if you left the threshold at -15 dB and increased the ratio to a setting of 10:1 as in the graph on the next page, the threshold might not be exceeded as frequently, but when it is far more compression is applied and the extreme ratio setting will ensure that the effect is far from subtle. More compression has been applied but in a different way, and with different-sounding results.

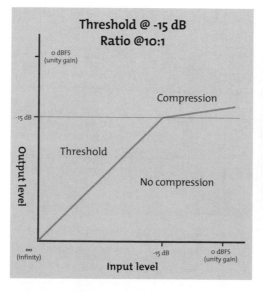

▲ The threshold is set to -15 dB and the ratio set to 10:1.

ATTACK AND DECAY

A lot of compressors feature controls for attack and decay, but while similar in principle to the controls of the same name found on synthesizers, they do not have the same effect on the sound.

The attack control determines how long it takes for the compressor to pass from no compression to full-ratio compression after the threshold has been exceeded. Small settings ensure

that even the shortest transient is caught and processed by the compressor, but also make the effect more obvious. Longer attack times are useful if you want a bit of the transient to get through before the compressor kicks in.

▲ Compressors commonly have attack and decay controls.

The decay control determines how long it takes for the compressor to return to no compression again after the signal falls below the threshold. Long decay times mean the compression effect drops off gradually, making it more subtle as a result, but also mean that signals below the threshold will be compressed if the compressor is still in a decay phase.

A lot of compressors have an auto mode where attack and decay settings are determined according to the nature of the input signal, and this will often provide perfectly usable results.

COMPRESSOR KNEES AND GAIN CONTROL

Believe it or not, compressors have **knees**. The name comes directly from the method of illustrating the results of dynamics processors on graphs as we are doing here. Notice in the graph below how the angle changes above the threshold and creates an angle a bit like a knee – this is where the name comes from. In our graphs, the change from no compression to full-ratio compression happens immediately, and a compressor capable of doing this would be described as being **hard knee**. More commonly, however, the transition from no compression to full-ratio compression is a little more gradual; this is called **soft knee**. A soft-knee compressor tends to deliver a more subtle and transparent effect

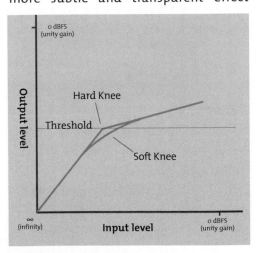

▲ The knee of a compressor is a measure of how it reacts to signals that are close to the threshold.

than its hard-knee counterpart. Most compressors provide you with both an input gain control and an output or make-up gain control.

The input gain simply adjusts the input signal level, although remember that this will affect the amount of compression being applied, as the input gain is independent of the threshold control; increase the input gain and the threshold is more likely to be exceeded.

The output gain control is often called the make-up gain because it makes up for the reduction in volume level that is a by-product of the compression process.

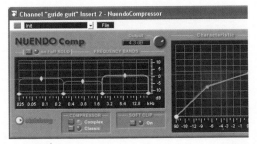

▲ Raising the output or make-up gain compensates for any loss in volume caused by the compressor.

As you are reducing the volume of the peaks in your signal when compressing it, the whole signal will appear to be quieter, which is where the make-up gain comes in – simply raise it to bring your overall level back up. Be aware that even though you have compressed your signal you can still cause it to clip, so do not get too exuberant with the make-up gain.

LIMITERS

A limiter is essentially a compressor that has a very high ratio, a hard knee, and a fast attack and decay time. As the name suggests, a limiter is used to limit the volume level of a signal.

▲ *Limiters are often included as part of a compressor plug-in.*

When the incoming signal exceeds the threshold of the **limiter**, a very high-ratio compression is applied. The onset of the compression is immediate because of the hard knee and fast attack time, and as soon as the signal peak has passed and its level has dropped back below the threshold, the fast decay time means the limiter immediately stops compressing the signal.

Limiters are often used in conjunction with a compressor; indeed, a lot of compressors actually have their own limiter stage. When used in this way, it is normal to set the limiter up so that its threshold is exceeded by only the loudest transients in the signal. This is because the very fast response of the limiter can reduce the level of these transients without your ears being aware of it.

You may sometimes hear people talk about **hard limiting**. This is where the threshold is set in such a way as to ensure it is (almost) constantly being exceeded by the incoming audio signal, causing constant limiting to be applied to the signal. While leaving your audio signal sounding rather squashed, hard limiting is still a useful effect. It is also particularly useful for processing an entire mix, where it imparts a hard, driving sound that is perfect for heavy rock, metal and the more extreme forms of dance music.

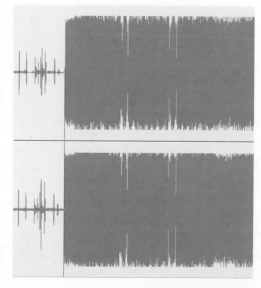

▲ *Hard limiting removes all the signal peaks from a part, but also creates a very squashed sound.*

NOISE GATES

A noise gate is a processor that is either on or off; that is, it either lets the signal through or it does not.

Noise gates work by monitoring the input signal. If the level of the signal exceeds the noise gate's threshold, the gate will open and the signal can pass through. If the input signal is below the threshold, the gate remains firmly shut, no signal is allowed through, and consequently no sound is heard. As the name suggests, this device was invented to reduce the amount of background noise in a recording by silencing a track when the instrument being recorded to the track is not playing. However, in the modern digital world this is less important, partly because you can adjust your audio parts to remove background noise, and partly because digital audio systems are inherently less noisy than analogue audio systems.

Nevertheless, a noise gate is still a useful tool, particularly when recording live instruments with a microphone. The microphone will pick up any background noise that is floating around in your studio – for example, the buzz of a guitar amp or the constant drone of a computer fan – and will also pick up a bit of noise in the analogue circuitry of your microphone pre-amp. Placing a gate into this signal chain

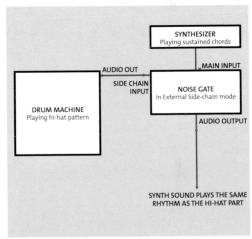

▲ *You can combine the rhythmic content of one part with the musical content of another using a noise gate.*

(hardware or software) will silence the channel while the instrument is not playing and open it when the instrument is played and the threshold exceeded. Gates can also be used to create rhythmic effects by feeding separate signals to the gate's input and **side-chain** input.

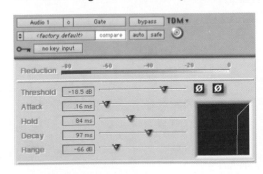

▲ *A noise gate only opens when the input signal is louder than the threshold.*

NOISE GATE CONTROLS

All noise gates have a threshold control – when the input signal level rises above the threshold, the gate opens; when it falls below the threshold the gate closes. However, many noise gates sport much more than this basic level of control.

For starters, some noise gates allow you to adjust the tone of the side-chain signal (that is, the portion of the signal that the noise gate "listens to" to determine whether to open or not); this makes the gate more sensitive to the low- or high-frequency components of the signal being processed.

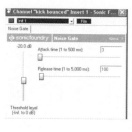

▲ *Some gates have very few controls ...*

▶ *... while others are a bit more complex.*

HOLD TIME

If your noise gate has attack and release controls, these determine how quickly the gate opens and closes in response to the threshold being exceeded.

It is also common for a noise gate to have a **hold time** control. This keeps the gate open for the selected amount of

time after the signal falls below the threshold level, and helps to ensure that you do not cut off the decay portion of the sound being processed.

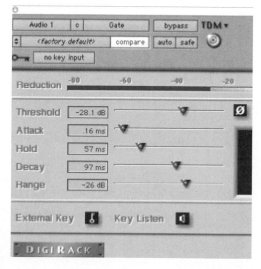

▲ *Pro Tools' standard Noise Gate lets you adjust the range of the gate.*

RANGE

A lot of noise gates work by being either open or closed, but some can simply turn down the signal rather than cutting it off entirely. This is done with a control called **range**, and is measured in decibels.

With this type of noise gate, the gate does not close when the signal falls below the threshold; rather, it turns the signal down by the selected range setting. This tends to yield results that sound more natural than the absolute silence created by a standard noise gate.

EXPANDERS

An expander is often described as being the opposite of a compressor; technically speaking this is true, but it can also be a misleading analogy.

A compressor acts when the input signal exceeds the threshold level, whereas an **expander** kicks in when a signal falls below the threshold. Also, an expansion ratio is the inverse of a compression ratio, so instead of ratios such as 4:1 – as found on a compressor – an expander will have a ratio such as 1:4.

This ratio is similar in meaning to one found on a compressor; that is, every 1 dB increase in input signal level results in a 4 dB increase in output level. However, because this volume adjustment is occurring below the threshold and not above it, the result is that the output level drops off more steeply when the signal is below the threshold (see graph below left). This is why expanders are often used in place of noise gates, as the drop-off of the signal level below the threshold produces a more subtle and transparent effect than the sharp cutoff of a gate. There is also a type of expander known as an **upward expander**, which works on signals that exceed the threshold level. These are only really useful for de-compressing an over-compressed signal.

An expander increases the dynamic range of a signal – in other words, it increases the difference between the peak and average signal levels. But because of the 0 dBFS limit, the expanded sound will appear to be quieter than the original unprocessed sound.

Threshold @ -15 dB
Ratio @ 1:4

0 dBFS
(unity gain)

No Expansion

-15 dB   Threshold

Output level

Expansion

∞
(infinity)

-15 dB   0 dBFS
(unity gain)

Input level

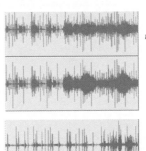

◄ *This audio part has not been expanded ...*

◄ *... here is the same audio part after being processed with an expander.*

◄ *An expander makes the volume level below the threshold drop off more quickly.*

THE SIDE CHAIN (AKA KEY)

For any dynamic processor to do its job properly, it has to monitor the incoming audio signal to determine when to process the signal and when to leave it alone.

To do this, a copy of the input signal is fed to a signal path within the processor known as the side chain (or the **key**), and it is this side chain that is monitored by the dynamics processor.

▲ *Filtering the side chain signal makes the processor less sensitive to the filtered frequencies.*

It is common to be able to filter or adjust the tone of the side-chain signal, and this has the result of making the processor more or less sensitive to different frequency components within the sound being processed. For example, filtering bass frequencies out of the side-chain signal of a compressor will make it less likely that bass-heavy components of the sound will cause the compressor's threshold to be exceeded. If this were done, say, on a drum loop it would mean the kick drums would be less likely to trigger the processor than the snares and hi-hats.

▲ *The rhythmic guitar effect in the Smiths' 'How Soon Is Now' demonstrates a classic use for the side chain.*

Some dynamics processors go a step further and allow you to process one signal with the dynamic characteristics of another. This is done via an external side-chain input, allowing you to feed separate signals to the side chain and main processor inputs. As well as making **ducking** and **de-essing** effects possible (see opposite), you can also create interesting effects by feeding a rhythmic track to the side chain of a noise gate or expander and feeding a different musical part through the processor. This creates a stuttering effect in the processed signal as the rhythmic signal opens and closes the gate according to its own transients – a classic example can be heard on the Smiths' song "How Soon Is Now".

DUCKING

Ducking reduces the volume of one audio signal automatically when another one is present.

This is mainly used in the broadcast world to automatically reduce, or duck, the volume of a music track to make space for a voice-over or similar, but it can be used in many music recording situations too.

▲ *Ducking is mainly used to duck a music track while a presenter is speaking.*

All you need to create a ducker is a compressor with an external side-chain input. In the typical broadcast world setup, the music track is fed through the compressor and mixed with the signal from the presenter's microphone. A second signal is taken from the microphone's channel (typically via an **auxiliary send**) and sent to the compressor's external side-chain input. The compressor's threshold is set so that when the presenter speaks the threshold is exceeded and the compressor kicks in.

However, the signal being compressed is the music being passed through the compressor, not the microphone signal arriving at the side-chain input. When the presenter speaks, the music is compressed and, as a result, becomes quieter.

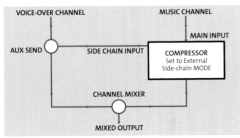

▲ *A typical ducker setup.*

A fast compressor attack time should be used so that the music ducks as soon as the voice-over starts. A longer decay time is best so that the music moves smoothly back to full volume when the presenter stops talking.

As well as for broadcasting purposes, ducking can be very useful musically. Where there is more than one sound playing at the same time in the same frequency range, one or more of the sounds can be automatically reduced in volume in order to let the most important sound stand out. Ducking guitar parts with a vocal is a common example; when the all-important vocal kicks in, the guitar part that was previously the focus of the track is lowered in volume to make room for it.

DE-ESSERS

De-essing is an effect specific to vocal recording and is used to reduce the harsh distortion that can result from sibilant sounds ("s", "sh", etc.).

When using a de-esser, the microphone signal is split into two identical channels. A compressor is inserted on the first channel and the output of the second channel is fed to an EQ and then into the external side-chain input of this compressor. It is the high frequencies in sibilant sounds (between 5 kHz and 10 kHz) that cause the distortion, so enhancing these frequencies in the side-chain signal via the EQ in the second channel will cause the compressor to be more sensitive to these sibilant frequencies. When the vocalist produces a sibilant sound the compressor will automatically reduce the volume of the signal, thereby reducing the distortion.

De-essing can be made even more effective if the signal passing through the compressor is delayed slightly, by up to 10 m, so that the side chain triggers the compressor before the actual sibilant sound arrives at the compressor's input.

You can also use a device called a **dynamic EQ**. This is essentially a compressor that only reduces the level of particular frequencies, not the entire signal.

MULTI-BAND DYNAMICS

A multi-band processor works by splitting the incoming signal into separate frequency bands and then processing these simultaneously but separately, before mixing the bands back together again for final consumption.

The benefit of this approach, particularly when working with full-range sounds, is that a far more subtle effect is obtained, even when heavily processing a sound. For example, a boomy kick drum will only cause the low-end frequency band to exceed its compression threshold and so the higher bands, where our ears are more sensitive anyway, will remain unaffected. Use **multi-band compression** and limiting to process entire mixes and full-frequency-range sounds such as pianos, because broadband processors will tend to impart a pumping effect to material of this nature.

▲ *Multi-band dynamics processors deal with each frequency band separately.*

MODULATION EFFECTS

Modulation effects are generally used to give a part a thicker, fuller sound, to add a shimmering ethereal quality to a part, or even to make a mono part sound like it is in fact a stereo part.

Modulation effects can be applied as an **insert effect**, but you should set the wet/dry balance of the plug-in so that some of the original signal gets through. You can also apply a modulation effect as a **send effect** (generally considered the norm), although in this scenario the balance should be set to 100 per cent wet.

An insert effect is an effect unit or plug-in that processes the entire signal. A send effect is an effect that is fed with signals from auxiliary sends and mixed back to its own channel(s). The wet/dry balance is the balance between the processed and unprocessed signals.

This family of effects works by processing the signal being fed into the plug-in's (or hardware device's) input with varying amounts of delay, pitch shifting and/or feedback. The amount of processing can be varied over time, turning the thinnest, dullest sound into a lush, rich, shimmering feast for the ears.

USE SPARINGLY

Modulation effects such as these are entirely synthetic and very rarely occur in nature, so if you slap your modulation effects around your recordings too much you will end up with an artificial, unnatural-sounding finished product. You may also find that even though this kind of effect can make a part sound wider in the stereo field, it also makes the part sound less distinct because your ears cannot pin-point the exact position it is coming from. Sometimes the synthetic or super-wide sound may be what you are aiming for – then lay it on with a shovel!

ADT

A common trick that is employed in the studio to make a part sound thicker or fuller is to record two or more versions of the part and pan them to separate positions in the stereo field.

This technique is called **double tracking**, and it creates its thickening effect through the slight pitch and timing differences that will exist between the two versions. The technique requires a fair amount of discipline on the part of the musician, as the two (or more) versions of the take have to be performed (practically) identically for the trick to work. Luckily, there are a couple of easier ways to achieve a similar result: **automatic double tracking** (ADT) and **chorus** (see below).

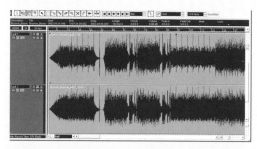

▲ *Manual double-tracking is a common method of thickening a part or sound, but it requires the ability to play accurately and consistently.*

If you do not actually have an ADT plug-in then do not worry – the effect is easy to create with your audio sequencer. Start off by recording a good take of the part you want to thicken and then copy it to a second track in your sequencer. Now apply a short delay (with no feedback) of between 10 ms and 50 ms to the copied part, or even simply move the part forward by a few milliseconds in your sequencer's edit window.

You can strengthen the effect by processing the copied part with a pitch shifter, although do not shift further than +/-10 per cent. Finally, pan your two parts so that they get a bit of separation in the stereo field, although panning them hard left and right is not advised as this will weight the sound to one side of the stereo field.

CHORUS

Without doubt the most frequently used modulation effect is chorus.

A basic chorus effect is achieved by applying a small pitch shift to the signal being processed and then slowly modulating the amount of pitch shifting with a Low Frequency Oscillator (LFO). A more pronounced effect can be achieved by adding a small delay of up to about 30 ms to the processed signal. The results of the processing are then mixed back with the original sound, typically with a 50:50 wet/dry balance.

▲ *A basic chorus is very easy to set up.*

A stereo chorus works in the same way, but applies slightly different amounts of delay, pitch shift and/or LFO modulation to the left and right channels respectively. This is a good way of making a

EFFECTS AND PROCESSORS

mono part sound like it is a stereo one. Some go a step further and take multiple copies of the input signal, applying slightly different amounts of delay, pitch-shift and/or LFO modulation to each copy. The result is a processed signal that is richer and fuller than anything a basic chorus processor can achieve.

Chorus processors tend to have very simple controls. The **depth** control determines the amount of pitch shifting that will be applied; the **rate** control sets the speed of the LFO that is modulating the amount of pitch shifting; the delay control adjusts the amount of delay being applied. Many chorus plug-ins allow the modulation rate to be synchronized with your song's tempo, although being in perfect time like this can enhance the effect's artificial nature.

FLANGING

Flanging is produced in a very similar way to chorus, although there are also some distinct differences.

First, a **flanger** always introduces a delay element to the processed signal. The pitch of the signal is then modulated by an LFO in the same way as with chorus, but this time a copy of the modulated signal is fed back to the flanger's input. This results in a very discernable effect that is often metallic sounding and always wholly unnatural; a flanging effect is practically impossible to produce acoustically.

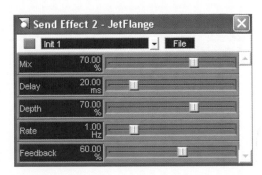

▲ *Flangers are easy to set up due to their having only a few parameters.*

Because the flanger sound is so distinctive and obvious when used, it has become quite clichéd and unpopular. You do not have to follow this trend yourself, of course, but you should only use flanging sparingly and only in the context of a special effect – a flanged rhythm guitar part running through an entire song would get very tiresome! Making settings on a flanger could not be easier, as there are only four controls and even small changes make a noticeable difference in the character of the effect.

DEPTH AND SPEED CONTROLS

The depth control sets the maximum amount of pitch shifting that will be applied, and the speed or rate control determines the frequency of the LFO that is modulating the amount of pitch shift.

Part Two: Reference

DELAY AND FEEDBACK

The delay control sets the amount of delay that is applied to the processed signal before it is fed back in with the unprocessed one, whilst the **feedback** (also known as **regen**) selects how much of the processed signal is fed back to the flanger's input.

PHASING

Take a look at the waveform of an audio recording in your sequencer, zooming in close so that you can see a single continuous line.

See how the signal oscillates above and below the centre line, creating **crests** and **troughs**. The pattern of these crests and troughs is the signal's **phase**. If you were to invert the series of crests and troughs, so that crests become troughs and vice versa, the resultant sound would be exactly the same.

However, if you mixed this phase-inverted signal with the original **in-phase** signal, the crests and troughs would cancel each other out, and you would hear nothing. Yes, literally nothing! This is called **phase cancellation**.

If you were to move the processed signal's phase slowly from an in phase to an inverted phase, you would hear the tonal character of the resultant sound change as different frequencies were cut and boosted in response to the varying amounts of phase addition and cancellation being created.

Phasing, then, is an effect that harnesses this method of shifting the tonal characteristics of a signal. The signal to be processed is fed into something known as a **phase-shift matrix** (or its digital equivalent), and the amount of phase-shifting applied by the matrix is modulated with an LFO. This creates a constantly shifting pattern of phase cancellation and results in a sound that is not dissimilar to flanging, but which lacks its intense, artificial nature.

Phasing is most effective when used on harmonically rich sound sources such as electric guitars, electric pianos, synthesizer pads and the like.

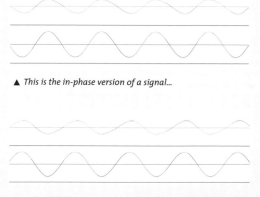

▲ *This is the in-phase version of a signal...*

▲ *... and the out-of-phase version of the same wave. They sound identical, but will cancel each other if played simultaneously.*

VIBRATO AND TREMOLO

Vibrato and tremolo are very similar effects, so much so that many people do not realize they are different.

It is normal to process an entire signal with these effects and not to mix the unprocessed signal back with the processed one as is done with ADT, chorus, flanging and phasing (that is, they should be used as inserts set to 100 per cent wet).

▲ *Vibrato simulates the effect of wobbling a string on a guitar.*

Both effects use an LFO to create them. A vibrato effect uses the LFO to modulate the pitch of the sound being processed, and is useful on long sustained sounds, such as a synthesizer pad. This effect should not be overused, as it can easily make a part sound out of tune. Tremolo, on the other hand, applies the LFO to the volume of the sound, and is often used to give a rhythmic quality to a part. Tremolo works particularly well on clean(ish) guitar tones, and is perfect for rockabilly and surf musical styles.

AUTO-PANNING

Auto-panning, as the name suggests, is an effect that automatically adjusts a part's position in the stereo field, constantly moving it from left to right and back again.

Auto-panners allow you to set the rate and width of the effect, and the centre point around which the pan effect will oscillate.

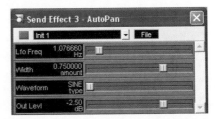

▲ *Auto-pan effects cause the processed signal to oscillate from left to right.*

You should be very cautious with auto-panning, viewing it as a special effect to be used sparingly and judiciously. Used in excess, the constant slewing of the signal from left to right can be quite disorientating and even nauseating to the listener.

SPATIAL EFFECTS

Delay and reverb are effects that are used primarily to create the impression that an instrument or part was played in a different acoustic space from the one in which it was actually recorded. In this context, the result of the effect processing tends to be seen as an embellishment rather than a constituent component of the part being processed.

Spatial effects can also be used in such a way that they become an intrinsic part of the sound being processed, particularly when used on synthesizer and lead guitar sounds. The use of spatial effects is practically unavoidable in the recording world, for unless you have access to a complex of differently sized rooms, all with good acoustics, the only way to create the impression of such spaces is with an effects unit or plug-in.

REVERB

When you make a sound in a room, or in an acoustic space, the sound waves produced travel outwards in all directions until something gets in the way to stop them, typically a wall.

When this happens, some of the sound wave will be absorbed by the materials in the wall, but some of it will be reflected back into the room, where it will keep travelling until it reaches another surface, where it is again partially absorbed and partially reflected. These reflected sound waves bounce around until eventually the walls absorb all of the wave's energy.

Because the sound wave propagates from the sound source in all directions, a very complex series of reflections will be created, and rarely will the reflections appear to be coming from any particular direction.

◄ *Sound waves are partially absorbed and partially reflected by surfaces they encounter.*

ABSORBED

DIRECT

REFLECTED

The tonal character of the reflections, and the time they take to fade, is determined by the size and shape of the room and the acoustic absorbency (or reflectivity) of the walls.

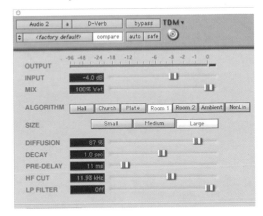

▲ *A reverb processor creates a virtual room for your audio parts to exist in.*

Reverb, then, is an artificial simulation of these sound reflections. You should apply a reverb unit or plug-in as a send effect, as this allows you to create sends from multiple audio tracks, thereby giving the impression that all the instruments were played in the same acoustic space. To create an accurate impression of the acoustic space, however, reverbs tend to have a lot of adjustable parameters. Let us take a look at them in detail.

COMMON REVERB CONTROLS

Pre-delay is a time delay between the initial sound and the onset of the reverb. In the real world, pre-delay is deter-mined by the distance from the sound source and listener to the nearest reflective surface, so a longer pre-delay requires a larger room. In the studio, pre-delay can be set separately from room size and can help to make a sound stand out from its associated reverberation.

Reverb time/decay is the time taken for the reverberations to fade back to nothing. This is analogous to the acoustic absorbency of the walls in a real-world acoustic space, with shorter decays giving the impression of greater acoustic absorbency.

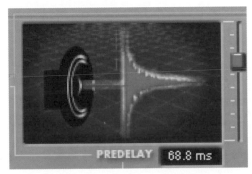

▲ *Pre-delay creates a pause between the initial sound and the onset of the reverb.*

Size determines the physical size of the simulated space. This also has a relationship with the decay time, although a smaller-sized room will tend to have a different tonal character than a larger one, even if the same decay time is set.

Part Two: Reference

Early reflection (ER) level determines the prominence of any individual reflections that can be heard before the onset of the main reverberations. In the real world, an ER can be caused by reflections from objects that are between the sound source and the walls where the main **wash** of the reverb is produced. Loud ERs give quite a snappy sound to a reverb.

Density relates to the texture of the walls in a real-world reverberant space. A very smooth wall will reflect sound waves in a more uniform direction than a rough or bumpy one, whose uneven surface will scatter the reflections in all directions, thereby creating a denser, more complex reverb sound.

High and **low frequency controls** are normally laid on to adjust the tone of the reverb sound. In the real world, all materials absorb different frequencies within a sound in different ways. A bare stone wall, for example, will absorb little but the very lowest frequencies, resulting in a bright, reverb sound, whereas plasterboard walls will absorb a lot of higher frequencies but be less effective at soaking up the lower ones. In a reverb unit or plug-in the high- and low-frequency controls allow you to simulate these real-world characteristics.

USING REVERB TO CREATE A 3-D SOUND FIELD

Imagine you are standing next to a speaker in a large, reverberant room. When a sound is played through the speaker, the direct signal reaches your ears before the ensuing reverberations – you are, after all, closer to the speaker producing the sound than to the walls producing the reverberations. However, if you were to move the speaker to the far end of the room, the situation could be very different; the reflected reverberant sound might be more prominent than the direct sound. This means that even if you were blindfolded you would be fully aware of the fact that the speaker had been moved farther away from you.

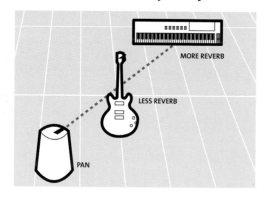

▲ *Adding a sense of depth to your mixes can help to separate sounds that occupy the same pan position.*

By applying this principle in the studio it is possible to create a stereo sound field that has both width and depth. The left-to-right position of a sound is easily set using a pan control on your mixer or sequencer channel while the near-to-far position can be set by adjusting balance between the direct signal and its resulting reverb.

Add more reverb and the part will sound more distant; reduce the reverb and the part comes closer again. You can enhance this effect by progressively rolling off high-end EQ from the direct signal, to make the sound appear farther and farther away.

There may be occasions when you want to apply a lot of reverb to a signal but also want it to stay in the foreground of the sound field, such as with a vocal or lead guitar part. The trick here is to apply a pre-delay to the reverb, thereby separating the direct signal from the resultant reverb.

It is advisable to avoid overdoing things with reverb, as using too much can make your mixes sound indistinct and mushy. But do not be too shy – the reverb sound should not be completely imperceptible. Trust your ears!

DELAY

Delay processing is at the heart of a number of different effects types, but it can be equally striking when used on its own.

A **delay** slows the signal that is being passed through it. There is, however, a little bit more to it than that. For a start, a feed from the delayed signal can be fed back into the input of the processor, producing multiple repeats of the original signal. Moreover, consider your stereo delay processors, which can handle the left and right channels in a number of different ways.

While delay is a relatively unnatural sound (caves and canyons excluded), it can still be used to create an impression of extra space and air in a mix. Short delays give a **slap-back** effect that are reminiscent of a sound being played in a small "snappy"-sounding room. Longer delay times can make even single notes take on a life of their own – just ask a guitarist!

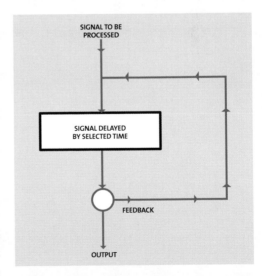

▲ *The signal path within a basic delay unit.*

DELAY TYPES

Mono delay is a straightforward delay processor as described above, with controls for delay time and feedback amount. It is most commonly found in guitar effects pedals.

L/R stereo delay is essentially a pair of mono delays with separate controls for the left and right channels. Setting a slightly different delay time on each channel creates a much sweeter-sounding effect than a mono delay.

LCR stereo delay is similar to an L/R stereo delay, except this time there are three separate delay lines: one panned to the middle and the others panned to the left and right channels.

Ping-pong delay only has a single delay line, but each successive repeat is played to the left channel, then the right channel, then back to the left and so on.

Multitap delay is more complicated. With this type of delay you can set a number of different delay times, depending upon the number of **taps**. Each tap is a single delay line. The first tap's delay setting determines the time between the beginning of the original signal and the beginning of first repetition. The second tap's delay setting determines the time

between the beginning of first repetition and the beginning of the second, and so on. Each tap's feedback signal is sent back to the beginning of the chain, where the whole process starts again. The tap's main signal can be panned to anywhere in the stereo field. Multitap delays can produce some interesting delay effects that build up over time, but can be tricky to set up.

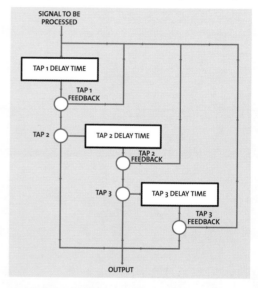

▲ *A typical multitap delay processor's signal path.*

Slapback delay is a very short delay (between 10 ms and 50 ms), typically mono and with only a tiny amount of feedback. It was very popular back in the 1950s and 1960s when it was a quintessential part of the rock'n'roll sound. Because of its historic roots, slapback delay always gives a retro feel to any part you use it on.

OTHER EFFECTS PROCESSORS

PITCH SHIFTING AND TIME STRETCHING

Pitch shifting and time stretching are very closely related effects.

Adjusting the pitch of an audio recording is a simple process, and involves nothing more than slowing down or speeding up the playback rate of the recorded part. But if you speed up a part to raise its pitch, its tempo will also speed up and this is often not the desired result. This is where **time stretching** comes in, an effect that was impossible before the days of digital audio. A digital recording is actually a string of individual samples replayed so quickly that our ears are fooled into thinking it is a constant sound.

This functions in much the same way as a movie does – a series of still images is played back fast enough to fool our eyes into thinking we are seeing a moving image. Sticking with the movie analogy, if each frame of the movie were played twice in succession, rather than just once, we would see exactly the same series of images but they would only be playing at half the speed.

▲ *Pitch shifting can be performed in real-time ...*

▲ *... but time stretching can only really be done as an off-line process.*

A time-stretch processor, then, adjusts the length of a part by repeating or skipping individual samples, thereby lengthening or shortening the audio being processed without affecting the pitch and overall content of the part. Used in conjunction with a pitch shifter, a time-stretch processor allows you to adjust the pitch of a part without altering its length or, alternatively, to adjust the length of the part without adjusting its pitch.

Time stretching produces a more natural sound when making small adjustments to a part's length. You should therefore consider breaking large time stretches up into a series of smaller ones.

EQUALIZERS

An equalizer (EQ) is a processor that adjusts the volume level of specific bands of frequencies within the part being processed.

Most sequencers use the same parametric **EQ** model as is found on a professional mixing console. This differs a great deal from the basic bass, middle and treble controls found on the average hi-fi. EQ is the most important effect in the sound engineer's arsenal. It can be used in a creative way to sculpt a particular frequency pattern into a sound, or it can be used to correct and improve imperfections in your recorded parts. It is important to understand that there are no hard-and-fast rules as to what frequencies you should boost or cut for particular instruments, as it always depends on the part in question and its context within the music you are creating. However, equalizing should not involve just aimlessly twiddling with the settings until you are bored; you should always have a goal in mind before you reach for the EQ controls.

A common mistake that is made when equalizing a part is to arrange the EQ controls so that the part in question sounds good when playing on its own

without the rest of the song to back it up. But what we think of as a good sound tends to be one with a full bass end and a sparkling top end. EQ all your parts like this and they will all end up getting in the way of each other (sonically speaking). When you EQ a part, therefore, you should always keep in mind the important tonal components of that sound – for example, bass for kick drums and bass guitar, mid-frequencies for vocals and guitars, etc., – as well as the part it plays within the context of the song you are producing. You should always check your EQ decisions in the context of your entire track, and be sure to test the equalized signal against the unprocessed original – this way you can be sure that it actually sounds better, and not simply a bit louder.

▲ *Many sequencers have console-style parametric EQ built into every channel.*

EQ TYPES

A **shelving EQ** applies a cut or boost to frequencies that fall above (**high shelving**) or below (**low shelving**) the frequency selected for the processor.

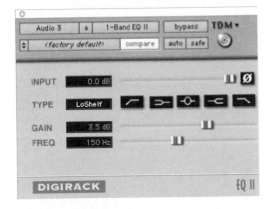

▲ A shelving EQ.

A **parametric EQ** has a selectable centre frequency, around which the signal is cut or boosted. The amount of spread from this centre frequency is governed by the Q or bandwidth control, with higher settings causing frequencies further away from the centre frequency to be affected than with lower Q settings.

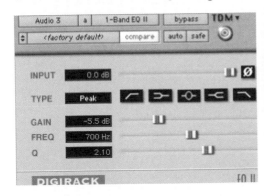

▲ A parametric EQ.

A **graphic EQ** has a number of fixed-frequency bands, with the bands arranged in such a way as to provide access to the whole audible frequency spectrum. The amount of cut or boost applied to each band is set by a fader, and the name graphic EQ is derived from the fact that the positions of these cut/boost faders give an accurate representation of the EQ curve being applied.

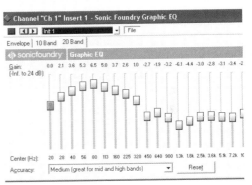

▲ A graphic EQ.

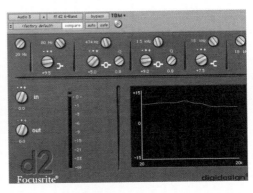

▲ If you simply boost all the EQ frequencies, you are doing little more than turning up the volume!

➡ What Is a Synthesizer? pp. 32–35; What Is a Sequencer? pp. 44–47; What Is an Effect? pp. 68–79; Finishing Off pp. 144–161; Synthesis pp. 268–287; Studio Layouts pp. 354–363

HARDWARE

HARDWARE

Before you rush off to the local computer supplier, take stock of what you really need to buy to create a good, workable home studio setup that is tailored to your needs – and budget.

MAC OR PC?

Ah yes, the age-old question: "Which should I get, a Mac or a PC?" This seemingly innocent question can turn brother against brother, friend into foe. The passion that users have for their platform of choice is legendary; thousands of hours have been spent arguing the issue in print, online and on television – with no end in sight.

But the truth is, it is not really all that bad, or even that big a deal anymore. A decade ago, which computer to use for recording music was simple: Apple Macintosh. The Mac was the computer with the more robust GUI, more stability and more multimedia savvy than Windows 3.1 (anyone remember that?), and most software for MIDI and recording was written for the Macintosh. That all started to change with Windows 95, and while the Macintosh still has the reputation for

being more user friendly, and more Macintosh computers that PCs are in high-priced professional studios, the Windows PC has become a truly viable music machine. Let us look at the current state of each platform for running music and recording software.

THE PC

Windows XP provided PC users with a modern, stable operating system that made up

▶ *The range and quality of the music-making software available for PCs means that function of the home computer does not have to be limited to creating spreadsheets and playing games!*

much of the ground lost to the Mac OS in previous years in the area of music production. The newest Intel microprocessors are now used by both PCs and Macs, further narrowing the performance gap (although Macs can now run both their own OS and Windows. See below.) Machines on both platforms are very fast, and there is an almost unlimited supply of music production software for Windows, which was not always the case. In 2007 Microsoft released Windows Vista, which has an entirely new audio architecture designed to further erase the differences that have traditionally made audio recording and programming more convenient and seamless on Macs. Many experienced users, however, chose to wait before committing to Vista until drivers for hardware were updated and the inevitable bugs were worked out of the system.

Although great strides have been made in convenience with new versions of Windows, administrative tasks, security settings and troubleshooting can still be time-consuming challenges on the platform.

THE MAC

The Macintosh may have lost the title of the only game in town, but it still has a lot going for it. Mac OS X is elegant, streamlined and very stable. Macintosh hardware is traditionally more expensive than PC hardware, although you tend to get a lot for your money. Apple's replacement of the Motorola/IBM-built PowerPC processor with Intel models (used in PCs) even allows Macs to run Windows, so the rare music-production application that only runs on PCs can be launched, converted, and perhaps even run simultaneously on a single Macintosh.

Macs also have far fewer problems with viruses and other security issues than PCs, and handles them more elegantly than their Windows counterparts. Ironically, the Mac security advantage may be the result of Apple's traditionally small market share overall, which finally is growing, thanks in part to Apple's other hardware triumphs, the iPod and iPhone, which has been predicted to be a major success in 2007.

In the music software market, of course, the major DAW applications Apple Logic Pro and MOTU Digital Performerare still exclusively Mac programs. The grandfather of pro-audio applications, Digidesign Pro Tools, though available for Windows, remains almost exclusively a Mac-based system in pro studios.

IT IS UP TO YOU

So in the end, the answer to the question "Mac or PC?" is: the computer with which you are more comfortable and that will run the software you want to use. If you want to use a program that runs only on one platform, the decision is made for you. If you have been using one platform for years and are really comfortable with it, there is no need to change for music. You can make brilliant music with either platform, and it really does come down to personal preference.

▶ *A Mac is a good, albeit pricey, bet for those who want to set up a home studio.*

HARD DISKS

Now that you have the machine, let us look at hard drives.

Because hard drives are so much larger and operating systems so much more stable these days, the occasional home recordist may do just fine recording to a

▲ *The Glyph GT051 is a portable external hard drive.*

single internal drive, as long as the drive remains optimized and defragmented and has plenty of unused space for work files that the audio program may generate. Burn the projects to CDs as soon as they're completed to free up hard-drive space. Most important: if your internal hard drive crashes, you lose anything that's not backed up.

With an external hard drive, you can access your projects quickly from another computer. External drives also are portable and a lot simpler to hook up than an internal drive.

These days, with FireWire (IEEE 1394) or USB 2 ports on almost every external hard drive, you simply plug the proper cable from your computer into your hard disk

and you are ready to go. In fact, some external drives are even capable of accepting their power over the FireWire or USB 2 bus, meaning that you will not even need an extra power supply. If you need an additional hard drive, therefore, we recommend you get an external one.

You will generally get better performance if your operating system and music applications are on one hard drive and your audio files are on another. In fact, some applications, such as Pro Tools, do not even support recording audio onto the system drive. Serious and semi-pro users should plan on adding an external hard drive to your DAW.

SPEED

How fast does your hard drive need to be? Simple answer – look for a hard drive that spins at a minimum of 7200 RPM (revolutions per minute) with a seek time of 10 ms or less. This will guarantee that your drive is fast enough to read and write a substantial number of audio tracks simultaneously.

SIZE

As to how large your hard drive needs to be, that depends on the size of two things: your music projects, and your wallet. The larger the hard drive, the more audio files it can store and the pricier it will be. Most hard drives these days are from £80 to £250 and range from category C to category D in price (see p. 2). If you have the money, it is probably safe to get the largest hard drive you can afford. If you are on a budget, you might want to stick to a 120-GB hard drive, or even smaller. Even 120-GB is a lot of track minutes' worth of audio at a 44.1-khz sample rate, so it will definitely serve you well.

As a general rule, you can assume that each minute of mono 24-bit audio at a 44.1- or 48-kHz sample rate requires about 8 MB, so that 120-GB drive will work out to about 15,000 track minutes. If you record at double sample rates (88.2 or 96 kHz), you can record half that many track minutes – or 7,500 track minutes – on your 120-GB drive.

To determine how much room that gives you based on how many tracks you use in your songs, you can divide the total track minutes by how many mono tracks of audio your songs normally require (count stereo tracks as two separate mono tracks). For example, if you normally have 48 tracks of audio recorded at 24-bit, 44.1-kHz in your songs, you would divide 15,000 minutes by 48 tracks and get about 312.5 minutes' worth of songs on a 120-GB hard drive. You can use the same formula for larger hard drives, to get the best drive for your needs.

SOUND CARDS

Your audio interface is means by which audio enters your computer and gets onto your hard disk. A built-in audio card that records and plays back 16-bit. 44.1 kHz audio may be fine for occasional recording, but most users will want to buy a dedicated interface to get higher-resolution audio into your computer.

▲ *The Edirol UA5 soundcard. This sound card connects to your computer via USB.*

Many different options are out there for nearly every conceivable price range and feature set. For example, there are simple stereo I/O sound cards more suited to video gamers than music producers that you can find for pennies (or already included in your PC) all the way up to a Pro Tools HD Accel system costing more than half a dozen computers and found only in the most professional studios.

TYPES OF AUDIO INTERFACE

Audio interfaces are connected to your computer in different ways, from PCI

Part Two: Reference

cards that you install inside your computer, to USB or USB 2 interfaces, to FireWire interfaces. Each type has its own advantages and disadvantages.

PCI CARDS

These are generally cheaper and often offer more inputs and outputs. The PCI bus also has more bandwidth than USB, USB 2 or the original FireWire (400 Mbits/sec.). Installation is more difficult than with external interfaces, however, and they are usually not compatible across platforms.

▲ *The RME Hammerfall DSP will interface with your computer via a PCI card.*

USB AUDIO INTERFACES

These are almost all cross-platform and usually very affordable. Not only that, but since USB is an external connection, these interfaces are truly plug and play. USB is not a very fast protocol, however, and USB interfaces tend not to offer too much in the way of high sample rates or lots of inputs and outputs.

FIREWIRE AND USB 2

These offer all of the advantages of USB, namely easy external connectivity and cross-platform compatibility. FireWire and USB 2 are faster than USB and often offer more input and output options as well as improved performance over USB. However, not all older Macs or PCs have USB 2 or FireWire ports, so this option may not be available without additional hardware.

WHAT TO LOOK OUT FOR

When choosing an audio interface, you need to take a number of things into consideration. First of all, be realistic about how many inputs and outputs you need. Do you need to record a whole band, or only one instrument at a time? Do you need digital I/O in order to interface with other hardware that has digital connections, or not? Do not just assume that having more I/O options is better; there is no reason to pay for more than you need.

Next, you need to take connectivity into account. What sort of expansion options do you have on your computer – PCI, USB, USB 2 and/or FireWire? Which of the advantages listed above are most important to you?

Give the specifications of the interfaces you are interested in a good once- over. Is it important to you that your interface be able to use high sample rates and bit depths? Does the interface boast a **dynamic range** that is acceptable to you? You cannot tell how good an interface is from the specs alone, but you can at least get a general sense of where an interface fits in compared to others.

▲ *This M-Audio Quattro is a good example of a high-quality USB audio interface.*

The dynamic range of an audio interface is the level at which the signal (your audio) will be louder than the noise floor of the converters. A audio interface with a dynamic range of 100 dB, for example, allows for 100 dB of volume before you will start hearing the hiss and hum of the instruments or other background noises.

PRICE

You can generally find an interface with the connectivity and I/O you need at almost every price range, but you can immediately rule out any units that are too expensive for your budget, to cut down the amount remaining to research.

Remember that an audio interface is one of the most important parts of your DAW, and not one to skimp on. Be sure to save a significant part of your budget for a quality audio interface, assess your needs and research which interfaces matching your requirements are currently available.

▲ *The M-Audio 410 FireWire audio interface offers more I/O options and a higher sample rate than comparable USB interfaces..*

SYNTHESIZERS

Almost everyone has seen their favourite band up on stage with one of the members playing one or more hardware synthesizers.

These sometimes take the form of racks filled with sound modules or, more often, a keyboard with knobs, sliders and perhaps a digital readout or two. Hardware synthesizers have been in use in rock and pop music for nearly three decades now. Even though software synthesizers are giving them a run for their money, they show no signs of going away anytime soon.

ANALOGUE SYNTHESIZERS

The original synthesizers were analogue synthesizers. This meant that their sounds were produced electronically. They sounded amazingly fresh and alive, but often had tuning problems and were prohibitively expensive. Some of the most revered synthesizers stem from this era, such as the Moog, Minimoog, and Polymoog from Moog Music; the Odyssey from ARP, and the Prophet 5 from Sequential Circuits.

DIGITAL SYNTHESIZERS

Digital synthesizers produce their sound inside dedicated signal-processing computer chips. The early digital synthesizers tried to include as many general purpose sounds (organs, pianos, trumpets and so on) as they could, with varying degrees of success. Perhaps the most famous digital synthesizer ever was the Yamaha DX7, but others were made by companies such as Roland (with its D-50), Korg, Emu and Kawai.

Today, hardware synthesizers are still most often based on digital technology. With the advances in chip design and

▲ *The Yamaha DX7, introduced in 1983, is one of the most influential synthesizers.*

software technology, however, many modern hardware synthesizers attempt to capture the sound and feel of the early analogue synthesizers without their drawbacks (for example, bulk, expense, tuning problems). These synthesizers are called **virtual analogue** synthesizers. The Access Virus, Clavia Nord, and Waldorf Q are popular models.

All synthesizers share a very basic architecture. First, some sort of tone generator produces a raw sound, either digitally or via one or more electric signal oscillators for a real analogue synthesizer. From there, a number of different processes, or **modules** act upon the tone.

Most synths contain one or more filters with which to remove certain frequencies from the original tone. **Modulation sections** modulate the tone to give it depth and motion. LFOs are used to oscillate the modulators. Finally, effects, such as delays, reverbs, pitch shifters and so on, put the finishing touches on the sound.

With software synthesizers becoming more and more popular in the home studio, it is possible to create convincing synthesizer parts without needing a hardware synthesizer. However, some hardware synthesizers still have an edge in sound quality and live performance use, so they still make a welcome addition to the home recording studio.

SEQUENCERS

Hardware sequencers are standalone units that have built-in sequencers, usually a disk drive or hard drive, and a number of MIDI I/O ports to allow the unit to control MIDI devices that are connected to it.

In the 1990s, many synthesizers began to include sequencers; these became the **workstation synthesizers** that included both tone generation and sequencing capability. Perhaps the most popular and successful of all such workstation synthesizer-sequencers was the Korg M1. The Korg Triton family of workstations has its roots back in that initial Korg offering.

Hardware sequencers also became popular in **groove box** style units. These devices often had limited tone-generation ability, such as drum samples and a groove machine or particular PCM synthesizer samples, but were more focused on their sequencing abilities. The Akai MPC series is the most popular groove box-style hardware sequencer.

These units are mostly useful in a live situation in which you want to use sequenced MIDI parts, but do not want to bring your computer onstage. In a home studio situation, having a computer-based sequencer gives you far more screen real estate, more robust graphic editing, integration with your audio and so on.

▲ *The Roland MC909 is an example of a standalone hardware sequencer/groove box.*

CONTROLLERS

Hardware controllers allow you to perform and record MIDI data into your computer sequencer.

Controllers generally do not make sounds themselves, and only generate MIDI events. MIDI events can be notes or control messages, such as pitch bend or program change, or simply a series of values that are assigned to a specified MIDI CC number, which is in turn assigned to a knob on a virtual synthesizer, for example. As the transmitted values increase, the knob will turn to the right; as they decrease, it will turn to the left. There are a number of different styles of controller, each for a different style of performing.

CONTROLLER TYPES

Drum controllers, or **rhythm controllers**, come in two basic types. These can be either a series of rubber squares called **pads** in a single hardware box, or a series of rubber pads that can be formed into an electronic drum set. Drum controllers allow you to tap or perform drum and rhythm lines either with your fingers (for units with multiple rubber squares) or by performing a drum part. Some offer USB ports and a direct driver into your computer system, while others connect via your MIDI interface's MIDI ports. Common examples of rubber pad drum controllers are the Akai MPD-16 and the Roland V-Drums for a drum kit/controller.

◄ With the Akai Professional MPD16 USB/MIDI pad control unit you can enter your rhythm or drum parts.

Keyboard controllers possess keyboards for performing keyboard parts, and usually some knobs and faders for sending MIDI messages. They do not generate their own tones, which is what separates them from synthesizers. Keyboard controllers come in all sizes, from two-octave portable controllers to full-sized 88-key piano-style controllers.

Recent keyboard controllers offer USB ports for direct integration into your computer system, but all of them offer MIDI ports for connection to your MIDI interface. M-Audio and Evolution make popular keyboard controllers.

Additional MIDI controllers are less-traditional MIDI units that also allow you to enter MIDI information. There are MIDI breath controllers that allow wind instrumentalists to input MIDI, the add-on MIDI-generating pickup systems for guitarists, and so on.

▲ You might find it easier to enter information into your computer using a controller such as this M-Audio Oxygen 8 Midiman.

Controllers offer the most natural way to input a MIDI performance into your computer sequencer. You will certainly want at least one type of controller, and perhaps multiple types. Even dedicated MIDI note programmers usually keep a keyboard controller around for those occasions in which they would rather perform than type in their part.

SOUND MODULES

Tone boxes, or sound modules, are basically synthesizers without the keyboards attached. They usually offer the same tone-generating possibilities, the same synthesis options, and the same effects as their synthesizer siblings, but offer a more portable package, and usually a lower price.

And for live performance, you may prefer bringing a few sound modules and a controller keyboard onstage rather than a laptop and controller.

➡ *Why Use a Computer? pp. 18–21; What Do I Need? pp. 22–27; What Is a Synthesizer? pp. 32–35; What Are Samplers pp. 40–43; What Is a Sequencer? pp. 44–47; What Is a Controller? pp. 56–59; How Do I Set Up My Home Studio? pp. 110–135; Synthesis pp. 268–287; Sequencing pp. 288–305*

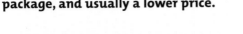

▲ *This is one piece of equipment you will not be able to find in a virtual format: the Emu Proteus 2000 tone box.*

▼ *The Akai Z8 tone box.*

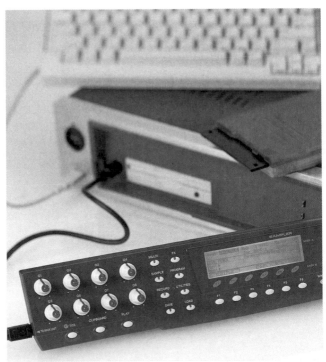

In some cases, however, a hardware **tone box** may not have an equivalent product in synthesizer form. Most hardware samplers, for example, could be considered tone boxes (once loaded with samples) and do not have synthesizer equivalents. Also, most Emu tone boxes do not have synthesizer equivalents.

In a world filled with excellent software synthesizers, you might wonder why there is a need for tone boxes anymore. First, you sometimes may prefer the sound a tone box makes to your available software synthesizers.

ANALOGUE RECORDING

As recently as 15 years ago, analogue tape was the standard for multitrack recording, in which sounds could be layered side by side, one after the other. Today it is the expensive option, but most engineers will tell you they prefer the sound of tape reproduction over digital, in much the same way that most audiophiles prefer vinyl to CD.

This is not to say that digital recordings are inferior to analogue ones; indeed it is the imperfections of analogue recording that provide its character, as they have the agreeable effect of mild compression and subtle warming on the program material.

MULTITRACK TAPE

This is made of layers within PVC. Beneath a top, protective layer lies magnetic oxide – tiny bar magnets all facing in random directions and invisible to the play head on the tape machine. A sound wave at the record head causes the magnets to line up, a process which is then detectable by the play head; this outputs a signal that is amplified back into a sound wave.

SPEED AND VARISPEED

For the tape to play back what was recorded it has to be kept at a constant speed and tension. Modern multitracks rely on motion sensors and tension-measuring devices to maintain ideal conditions. This type of computerized control also makes it possible to synchronize analogue multitracks to other media via time code.

The faster the tape can travel, the better the frequency response of the tape. Modern machines run at 30 **ips** (inches per second) and, coupled with noise reduction, can perform to very high standards. The repro playback head is only used during mixdown, in order to prolong its life and keep quality high.

Some analogue machines can be made to run faster or slower. This is known as **varispeed**. Artists as diverse as Led Zeppelin and Prince have used this function to record music and vocals at higher and lower pitches than are humanly attainable. Another effect that varispeed can be used for is **glissando** (a sliding sound). The amount of varispeed can also be recalled, so that drum tracks

▲ *How it used to be done: the Otari MTR90 24-track recorder.*

can be sped up or slowed down before everything else is added.

OVERDUBS

Once you have made a recording of the basic tracks, you can put the tracks in safe mode to avoid recording over them. New tracks can then be **armed** (set up for recording), for adding overdubs or extra parts. On an analogue machine, overdubs are performed in **sync** mode, in which the record head also acts as a playback head and the part being recorded is monitored in sync with the existing backing track.

DROP INS (PUNCH-INS)

Mistakes made in small sections of the take are far easier to correct with digital cut-and-paste functions. The limited amount of space on analogue tape means that corrections need to be done by **dropping in** on the incorrect section. In other words, the track is played and the artist performs alongside his or her previous take. At the punch-in point, the engineer flicks the tape machine into record mode on the channel in question, and then punches out again, making sure that the good performances on either side are left intact. This is a fairly tricky process and can be quite stressful; successful drop-ins still earn a pat on the back all around.

COMPING AND BOUNCING

If there are enough free tracks on the tape, a singer can try different takes on different tracks to avoid erasing a good one. The best take can then be **bounced** (recorded to another track of the tape) to form a **comp** (or composite) on one master track. If space is getting tight, all the drum tracks can be bounced down to a stereo pair of tracks – freeing up more space to record.

LEVELS

When recording digitally, the signal is either distorted or it is not – and when it is distorted, the sound is dreadful. In an analogue signal path it is possible to distort a signal gradually and at different points in the path. A signal can be **hot** (overloaded) coming into the desk and then printed hot onto tape. The result will be distorted, but in a way controlled by the engineer.

METERS, HEADROOM AND GAIN

Volume unit (VM) meters are designed to match the average levels of a signal to our ears' perception of loudness. This means that, unlike the super-fast peak level meters, VU meters do not show brief peaks in the signal. These peaks could be as much as 14 dB above 0 VU, where 0 VU represents the average operating level (+4 dBm signal or 1.228 V in a 600 ohm circuit). This level is what is

Part Two: Reference

referred to when analogue equipment is said to be lined up at "+4".

To accommodate the possibility of big transient peaks, the equipment has to be made so that it only actually distorts at a level greater than 0 VU. The level at which the sound distorts is described by the equipment's **headroom**; for example, if it distorts at 26 dB above 0 VU, the equipment is said to have a headroom of 26 dB. This figure is typical of a high-quality mixing console.

Gain is another word for amplification and is measured in dB. Gain structure concerns the input and output levels of a signal through a chain of components, maximizing signal level and minimizing distortion in each component.

NOISE REDUCTION

To avoid distorting tape, a signal with occasional high peaks would have to be recorded at a low level. To then listen to that low-level material, it would have to be turned up loud – which would also make the tape hiss noise louder.

Tape hiss is always there, but when a good average signal level is maintained it is barely noticeable in the background. To combat the problem of tape hiss, various noise-reduction systems were invented, the most important of which is Dolby.

Dolby compander systems take an incoming sound and compress it into a narrow dynamic range. This controls peaks in the signal so that it can be recorded at a much higher level than usual, without distorting the sound. On playback, this loud sound is expanded and played back at its normal (quieter) level; the apparent level of the tape hiss that has been picked up along the way is greatly reduced.

DOLBY SPECTRAL RECORDING (SR)

SR is superior to the cheaper A-, B- and C-type noise reduction. Each tape track has a module of its own and when there is no sound, SR applies a filter so that no hiss or other interference can be heard. When the signal arrives, a small number of filters respond to the shape of the incoming signal so as to affect only the parts of it that are most in need of noise reduction. When combined, these filters are capable of infinite configurations that exactly suit the signal, and the opposite configurations are applied to the sound on playback. The result is a uniquely companded signal, in which the tape hiss is almost 24 dB quieter.

EDITING

Rearranging the order of things or joining different takes together on an analogue tape means literally getting out a razor blade, cutting the tape up and sticking it back together with splicing tape. This may sound terrifying, but it is still the method employed on many albums, such as Radiohead's *OK Computer*.

The tape is rolled back and forth over the playback head and a chinagraph (or grease) pencil mark is made on the back of the tape at the point just before the signal starts. That is the point where the tape will be cut. The cutting is done on an editing block; this holds the tape firmly in a groove where two cuts, usually diagonal, can be smoothly rejoined with splicing tape on the back of the tape.

It is standard practice to insert plastic leader between each track on a multitrack master – this makes finding the tracks easier and also saves on expensive tape.

When recording onto analogue tape, it is also advisable, if you have the equipment, to transfer the tracks into a digital workstation such as Pro Tools when the recordings have been completed. It is quicker and much safer to do the editing in this environment.

PRINT-THROUGH

Print-through is the transfer of a magnetic signal from one layer of tape to an adjacent layer, while stored on a reel. This induced signal creates an echo onto the outer layer, which can be quietly heard either before or after the original signal, depending on how the tape was wound off the machine. Of the two, an echo after the original signal is preferable, as it tends to be masked by the original signal and can even add to a reverb effect. Storing the tapes **tail out** ensures a post- rather than a pre-echo. Storing a tape tail out means that the tape should be played right to the end and then left on the take-up reel (rather than on the supply reel).

MAINTENANCE

"Temperamental" is a good word to describe analogue tape machines. Rather like most of their owners, their well being alters with humidity, temperature and age, and so they require constant care and attention if they are to produce good results. Also, the tape itself sheds particles of oxide, which must be constantly cleaned away.

In well-run studios, a full maintenance drill is carried out at least once a day. Isopropyl alcohol is used to clean up the metal tape heads and transport guides, as even the smallest amount of oxide can reduce the high-frequency performance by half. Over long periods, the tape heads will pick up a residual magnetism, which will also impair high-frequency performance. A **degausser** is a handheld, rubber-tipped probe that plugs into the mains and is run across the heads and then moved away very slowly when the procedure is complete.

➜ *Digital Audio Workstations pp. 350–353*

Part Two: Reference

DIGITAL RECORDING

▲ *This analogue-digital/digital-analogue converter turns analogue sound waves into computer-friendly code.*

Analogue recording is still considered by purists to sound better than its digital counterpart. In reality, however, you are unlikely to find much difference between the two unless you are listening to highly dynamic classical recordings on a spectacular hi-fi in a silent room. By the time most pop music gets to our CD players, only a few golden-eared audiophiles would be able to tell one from the other.

DIGITAL VS ANALOGUE RECORDING

Digital recording differs from analogue in that it recognizes sound in slices instead of as a continuous signal. The first link in a digital audio recording chain is an analogue-to-digital converter; this filters and encodes the analogue sound wave into a computer-friendly set of ones and zeroes, which can be stored and then retrieved and decoded later.

Digital recording is very practical if you are short of space; rather than having to find room for endless reels of magnetic tape, you can store your digital recordings on a compact hard drive, capable of holding many times more audio.

SAMPLE RATES

Sample rates are measured in kHz and describe the number of sound samples that are taken every second; for example, a digital recorder working at 44.1 kHz will take 44,100 samples each second. The sample will measure the amplitude of the sound wave at a particular point in time (see the diagram below).

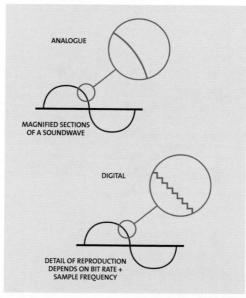

ANALOGUE

MAGNIFIED SECTIONS OF A SOUNDWAVE

DIGITAL

DETAIL OF REPRODUCTION DEPENDS ON BIT RATE + SAMPLE FREQUENCY

▲ *A closeup view showing how bit rate and sampling frequency affect the quality of the digital recording.*

A sound wave that lasts a second will be stored as 44,100 amplitude measurements. The original waveform would have been smooth, but the digitally encoded waveform will be made of tiny little steps each lasting 1/44,100 of a second.

BIT RATES

The other term used to specify the resolution of a digital system is the **bit rate**, which tells you how many ones or zeroes are used to describe a sample. Each sample describes the amplitude or height of the wave; the higher the bit rate, the more accurate the measurement will be, and the more accurate each measurement is, the closer the sample will be to the original sound signal. As an analogy, if you wanted to measure the height of a building in meters you could do so most accurately if you used more digits, for example, 3.764 m. If you were only using one digit then you would get 4 m, which would only be an approximation.

A 48-kHz, 24-bit recorder will take 48,000 samples, each of which comprises a string of 24 ones and zeroes. This string of digits is called a **word**. **Word clock** is the device that tells interconnected units

of digital audio equipment to begin their words at the same time. Under some circumstances, distortion will occur if there is no word-clock synchronization.

Old eight-bit samplers are still loved by many for their old-fashioned, crunchy sound. When using eight-bit sampling, there is a resolution of 256 steps with which to measure the wave – this is not much by today's standards. To give you a comparison, 24-bit sampling allows for a resolution of 16,777,216 steps, which makes for a much more detailed sound image.

Of course higher bit and sample rates amount to larger files that require more storage capacity. With most people still listening to CDs (16-bit, 44 kHz resolution) and even lower-resolution and highly compressed MP3 and AAC files, the industry by 2007 had mostly standardized on a 24-bit word length in recording gear, with some engineers preferring different sample rates for different tasks.

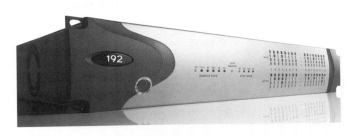

▲ *This ProTools HDS 192 interface offers the ultimate sampling resolution.*

TRANSFERRING DIGITAL AUDIO

Manufacturers have developed different digital formats for different purposes.

STEREO

The first digital audio connections carried stereo signals on a single cable for both channels of input or output. Still common today, they're labeled **S/PDIF** (pronounced "spidif" or "spee-dif") or **AES/EBU**. S/PDIF travels on either RCA (phono-type) or Toslink (optical) cables. Cable runs are limited to five to ten metres. The S/PDIF protocol is common on consumer CD and DVD players.

AES/EBU uses XLR (microphone-type) cables, though AES/EBU cables require a higher impedance (110 ohms). These cables can stretch to 100 metres. AES/EBU carries its own word-clock reference, so you don't have to worry about establishing clock synchronization.

MULTICHANNEL

Alesis' ADAT **Lightpipe** format can transfer as many as eight channels of digital audio simultaneously (in one direction) through a single cable at up to 24-bit, 48 kHz resolution.

For higher sample rates, a derivative of Lightpipe has emerged in recent years, known as **SMUX**. This scheme typically provides four Toslink connectors, two each for input and output. Units with SMUX implementation use the first connector for channels 1–4 and the second for channels 5–8 in each input or output section.

Tascam's competing **TDIF** (pronounced "tidif" or "tee-dif") can carry up to eight channels bi-directionally, on 25-pin D-Sub cables (like serial-style PC cables) that conform to special TDIF specs.

COMPUTER FORMATS

In modern home studios multichannel digital audio is usually transferred on **USB** or **FireWire** cables. Incoming analogue signals, such as vocals, guitars or other miked instruments, are digitized in the audio interface and transferred to an audio application in the digital format used by the interface and recognized by the application, either internally over a PCI-card connection or externally over FireWire or USB.

Whatever the format or connections used, if digital audio is imported into a recording program, the audio's bit rate and sample rate has to match that of the target project, which is determined when the project is set up. The audio must be converted if the resolutions don't match.

DISTORTION

When you are working with analogue equipment, distortion is very much part of the picture, and quite often a welcome colour that can lend warmth and punch to the sound. In the digital domain, distortion is absolutely unwelcome.

If you distort the inputs or outputs of a digital device, the resulting noise is horrible and will ruin your recording. There is no middle ground; if you get past the red section at the top of your meters you will face distortion and that is that. This is easy to avoid by not recording at too high a level, and not overloading your outputs on playback.

OTHER DISTORTION

There are situations in which sample-rate and bit-depth mismatches or word-clock synchronization problems can affect the signal in less obvious ways than the noise of digital overload. Sometimes the sound can be thin and strange zipping noises will be lurking in the background, or there will be a **spike**, or rogue sample, every now and then.

If you are using a master clock that is set up incorrectly, the music can play at the wrong speed. You may only realize this when a CD of the session plays fast or slow. Vigilance will eventually become a habit!

CALIBRATING DIGITAL RECORDERS

When using an analogue desk with a digital recorder, the inputs of the recorder are normally lined up to around -16 dB. This means that a test tone at 0 VU sent from the analogue desk should meter at -16 dB on the input of the recorder. This is because VU meters measure an average signal; you can actually pass a signal that is 14 dB *louder* than 0 VU before analogue distortion occurs at the output of your desk. Lining up in this way means you can rely on your VU meters to prevent the occurance of digital distortion.

FILE TYPE

If you know you will be exchanging files with other musicians or taking your work to a big studio to mix, make sure that you are working in a file format, sample rate and bit depth that is not going to cause problems and use up time at the other end. Speak to the engineers well in advance. You do not want to pay £30 ($50) an hour waiting for files to be converted.

▲ *Before you start, check your session setup details: pictured is ProTools' setup window*

DIGITAL AUDIO WORK-STATIONS

A large enough range of equipment is out there for you to tailor-make a digital audio workstation to fulfil your needs.

In all probability, this will comprise a mixture of analogue and digital gear, as well as MIDI and word-clock sync systems that all need to run in perfect harmony. It is vitally important that you are clear on how you want your setup to perform, and what level of flexibility and integration you require with the outside world.

THE STANDALONE DAW, OR PERSONAL DIGITAL STUDIO

Many people are not interested in the potential headache of having to understand the complexities of combining all these different systems. They will only need a certain amount of flexibility, as long as they can record songs to a high sonic standard, with good effects, and be able to make CDs at the end of the recording process.

In these cases, a self-contained workstation is the obvious choice, for the following reasons:

- These machines are a one-stop recording studio, mastering house and pressing plant, and have a number of advantages over multi-component modular studios.
- They take up a lot less space than multi-component modular stations.
- There are no problems with differing digital audio formats between components because everything is inside the box and all routing occurs in built-in software.
- There is no need for separate audio or MIDI interfaces; all the sockets you need are at the back of the unit.
- All session data, mix automation and snapshots are stored in-house with the session.
- There is a control surface with faders and sometimes flying faders, which some find easier to use than a mouse.
- There is the portability factor: you can put your entire studio in the car and take it to a mountain hideaway!
- There are standalone solutions to suit all pockets out there. The giants include the Roland VS-2400 CD and the Yamaha AW-4416. See p. 11 for price guides. Certain manufacturers have created full lines of personal digital studios and expanded their offerings over the years:

ROLAND VS SERIES

Roland's V-Studio series now centres around the VS-2400 and its beefed up descendants, the VS-2480CD, VS-2400CD and VS-2480DVD, which adds version 2 software and the ability to use a keyboard and mouse. All have expansion options for features like more channels of simultaneous recording or for more effects, such as with the VS8F-3 Plug-In Effect Expansion Board.

▲ The Roland VS-2400 CD.

The Roland VS-2400CD can record up to 24 tracks of 24-bit/48-kHz audio simultaneously. As well as having the 24 audio channels on the mixer, there are another 16 for any MIDI modules that you may want to run live with the mix, and another 8 FX return channels.

The VS series also offers on-board effects including Roland's COSM virtual amp modeling and the company's RSS 3D panning. There is also the option to record at 96 kHz, although in that case you are limited to eight tracks at a time. (www.roland.com)

Price band F+

BOSS BR SERIES

Roland's Boss division offers entry level PDSs that often appeal to guitarists and songwriters, from the 8-track BR-600 up to the 16-track BR-1600CD, which offers eight XLR inputs for simultaneous recording, pro-grade effects, Version 2 software, COSM bass amp models from Roland's GT-6B, enhanced vocal tools, and MIDI sync capability. (www.bossus.com)

▲ The Boss BR-864.

YAMAHA AW AUDIO WORKSTATIONS

Yamaha's AW1600 and AW2400 are full-featured studios in compact boxes. The AW2400, the new flagship of the AW line, allows 24 simultaneous tracks of

▲ *The Yamaha AW-4416.*

playback, motorized 100 mm faders, and the same expansion slot found on Yamahas digital mixing consoles for connecting the AW to professional studio gear.

The AW2400 has 16-input, 24-track recording of uncompressed audio at 16-bit or 24-bit resolution at 44.1 or 48 kHz sample rates.(You get 12 tracks when

▲ *The Akai MPC 4000.*

recording 24-bit audio.) Like the Roland and Boss units, you also get virtual or work tracks, which allow you to store extra takes or parts that can be selected later for inclusion in the final mix. (www.yamaha.com)

Price band F+

THE AKAI MPC (MUSIC PRODUCTION CENTER)

This series of samplers with built-in MIDI sequencers has proven its worth over and over again, both on the road and in the studio. The reputation of these models for ease of use and rock-solid timing put them at the heart of many hip-hop and dance records. From the original MPC60 to the compact MPC50 and top-of-the-line MPC4000 Plus, their evolution is evidence of their success, and they form the beating heart of many studios. (www.akaipro.com)

Price band F+

COMPUTER-BASED WORKSTATIONS

The most advanced and flexible workstations are built around computers, be they Windows, Mac OS or (less commonly) Linux-based machines.

To build studios with computers, you need equipment and software from third parties. These items come in the form of PCI cards which slot into the motherboard of the PC, or external devices that connect over USB or FireWire.

DIGIDESIGN PRO TOOLS

You cannot talk about computer-based audio without talking about Digidesign's ubiquitous digital audio/MIDI sequencer Pro Tools. It is a little different from most of the rest because you cannot use the excellent software without Digidesign's hardware, which is very expensive if you want the best model.

Digidesign now offers three different versions of Pro Tools software and a multitude of hardware interfaces at all price levels, thanks to their union with M-Audio (see p. 244). At the upper end of the spectrum is Pro Tools HD. These systems use a technology known as TDM, Which uses customized hardware connected to the computer by PCI cards to achieve the highest possible quality in terms of system performance and audio fidelity. TDM plug-ins rely on the external hardware to process audio smoothly and without taxing the computer's processor.

RTAS plug-ins, on the other hand, use Digidesign's DAE software architecture, but use the host's computer power rather than Digidesign hardware, and work with all Pro Tools versions.

You can use other audio sequencers with Digidesign hardware – Logic Audio and Digital Performer can also tap into its DAE and TDM power. (www.digidesign.com)

APPLE LOGIC PRO

Apple's audio/MIDI sequencer Logic Audio has traditionally been favoured by writers and musicians rather than by engineers, because of its superb handling of MIDI information and the ease with which sections of a song can be edited.

Besides its Logic Pro 7 lets you tap networked computers for more DSP processing power – up to 128 stereo streams. The newest version also adds several software synthesizers and effects and supports sample rates up to 192 kHz.

Home studio owners may find that Logic Express 7, a version with a reduced features set, meets their needs for about a third of the cost of Logic Pro 7. (www.apple.com)

OTHER PACKAGES

There are plenty of other computer-based audio packages that you should look out for, including Steinberg Cubase and Nuendo, MOTU Digital Performer, Adobe Audition, Sony Acid Pro, Cakewalk Sonar, Propellerhead Reason and Ableton Live.

➡ *Software: Sequencers pp. 220–233;*
Software: Plug-ins pp. 234–247

STUDIO LAYOUTS
ESSENTIAL SETUPS

CREATE A GOOD WORKING SPACE

Your studio should be your haven away from the realities of life – somewhere you can hide away and allow your creativity to flourish. The last thing you need when you are working is friends and family tramping through your workspace on their way to the

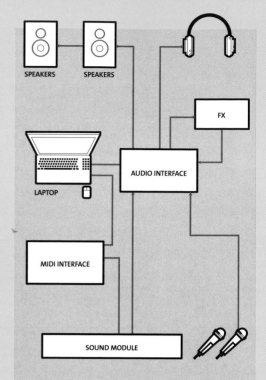

▲ Correct speaker placement.

washing machine! If you have the luxury of being able to choose a room, then make sure it is out of the way so that no one will be affected by your noise (and you will not be affected by theirs). Modern housing provides little internal sonic insulation, and low frequencies

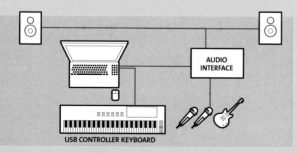

▲ A range of studio setups from simple (above)

to complex (top right).

travel farther than you might think – a moderate volume in one room can sound like a nightclub in the next.

Place your speakers on solid stands – concrete blocks on neoprene mats if possible. This will help to prevent low frequencies from being physically transmitted through the building. Place the speakers with the tweeters (the speaker's high-frequency driver) at ear height, forming an equilateral triangle with your head as the third corner (see the diagram above left).

Get yourself some good-quality headphones for late-night work – try as many pairs as you can before you choose, as you may be wearing them for hours at a time. Open-backed headphones sound better, but if your budget is tight you may have to get a closed pair that will double as recording headphones and prevent headphone spill when recording vocals. Buy the best set that you can afford; you will thank yourself later when you are recording vocals with a deep, rich and three-dimensional headphone mix that inspires you and your singers or players.

ORGANIZING YOUR SYSTEM

If you own a mixing desk or console and work on a computer, there is a tough decision to be made. What should go between the speakers – the console, or the screen, mouse and keyboard?

The chances are that you will do most of the balancing and sonic sculpture within your computer, in which case it is best to position the speakers on either side of the computer. However, if you use your computer more like a tape machine (that is, for recording, playback and basic editing) or if you are using a tape machine, all your balancing and tweaking will happen on the console. In this case, you should place the speakers around the console.

On this page and the previous page are three flow diagrams showing studios of increasing complexity and without **patch bays** (hardware devices that amalgamate all your input and output sockets into one unit). They show the basic audio and MIDI systems, which will vary according to the specific equipment that you use. Drawing up plans like these will help you to work out which cables and plugs you will need, how long they will need to be, your power requirements and where everything will plug in.

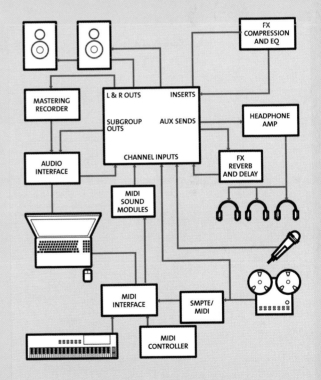

▲ *This final, most complex, setup is really in need of a patch bay.*

When you work at home, floor space is at a premium. With the recent increases in computer technology it is now possible for a laptop computer to out-perform the kind of setup that would have filled an entire room only 10 years ago. However, you may still wish to use outboard gear, MIDI modules and keyboards in your setup.

The diagrams below and on p. 357 show two extremes of home studio setups. The first is laptop based, with a USB keyboard controller. The second incorporates multiple MIDI controllers, outboard racks and a patch bay. This is a practical way to design a one-person pod-style studio. (If you are left-handed, reverse the setup.)

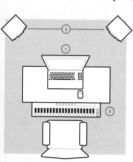

1. Computer
2. USB/MIDI controller keyboard/synthesizer
3. Monitors

▲ *A plan of a simple, one-person studio.*

SYMMETRY

Try to have some symmetry in the environment around your monitoring position – this will help with imaging, that is, creating a balanced stereo sound image between the left and right speakers.

MIDI AND ELECTRICAL SET UPS

The diagram on p. 357 demonstrates a little logical thinking. All MIDI controllers are in the same area as the MIDI modules and samplers, etc. – this enables you to tweak the sounds as you play them. The console sits to the right of the master keyboard, so that you can set the levels while playing the sound you are working on. The FX rack is near the desk so that the levels on both can be adjusted simultaneously. Planning ahead will make it so much easier to get on with the job in hand and have fun, rather than balancing on furniture and knocking things over all the time!

As well as the audio and MIDI layout of your studio, there is the electrical layout to consider. Power cables can interfere with your sound, so a certain amount of thought needs to go into cabling and distribution.

Assuming you are not a professional electrician, you will have to put up with a domestic supply and probably about four outlets to run all your gear. This should not present many problems unless you are running huge amps or an enormous mixing desk.

Most modern equipment runs on milliamps, so you should be able to run several power distribution boards with no problem. Once you have installed the gear in position, plug in the electrics first and try to keep all the power cables as tidy and together as possible. When you start setting up the audio cables, try to keep them as far away from the power cables as you can, to prevent electrical interference from affecting your audio signals.

LABELLING

Label your mains, audio and MIDI plugs so that you know what you are unplugging. An hour spent with a label maker will save you from crawling around on the floor tracing wires by hand when you could be making music.

TRICKS OF THE TRADE

• Have a sofa in the room – it will be comfortable for your guests and will prove useful for low-frequency absorption.

• Make sure that the power for the speakers or their amplifier is within easy reach. This way, it is easy to turn off the monitoring when recording using microphones.

• Keep a long microphone lead and a long headphone extender close at hand, so that you can record in another room if necessary.

• Fill your racks with the deepest units at the bottom – otherwise it can be difficult to reach the connectors at the back of the shallower units.

• Leave enough room to enable you to access the back of your equipment easily; you will need to do so constantly. If there is not enough space to do this, you will need to arm yourself with a mirror and a flashlight.

• Try using a patch bay – it will make things simpler and will give you more flexibility.

• Research your wiring. Do not be afraid of the soldering iron! If you can get your head around a sequencer and a studio, you can easily grasp the basics of balanced/ unbalanced connectors and earthing, or grounding. You do not need a diploma in electrical science; a bit of basic knowledge will save you hours of frustration with hums and buzzes, and a potential fortune if you can make your own cables.

• Be nice to yourself! It is vital to make a comfortable studio. You will spend hours at a time in there, so it is worth buying a decent chair. Do not put up with a forgotten stool that happens to be free. If you feel good, you will have fun and make great music; backache will make you irritable and difficult to work with.

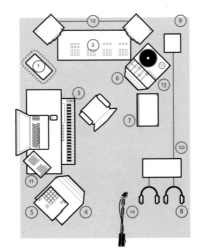

◄ *A plan of a fully equipped one-person studio.*

1. Computer (possibly in a noise-reducing cabinet)
2. Mixing desk
3. USB/ MIDI controller keyboard/synth
4. Rack of MIDI sound modules/samplers
5. MIDI controller/sampler with pads (e.g., Akai MPC)
6. Rack of effects and outboard (compressors, gates, EQ, etc.)
7. Patch bay
8. Headphones
9. Headphone amplifier
10. Headphone distributor box
11. MIDI controller
12. Monitors
13. Turntable and mixer
14. Microphone

MIDI CHAINS

If you are working on a laptop and USB controller keyboard only as in the diagram below, you may not even have to think about MIDI connections. Those of you who possess more than one MIDI controller, external MIDI sound module, sampler, synthesizer or tape machine will have to build a MIDI network, so that all your pieces of equipment can communicate with each other.

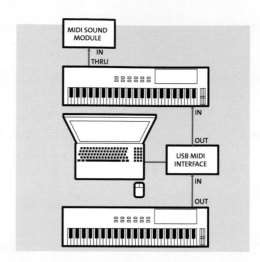

▲ *A laptop and single-port USB MIDI interface setup.*

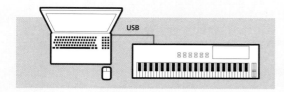

▲ *A simple setup consisting of a laptop and USB controller keyboard.*

The diagram above shows a basic 1 in 1 out or 1 port MIDI interface connected to the USB port of a laptop. In this case, the MIDI keyboard controller connects to the single MIDI input on the interface, while the single output of the interface connects to your external MIDI modules.

Any further modules, synthesizers and samplers are connected in a daisy chain from the MIDI thru port of one module to the MIDI in port of the next. This is an acceptable system, but long chains can result in MIDI delays, so it is best to have modules supplying rhythmic sounds (which obviously need to be accurate in terms of timing) as close to the interface as possible.

In the event that the controller keyboard is itself a sound source, the MIDI thru of the last module in the chain would connect to the MIDI in of the controller keyboard. In this case, you will need to switch off the local control in the MIDI menu of your controller keyboard. With a 1 in 1 out interface, no matter how many modules you have, you are limited to 16 MIDI channels. This means you could use 16 separate MIDI modules, or use every voice in a 16-part multitimbral module.

MULTIPLE MIDI

The diagram on p. 359 shows a fully loaded 8 in 8 out multiport MIDI interface at the heart of a complex MIDI setup. There are multiple MIDI sound modules available and each has its own dedicated output port on the interface. This will cut down on MIDI delays created by daisy chaining. Each output port on the interface has its own 16 channels of MIDI, offering 128 MIDI channels. Furthermore, each output port can still have its own daisy chain.

GOOD PERCUSSION PARTS

The multiple MIDI inputs make it easy to incorporate and switch between MIDI input methods and sources. A MIDI drum kit, for example, enables a drummer or percussionist to play along with the track, resulting in a MIDI part with a human feel. But because it is MIDI, the part can then be quantized or otherwise tweaked if it turns out to be a bit too human!

The AKAI MPC, an excellent sequencing sampler in its own right, is the middle ground between keyboard and drum pad. Many drummers swear by the rubberized pads of an AKAI MPC sampler as a way of playing percussion parts, and for non-drummers it certainly makes for a more intuitive input device for drum parts than a keyboard.

An audio-to-MIDI trigger, such as the AKAI ME35T, is a great way of turning a live drum or percussion part on tape into a series of MIDI notes in your sequencer.

An example of when this might be useful would be for rescuing a live drum take with a great performance but bad sound. A kick and snare drum sample could be combined with the kick and snare drum from the tape, resulting in the big fat drum sound that you always wanted.

A SMPTE to MIDI converter allows the sequencer to be synchronized to an analogue tape machine while you play along on the keyboard. The scenario below offers the most flexibility.

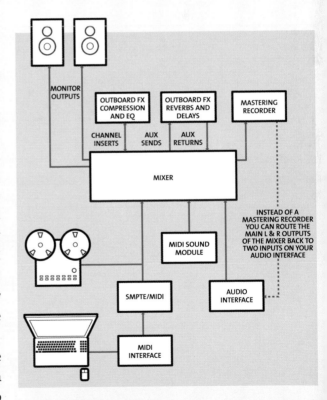

▲ A multiport MIDI interface setup.

FX SENDS AND RETURNS

Whether you work entirely within your computer or use a mixing desk and outboard, there are some universal methods of making the most of your effect units. Software effects are theoretically unlimited in number, but the power used by processors will limit the number of plug-ins you can run simultaneously. Hardware effects are limited only by the number of units that you own.

REVERBS AND DELAYS

The most efficient way to use this type of effect is by using auxiliary sends and returns, enabling you to use the same effect on several different sounds at once.

Imagine three channels of drums, guitar and vocals on a mixer (hardware or software). On each of these channels there is provision for a send, usually called an auxiliary send or a bus. This will usually take the form of a rotary pot, and by turning up the send on each of your channels you will send varying amounts of drums, guitar and vocals down this auxiliary send.

On a hardware mixer, there will be an output on the back of the desk called aux 1 send. This is where the mixed-up signals arrive, and this output needs to be connected to the input of a reverb unit, delay or other send-based effect, as in the diagram below left.

On a software desk, there will be a channel called bus 1 (if there is not, you can create an auxiliary input channel and assign its input to be bus 1), which is where your mixed-up signals will arrive. You can then call up the effects plug-in over that auxiliary channel. Alternatively, you can use an analogue output on your audio interface if you want to use a hardware reverb, as in the diagram below.

You now have a little of each sound going to the one reverb unit – all that you need to do is hear it back.

AUX 1 SEND
(DESK OUTPUT)

AUX 1 MASTER SEND LEVEL
(CONTROLS THE OVERALL LEVEL OF THE MIX OF DRUM, GUITAR AND VOCAL)

TO REVERB

DRUMS GUITAR VOCAL

▲ *How to connect an auxiliary send to the input of a reverb unit.*

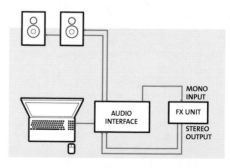

MONO INPUT

AUDIO INTERFACE

FX UNIT

STEREO OUTPUT

▲ *Using analogue outputs from your audio interface to incorporate a hardware effect unit.*

BRINGING THE EFFECTS BACK

On your software desk, there is an auxiliary channel with an effects plug-in that is receiving a mix of your three sounds. To include it in your main mix, all you need to do is set its output to out 1 and out 2 (or whichever ones you are using as the main outputs).

On the hardware desk, you have the choice of plugging the outputs of the effects unit into normal channels on the desk, or into auxiliary returns, which are very simple inputs, usually with volume and pan controls, routed straight to the main left and right outputs of the desk as in the diagram below.

Whichever unit the reverb is plugged into is called the reverb return, and by mixing this effect with your original dry sounds, you can create the illusion of all three sounds being in the same reverberating space.

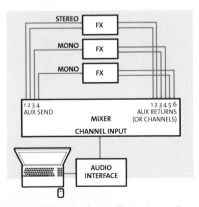

▲ *Routing to and from hardware effects using auxiliary sends and returns on a mixing desk.*

COMPRESSION AND EQ

Although groups of sounds can be sent to these types of effects, it is common practice for them to be used over one sound at a time.

The usual way of applying compression or EQ is to use a channel insert. Imagine a channel of vocals on your mixer. On each hardware desk channel will be an insert send and insert return socket. Connecting the send socket to the input of the compressor silences the vocal until you connect the output of the compressor to the "return" socket, at which point you will hear the vocals again, but now they will be compressed.

On a software mixer this operation is as simple as calling up a compressor plug-in on the vocal channel.

PATCH BAYS

A patch bay is a way of making your studio tidy and flexible. It will end your days of constantly reaching around to the back of your equipment in order to plug things in.

Many people are put off by the patch bay, which is the item at the end of big studio mixing desks that looks like a complex telephone switchboard covered in wires. However, it is possibly the simplest and most useful part of any studio.

INPUTS AND OUTPUTS MADE SIMPLE

Imagine looking at all your gear from the back and seeing all those input and output sockets. A MIDI sound module might have eight outputs; an audio interface may have eight inputs and eight outputs; your mixer will have countless mic inputs, line inputs, sends, returns, and so on. A patch bay takes every single one of these sockets and presents them to you on a single flat surface, with uniform connectors, conveniently placed, logically organized and labelled.

LEADS AND PLUGS

If you want to connect a synthesizer to a distortion, then to a delay and then to an audio input on your computer, instead of going round the back with three long leads, you can use three 30-cm- (12-in-) long patch leads and connect the relevant sockets on the patch bay from the comfort of your chair.

Patch bays in big studios are usually on bantam plugs, which are small but expensive. The cheapest are ¼-inch jack-plug patch-bays, which can be plugged up at home.

NORMALLING

Patch bays can be set to default to certain connections, for example, the subgroup outputs on your mixer can be normalled

to the audio inputs of your computer. Therefore, subgroup 1 output always feeds audio input 1 unless you interrupt that connection by patching something else to audio input 1 instead. This means that with a blank patch bay your studio is fully connected and functional, yet you can interrupt and change the routing at any time with short patch leads. When recording back into your computer make sure that you mute the tracks you are recording on. If you do not, and the tracks are routed to the main left and right mix, you will get hideous digital feedback that could blow your tweeters.

➔ *MIDI pp. 252–267*

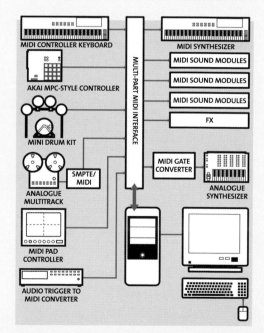

▲ *The patch bay can be the heart of your studio, where everything is connected to everything else.*

GENERIC MIX ROUTING

When it comes to mixing, you will test your studio to its limits. If you are running a self-contained laptop studio, you'll have loads of tracks on the go and be on the point of maxing out your CPU with plug-ins, software synthesizers and samplers, and then you will have to bounce your mix on top of that (see the diagram below left).

If you are running MIDI hardware, outboard, a mixing desk and a tape machine, then you are asking all of these systems to work happily side by side, so you can capture the results for posterity. By this stage, all your MIDI modules will be coming in to channels on the desk, along with any audio from your computer and/or tape machine.

Compression and EQ will be patched in to channel inserts where necessary, and the auxiliary sends will be feeding your reverbs and delays, which will either be returning in to channels or auxiliary returns. Either way, the main mix will be coming from the main left and right outputs of your mixer.

HOW DO I RECORD MY MIX?

Today most mixes stay in the digital domain, although some engineers still prefer to mix down to analogue tape. Other engineers prefer the sound of certain DAT (digital audio tape) or direct-to-CD recorders.

Record your mix back into two tracks of your software (see the diagram below). This way, your stereo mix is in sync with the multitrack session and easy to edit, tidy up and export in a suitable format.

You can also mix down to a compressed audio format like MP3 for transmitting to an iPod, or for sharing over the Internet. Bear in mind that these formats sacrifice subtle details in audio quality in order to achieve a smaller file size, and so aren't ideal for your final mix.

→ **MIDI pp. 252–267**

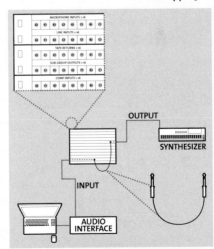

▶ *This shows the general rule of how gear should be set up for a mix, and how to use your computer as the mastering machine.*

READING MUSIC

If you are making music on a computer, is it necessary to read music at all? The very fact that you are reading this suggests that you are at least considering the possibility.

One argument for learning music is that it is one aspect of musicianship – the full understanding of music, practically and theoretically – and in learning to read you will be equipping yourself with a better knowledge of scales, chords and rhythms. Another reason is that you may at some point need to communicate with reading musicians – a string section in a recording studio, for example – and the ability to put down on paper precisely what you want them to play is a great asset.

A third argument for reading music is that it opens up the possibility that you will be able to decipher music written by other people without having to ask someone else to play it for you.

All these considerations aside, in this section of the book we are not trying to persuade the reluctant, but to advise those who would like to learn how to read and understand musical notation.

FIRST THINGS FIRST

There are perhaps two points to make first:

• You cannot expect notation software to do the job for you; to use a score writer effectively you really need to know how the music should look.

• Learning to read music requires application and patience but is not that difficult really! The fact that you are reading this page proves that you have already accomplished something harder, namely, reading English.

Many people are put off learning to read music by teachers who expect them to learn notation and an instrument at the same time. Here we are not addressing the business of instrumental technique – that will be left up to you – but simply looking at how musical ideas may be recorded on paper as well as on hard disks. Please do not expect to be able to read music after glancing through a few pages of this book. It does take time, but here we can look at the learning process and see how you can accomplish it as painlessly as possible.

RHYTHM

Rhythm is an essential part of virtually every musical style, and rhythmic notation is common to all instruments.

The basics of rhythmic notation are simple.

• Most music has a regular pulse – the beat – which can be hammered out or subtly implied.

•Most musical rhythms are patterns based on simple mathematical divisions of this beat.

In music applications we tend to use the US nomenclature for rhythms rather than the UK one, so we will say that the pulse, or beat, is usually represented by a series of quarter notes (or crochets), which are grouped together in measures (or bars) of equal length. The most common pattern is four beats to the measure, otherwise known as 4/4 time.

We count measures like this: "1, 2, 3, 4; 1, 2, 3, 4," etc., and it is vital that you keep a steady beat. It is better to start reading rhythms fairly slowly rather than rushing and then hesitating.

Notes that last for two beats are called half notes (minims) and look like hollow quarters:

This pattern would still be counted "1, 2, 3, 4" but the note on the third beat lasts through the fourth beat too.

Notes exactly half a beat long are called eighth notes (quavers) and are joined with a heavy beam .

This pattern would be counted "1, 2, 3&, 4&" with the numbers representing the beat kept steady and the &s fitted between them. Try tapping your foot on the four beats and clapping the rhythm with the eighths.

A quarter note may be tied with a curved line to an eighth, glueing the two notes together so they become one note with a combined length of one and a half beats. This rhythm is also often notated by adding a dot to the right of the quarter, adding on 50 per cent of its length. At the end of the measure below, the isolated eighth is shown with a flag, as there is no other eighth to beam to. The two halves of this rhythm sound the same.

This measure should be counted "1, 2&, 3, 4&". Take care that your foot tap does not stray onto the off-beat eighths!

SCALES

Scales are all the notes in a key played sequentially. Most music is based, however loosely, on some kind of scale.

This can be thought of as a ladder of notes, from which the melody, chords and bass notes are chosen. They can be thought of as purely technical exercises, but we are going to consider them as a means to understanding melody.

Perhaps the most familiar scale (and the easiest to come to grips with) will be the white note scale on a keyboard. This is known as the C major scale and is notated in the treble clef like this:

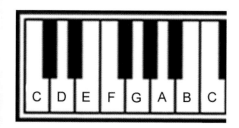

Each line or space on the five-line stave represents the next note above or below, and time is read from left to right, rather like a graph.

This corresponds well to how we hear tunes. Even if you have never learned to read music at all, if you know the melody "Baa, Baa, Black Sheep" you will be able to recognize its contours in the notation.

The black notes on the keyboard are notated by relating them to the nearest

white note above or below. The note between C and D can, therefore, be called either C♯ (C sharp) or D♭ (D flat). On the stave, the sharp or flat comes before the note.

MEMORIZE IT!

When learning to read pitches (notes), resist all temptation to write the names of the notes below the stave – you will come to rely on the letter names and slow down your progress.

Get one note fixed in your mind, perhaps the first note of the scale, and read the pattern of notes from that.

CHORDS

Chords are groups of notes, often relating to the same scale, which sound good together. They are going to be examined as building blocks for songs and other pieces of music.

A common pattern used in making chords is choosing alternate notes from some scale or other. Here is the C major scale from the previous page and we are going to base our chord on the note F, taking every alternate note from the scale.

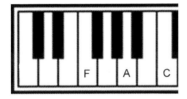

The notes used here are, F, A and C (leaving out G and B) and the chord is called F major. This chord is represented in stave notation by placing all the notes one above the other, which tells you to play the notes simultaneously.

For an F minor chord, lower the middle note to the next lowest on the keyboard which in this case is A s, a black note. It is this middle note, the third, which governs whether the chord is major or minor.

CHORDS FOR GUITARISTS

There is another way of notating chords, known to guitarists, which names the lowest note of the chord (the root) and then a series of abbreviations that tell you which notes to add. Our F major chord would be indicated simply as F, because we assume that the third and fifth note in the scale above the root are present. To indicate our F minor chord we would write Fmin, Fm, or F–. All these abbreviations mean the same thing.

SPECIALIZED NOTATION

DRUMS

A percussion stave is used where the lines and spaces are used to represent different parts of the kit, rather than any particular pitch.

Kick (bass) drums usually occupy the lowest space on the stave, with note stems pointing downward. Snare (side) drums are usually situated on the second space down, with stems pointing up.

Cymbals are often differentiated from drums through their note heads being written as crosses. The kick and snare rhythm in the first example would probably be accompanied by a steady eighth pattern on a hi-hat, written with crosses and stems up. In this case, the snare might have stems down, especially if its rhythm can be seen as forming a continuous pattern with the kick drum.

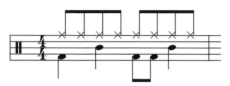

For your drum parts, just put in the essential rhythms and indicate repeated measures with the standard dot and slash notation, which simply means "repeat previous bar".

▲ *The first measure is played four times in total.*

GUITAR TABLATURE

Some guitarists will be familiar with a specialized form of notation commonly known as tablature or TAB. Using TAB will probably be relevant in two situations: where you are writing for a guitarist who only reads TAB, and when the guitarist is entering music into a sequencer by means of TAB.

TAB works by indicating the position of notes on the guitar fretboard (the action) rather then the heard pitches (the result), and so is rather difficult to follow for non-guitarists. The six lines represent the strings and the numbers indicate frets. Most notation applications and score-writing windows in sequencers will be able to display MIDI parts in TAB.

▲ *The beginning of "Baa Baa Black Sheep" notated in TAB.*

FINALLY ...

If you have read to the end of this section you may be seriously thinking about learning to read music. You can study it yourself but will benefit immensely from playing regularly from notation with another musician – either a teacher or a friend who reads well, or at least reads better than you do. It is difficult to sight read – playing a piece or passage through without practicing first – if you try to do it alone, so a class may be more helpful here than individual lessons.

It is worth stressing, however, that reading music is better absorbed from a good teacher, whether individually or in a class, than through books or web sites.

GETTING YOUR MUSIC OUT THERE

THE PRESS KIT

Whether you are trying to get signed, get gigs, find a manager or promote a self-release, you are going to need to put together a press kit. This is the first thing people will see. As a first impression, it influences their preconceptions of what they are about to hear when they put on the CD. So it has to be good. Very good.

The overall effect of a good press kit is to express the creative image and vision of the band, while at the same time providing information on who you are and what music you make. Traditionally it contains three things: a press release, photos and a CD. A bonus would be a short DVD of the band in action.

The press release needs to be snappy to allow for the short attention span of most people who will be reading it, covering the salient points of your musical history to date, your present musical intentions and your future ambitions. Most importantly, it should display your band logo as a bold header,

and equally loud contact details: phone, e-mail, web site. Date it as well for currency, include an upcoming gig list and add a couple of good press quotes. Ideally, find a skilled writer to shape it for you once you have decided on the content, and keep it up to date.

The photos are the hardest part because they really do create rock-solid preconceptions and there is nothing more damaging than a bad set of snaps. Consider the images you want to portray as carefully as you considered the music on the CD, and get a professional or a photographer you know and love to do them. Put your band name and contact details on each of the photos.

If you are sending out a demo, include no more than four songs on it and always put the best song first. Imagine you are the one receiving it and ask yourself if it is worth editing the songs down in length for first-impression impact. Do a rough mastering job on them so that all the songs are evenly loud and of similar tone. Put contact details on the CD artwork.

GETTING SIGNED

For many young aspiring rock stars the focus of their ambition is the elusive record deal, and often once that is achieved they think the job is done, they have made it and it is time to relax and celebrate. To their disappointment many stars find that the deal is just the starting point for the hard work to come – a fact not too surprising because getting the deal is such a deal in itself.

So what can you do to ease the process? Apart from strokes of luck there are really no shortcuts, just a fastidious approach driven by single-mindedness that starts with identifying the record companies you would consider signing with. This involves a lot of research into stylistic preference, current bands on the label, the success and stability of the company's A&R (Artists and Repertoire) department and funding. Identifying the A&R people can be hard if you do not have money to spend; not much accurate, up-to-date information on the Internet is up for grabs, but it is worth a search. Music Connection in the US is a good source (as of course is Billboard) to help you keep your finger on the industry pulse. In the UK there is Music Week, but few other publications of note. If you have money to spend, then go to www.musicregistry.com for its definitive A&R directory, updated every eight weeks, and the latest news from within the record companies. Try a call to a specific A&R person whom you think might like your stuff. Usually you will be fielded by an assistant, so turn on the charm and try to fix a meeting to play it

person to person – a long shot, but it has been known to work. If that is not successful, ask if you can send in a press kit for his or her personal attention. Follow it up with a call a week later, and after gauging the reaction try for a meeting again, or get the person to come down to a gig or a rehearsal. If it is colder than that, try to encourage him or her to send a scout. And if it is colder than that, go fish somewhere else.

Apart from the direct approach, several avenues are open to expose you to labels' attention. It is very crowded out there, but they rightly work on the principle that the cream floats to the surface. Executives often pay attention to magazine reviews of unsigned bands, radio shows of the same, and local scouts who go to a lot of gigs (for "scout" read "friend") and pass on tips. So get your demos out there and see if they float. If they do not, then learn from the feedback and try again.

SELF-PROMOTION

So you have finished the record and you are releasing it yourselves. Now for the hard bit – getting people to buy it. Before they do that they have to hear it. There is nothing more offputting than being told to like a band, or having a band name, gig, radio appearance or record release shoved down your throat. It may work for teen bands and the under-10s market, but for a credible band it does not work, never has and never will – so do not be fooled into thinking it will work for your music just because you love it. The only way people are going to pick up on it is if they feel that they have discovered it themselves or if they have been turned on to it by someone whose taste they respect. It is a hard call because you cannot release a record, especially a debut record, and expect it to break without any promotion yet; if you are seen to be trying too hard it is all over.

A promotional strategy – and you definitely need one – has to be very cunning, coming in under radar and capturing the public's attention almost without their being aware of it. Of course, you will not have any budget to pay for marketing; you will have to take the sweat-and-toil route with guerrilla marketing tactics. If you have a manager it is his or her job to carry your plan out, but if not it comes down to you. The first thing to do is draw up the plan, which should start with asking yourselves what your music is and who your potential target audience is, and work backwards from there. What magazines do they read? What radio stations do they listen to? What TV shows do they watch? What DJ would want to play it? What record shop would sell it? Identifying all these factors can avoid wasting time and

money and can get your record to the right starting place. Once it gets there, a lot of the work begins to get done for you.

If you have been following this guide, you should already have a good press kit together. The next thing to do is to send it out to the right people, the people who can do something for you. Here are some places to start:

• Radio stations – Find out the names of the producers and presenters of radio shows that play unsigned acts and feature similar artists and send copies directly to them.

• Music magazines and papers – Identify magazines that foster your style of music and furnish them with a copy. Ideally target specific music journalists within those publications who favour your genre and invite them to a gig, do a bit of schmoozing and try to get a review of the gig and record out of it. Getting someone else to shout for you is the perfect scenario.

• Distributors – If you are fed up with hawking your independent release around record shops, you can send distributors a copy to try to raise the release profile.

• Record companies – These will be your first stop if you are after a recording deal, but you might think about doing the same if you want to go for a licensing deal on a finished record to get the advantage of major record-company promotion and distribution. It involves the same thankless task of wading through A&R departments, though. As further proof of the Internet's power, in 2007 some record companies announced that they would only review demo material that had been posted online at a personal web site or commercial site such as MySpace or iTunes. The days of a record company's initiating a relationship with an artist because of an unsolicited demo may finally be over for good.

GIGS

Arguably the best advertisement for a band should be its music, so the best thing you can do as a band to promote your record is to play gigs – as many as you can. Gigs require promotion, which is time consuming. Place flyers in pubs and bars frequented by your target audience, put listings in local papers and magazines, contact local radio shows that publicize gigs, and alert local Internet sites that do the same.

WEB RELEASING

There is no doubt that the world of music distribution has been revolutionized by the Internet. This can only be the start of much bigger things. The Internet provides such immediate direct contact between artist and listener that it is hard to see any other solution surviving. Several artists have chosen to release records solely online, a much easier policy if you are an artist with an existing profile because fans know to look for you. The hard task is launching and promoting yourself as an artist that no one has ever heard of, a task made that much harder because of the sheer number of others trying to do the same.

Base the whole campaign around your website; this is a natural hub from which everything can emanate and where people can buy your CD when they have heard it and decided they love it. Get yourself a PayPal account so you can collect money from purchasers (www.paypal.com). You will also need to get the CD stocked at places like Amazon, CD-Wow.com (UK) and CDUniverse.com (US) for eventual links from other places. On your website, have free membership for people to sign up for; this can be the start of your fan database, which can then be the first to receive monthly bulletins, gig lists, etc., automatically. You might be tempted to send e-flyers to addresses you have picked up from magazines, directories, etc., but this is akin to spamming and most people will get turned off. Host a message board on your site from which you can get information about fans' habits and haunts. This can lead to ideas for targets and associations.

Find Internet streams that play your style of music. There are thousands at www.shoutcast.com. Contact individual netcasters and try to get playlisted. You will not get paid anything for the plays, but by law netcasters have to publish on their websites a playlist of what has been featured, as well as a link to where you can buy it. This is going to be one of the major conduits for getting heard and hearing new music, because the stream server acts as a stylistic filter.

Identify forums and other general sites related to your genre and become active there, posting constructive views rather than blatant self-promotion. Aim at getting links to your site from these and also sites of similar bands, accommodating links to theirs in return.

Have a stream of your music on your site and a short MP3 sample to download as a giveaway. Think about other things you can sell and give away, too, like T-shirts, caps and stickers.

FORUMS AND MESSAGE BOARDS

Many bands think they are so great that they just have to record a demo and sit back to wait for the world to discover them. It never works like that and every band has to work to get itself heard. Finding like-minded people, swapping ideas, discussing techniques, and sharing resources and skills are all things that can help you on your way.

The Internet is now the key source for information and you will find plenty of useful sites for unsigned bands on pp. 400–403. You will also find plenty of forums based on specific recording gear or techniques, especially sequencers. Forums for Cubase, Logic and Cakewalk users are great for all skill levels. Got a problem with a bit of software and cannot get through to the help desk? Try posting a question on one of these forums.

The Internet tends to be a bit global for certain needs, and local message boards perform a similar function on a small scale. They are ideal for things like finding a new drummer, but you might also fin a useful local web community. Find these in music shops, record shops, rehearsal rooms and hip cafés.

SAMPLES AND THE LAW

Few people fully understand the copyright laws concerning samples and even fewer seem to pay them any attention, but the bigger the world of sampling gets, the more likely it is that laws will be more fastidiously policed. Ignorance of the law is no defence.

There are two areas of sampling copyright to know about: sampling other people's records and using sample CDs. Contrary to popular urban myth, you cannot legally sample five seconds or less of someone else's record, nor can you sample three notes or fewer. The reality is that you cannot sample any part of a copyrighted recording without permission, however short it may be.

It is also a popular misconception that sampling is allowed as long as your tune is not generally released; the surprising truth here is that as soon as you take a sample of someone else's record without permission, you are infringing on copyright. Your only defence in court is to prove fair use, a complicated legal argument, but it is one that is unlikely to hold water if it was for a commercial release.

You could find yourself in even greater difficulty if you are signed to a label, because you have probably agreed to some clauses that make you personally responsible for copyright infringements. This could mean you are liable for the court and legal costs of your label, and the costs to distributors and shops for withdrawing the record. And that is after you have paid anything up to £100,000 ($200,000) to the copyright owner for willful infringement. The usual outcome is that you have to sign away a proportion of the royalties to the copyright owner, sometimes 100 per cent; we all remember the Verve and its track "Bitter Sweet Symphony" that sampled Andrew Loog Oldham's strings.

The wise thing to do is to seek permission from the legal department of the publishers and record company that own the copyrights before you release a record. The agreement you reach then is going to be more favourable than if you try to reach an agreement in hindsight on a record that is already in the Top 10.

COPYRIGHT LAW

Copyright law varies from country to country, and it never does any harm to try to gain a basic knowledge of the issues involved. Check the Internet for information.

UK
PRS (Performing Rights Society)
MCPS (Mechanical Copyright Protection Society)

US
ASCAP (American Society of Composers and Performers)
BMI (Broadcast Musicians Incorporated)

The law surrounding sample CDs is different because these are records released with the intention of being used as part of other commercial releases. The main thing to be aware of here is that when you buy a sample CD you do not own the music; you are simply buying a license to use the samples. The sample CD company or original creator still owns the copyright. It is a single-user non-transferable license, which means it is an infringement of copyright to let someone else use a sample on his or her record, even if he or she is your best friend. It is also an infringement to burn copies of the CD or even to give individual samples away, so when you get into those sample swap sessions be aware that you might be breaking the law. It is also an infringement to resell the CD when you have had enough of it. Conversely, if you buy a second-hand sample CD you are not at liberty to use the samples for commercial releases because you are not the licensee.

One exception to all this is that if you are a producer, you are allowed to use your sample CDs on other people's records if you have a creative credit. The best advice is to keep the purchase receipts of any sample CDs you buy to prove you are the licensee just in case you use one on a massive hit.

ABOUT MEDIA

It's hard to believe you can transfer music from a digital audio application like Pro Tools or Cubase directly to a digital music player like an iPod.

With improved compression formats like AAC, a producer can mix down a song with little or no apparent loss of fidelity and send it over the Internet instantly.

Nevertheless compromises are made with compression formats like MP3, including some loss of the original audio information. For full-resolution audio, you still must burn your mix to an audio CD using a recordable CD or to the audio tracks of a DVD with a DVD recorder. The latter is essential for anyone who wants to preserve a multichannel surround mix in hi-resolution format. You can find CD-Rs in supermarkets as well as computer stores. DVD-Rs are available in bulk from hundreds of online retailers and in mid 2007 cost about a £1 (around $2) per disk.

But the forward-thinking computer producer might just as easily take a music project to another studio on a 4 GB USB keychain flash drive (about £30/$50 in 2007).

INTERNET SITES

MACINTOSH AUDIO SITES

www.macmusic.org
Excellent web site for Macintosh computer music devotees. Includes software downloads, troubleshooting forums, news and articles on digitally created music.
www.mashine.com
Tuition resources for Macintosh-generated music.

PC AUDIO SITES

www.music-utilities.com
Offers a wide range of computer software for the PC.
www.sonicstate.com
Comprehensive site that features classified ads, articles, user reviews, and discussion groups, all related to music, MIDI and digital recording.

GENERAL AUDIO SITES

www.harmony-central.com
Massive site offering MODs, MIDI files, discussion forums and extensive links.
www.analogx.com
Offering free downloads of plug-ins, original MP3 music and MIDI software.
www.audiomelody.com
Featuring audio software, samples, SoundFonts, tutorials and links.
www.audio-recording-center.com
Covers all aspects of analogue and digital recording.
www.hammersound.net
Offers news, forums and SoundFonts.
www.soniccontrol.com
Vast site offering reviews, features, scores, links and digital audio resources.
www.wfmu.org/~jhhl/sinth.html
Online synthesizer that allows you to adjust perimeters to create electronic sounds.

HARDWARE

http://www.pctechguide.com/11sound.htm
Discussion of sound cards and PC audio.
www.soundcardcentral.com
Offers reviews of audio interfaces and extensive links to audio interface manufacturers.

SOFTWARE

www.arturia.com
Find information on here about Storm and other Arturia products.
www.cakewalk.com
Homepage of the makers of Sonar Studio Edition, also with details of Project 5 and Sonar Home Studio.
www.sonikmatter.com
Discussion forums, news and reviews.
www.digidesign.com
Homepage of the makers of Pro Tools.
www.ecma.co.uk
Music instruction courses, degree.
www.apple.com/logicpro
Homepage of the makers of Logic Audio.
www.finalemusic.com
Information about Finale Guitar, which can cope with all your tabbing requirements and is also a good-value all-round score writer for staff notation.
www.fruityloops.com
Homepage of the makers of FL Studio.
www.magix.com
Visit this site for an entry-level application that will help with score writing.
www.MP3-converter.com
MP3 programs and converters.
www.propellerheads.se
Homepage of the makers of Reason.
www.sibelius.com
Sibelius' G7 application is specifically for guitarists.
www.sonicspot.com
Large repository of all types of computer audio software.
www.steinberg.net
Homepage of the makers of Cubase.
www.synthzone.com
Extensive keyboard and audio-software site.
http://tkplugins.free.fr
Collection of free audio software plug-ins.

SAMPLES, LOOPS AND GROOVES

The following sites all offer downloadable free audio samples:
www.abstractbeats.com/
www.acidfanatic.com/
www.bassculture.org/
www.beatcreator.com (Seamless Looper)
www.bias-inc.com
www.bitshiftaudio.com
www.creativesampling.com/
www.deltaz-palaze.de/
www.djmixsource.com/
www.d-soundpro.com
www.ez-editor.com

www.flashkit.com/soundfx/
www.fortunecity.com/tinpan/funkadelic/808/
www.geocities.com/SunsetStrip/Studio/5821/samples
hem2.passagen.se/lej97/kalava/
www.humanworkshop.com/
www.killerbeats.com/
listen.to/the.zone
www.loopasonic.com/
www.looperman.com
www.loopers-delight.com/loop.html
www.lysator.liu.se/~zap/ldb
machines.hyperreal.org/
matrix-12.tripod.com/home.htm
www.members.tripod.com/hakachukai/samples.html
members.tripod.com/~professorkermit/
www.mp3.com/
www.musicbootcamp.com/audio_sample_library.shtml
www.musicstuff.de/
netvet.wustl.edu/sounds.htm
www.northernsounds.com/
www.olscratchrecordings.com/
www.oneshotsamples.com/
www.phatdrumloops.com/
www.powerfx.com/
powersamples.free.fr/
www.propellerheads.se/
www.pyraplastic.com/
remixer.com/drumloops.htm
www.samplearena.com/
www.samplecraze.com/
www.samplehead.com/
www.samplenet.co.uk
www.samplepoolz.de/
www.samples4u.tk/
www.samplez.de/
www.sonicfoundry.com
www.sonichound.com/
www.soundamerica.com/
www.sounddogs.com/
www.squarecircle.co.uk
www.sseyo.com/downloads/freemp3samples/mp53/
www.stonewashed.net/sfx.html
hwww.synthzone.com/drums.htm
www.synthzone.com/sampling.htm
www.thecheatmen.cjb.net/
www.thelooplibrary.com
tinpan.fortunecity.com/aphex/113
tinpan.fortunecity.com/morrison/840/
www.vionline.com/sound
www.virtualbassplayer.com/
www.wfmu.org/~jhhl/sinth
www.worrasplace.com/
www.xelenio.com/
www.xs4all.nl/~avg/avsound/avsound.html
www.zero-g.co.uk

FORMATS: MIDI

www.classicalarchives.com
Enormous archive of classical music in the MIDI format.
home.epix.net/~joelc/midi_git.html
Resource centre for MIDI guitarists.
library.wustl.edu/~music/internet/online_journals.htm
Offers extensive links to online music journals.
www.midibase.com
Featuring MIDI files and software, samples and MODs,
and a MIDI knowledge base. MIDI information and files.
www.midiworld.com/index.htm
Offers downloadable MIDI files and software, as well as
discussion forums.
www.musicrobot.com
A search engine for locating rare MIDI files on the web.
www.perspectivesofnewmusic.org
Research journal for composers and performers.
www.ucpress.edu/journals/mts
Twice-yearly journal devoted to music theory.
www.ultimatemidi.com
News, software and extensive links to MIDI web sites.

FORMATS: WAV

www.free-food.net/wavfiles.html
Offers links to free downloadable WAV files.
www.thefreesite.com/Free_Sounds/Free_WAVs
More links to free downloadable WAV files.

FORMATS: MODS

www.castlex.com/modfaq/1-3.html
MOD frequently asked questions.
www.geocities.com/SunsetStrip/9879/music1.htm?80,25
Techno and ambient MOD files for free download.
www.synt.nu/mods
A large collection of synthpop MOD files.
www.united-trackers.org
Discussion boards and links for MOD files (login
required).

FORMATS: CD

www.cd-info.com/
Information centre devoted to CD technology.

FORMATS: MP3

www.howstuffworks.com/mp3-player.htm
Information on the technology behind the MP3 format.
www.mp3board.com
An MP3 discussion board.
www.mp3.box.sk
Features MP3 software and an MP3 search engine.

www.mp3-2000.com
Large site offering MP3 tutorials and links.
music.lycos.com
Search for and download MP3 files.

PUBLISHING YOUR MUSIC

www.ascap.com/ace/ACE.html
Vast database of songs, including information on the songs' composers and those who performed them.
www.lib.washington.edu/music/records.html#sounds
Links to online historical recordings collections.
www.mpa.org
A comprehensive worldwide list of music publishers.
www.mpa.org/crc.html
Learn how to copyright your music.

PUBLICATIONS

www.emusician.com
Homepage of the US magazine *Electronic Musician*.
www.futuremusic.co.uk
Homepage of the UK magazine *Future Music*.
www.keyboardmag.com
Homepage of the US magazine *Keyboard*.
www.musictechmag.co.uk
Homepage of the UK magazine *Music Tech*.
www.recordingmag.com
Homepage of the US magazine *Recording*.
www.soundonsound.com
Homepage of the UK magazine *Sound on Sound*.
www.yale.edu/jmt
The Journal of Music Theory at Yale University.
www.songwriter101.com
BMI-sponsored website featuring articles about recording, composing and more.

ORGANIZATIONS

ccrma-www.stanford.edu
Stanford University's centre for computer research in music and acoustics.
www.emf.org
Homepage of the Electronic Music Foundation.
library.wustl.edu/units/music/necro
The Washington University music library.
www.library.yale.edu
Online music resource from Yale University in the US.
www.lib.washington.edu/music/jazz.html#Blues%20and%20Jazz
Extensive jazz library, including performer biographies and links.
music.columbia.edu/cmc/history/
State-of-the-art computer music facility.

HISTORY

ccrma-www.stanford.edu/~jos/kna/kna.html
Provides a complete history of the digital synthesizer.
www.mellotron.com/history.htm
Details the history of the Mellotron.
www.moogarchives.com
The history of the Moog synthesizer.
music.dartmouth.edu/~wowem/electronmedia/music/eamhistory.html
Features the history of electronic music.
www.obsolete.com/120_years
Timeline of electronic music from 1970 to 1990.
www.synthmuseum.com
The history of and extensive links to synthesizer manufacturers.

MUSIC GENRES

www.electronicmusic.com
Devoted to electronic pop music and featuring links to popular electronic classics.
www.jmwc.org
An online forum for academic, organizational and individual activities in Jewish music.
www.libraries.rutgers.edu/rulib/abtlib/danlib/jazz.htm
The Institute of Jazz Studies.
www.lib.washington.edu/music/film.html#Film%20Music
Directory of music resources relating to film and TV.
www.music.indiana.edu/som/lamc
Huge resource relating to Latin-American music.
www.tulane.edu/~lmiller/JazzHome.html
Enormous online resource on jazz.

ONLINE MUSIC SCORES

www.cpdl.org
Download choral music scores.
www.musedata.org
Download free classical music scores.
www.mutopiaproject.org/piece-list.html
Free classical and popular music scores to download.

READING MUSIC

www.notation.com
Music notation software from Notation Software, Inc.
www.cleverjoe.com/articles/why_learn_to_read_music.html
Aimed at guitarists but worth reading even if you are not one.
datadragon.com/education/reading
Provides basic introduction to reading music
www.musictheory.halifax.ns.ca
Easy music theory course.

ACKNOWLEDGEMENTS

PICTURE CREDITS

Apple Computers Inc.: 332
Arbiter Group plc: 140 Akai Professional M.I.
   Corp: 58 (bl), 340 (l), 341 (br), 352 (b)
Crown Audio / audiogear.com: 123 (b)
Digidesign: 199, 347
Edirol Corporation: 335, 336
E-MU Systems: 341 (tl)
Event Electronics: 25, 124
Focusrite Audio Engineering Ltd: 130, 135 (t)
Foundry Arts: 14, 23, 29, 110, 111 (t), 121, 127, 131,
   146, 147 (all), 164, 166, 268
Glyph Technologies Inc.: 34
Hammond UK Pro Music Division: 96
KLPR: 191
Kobal Collection Ltd: Institute for Regional
   Education: 17
Korg UK: 58 (t), 181
LaCie UK: 180 (t)
M-Audio: 37, 133 (all), 337 (all), 340 (r)
MIDI Manufacturers Association: 264 (t)
MoogArchives.com: 20, 32
Music Industries Corp. Inc.: 66
Neutrik: 134
Numark: 201
Osborne Creative Services: 342
Prism Media Products Ltd: 346 (t)
Redferns: Michael Ochs Archives: 99 (t), 138, 143,
   163 (b); Paul Bergen: 205; Chuck Boyd: 184,
   198; Richard Ecclestone: 118 (l & r), 119 (tl &
   tr); Suzie Gibbons: 306 (l); Mick Hutson: 86,
   185; Simon King: 113; Michel Linssen: 186; Paul
   Massey: 16; Ebet Roberts: 115 (b), 136; Nicky J.
   Sims: 196; Jon Super: 204
Roland Corporation: 190, 339, 351 (all)
S.I.N.: Gilbert Blecken: 87; Martyn Goodacre: 15
Sennheiser: 120, 122, 123 (t), 128, 140 (t)
Shure Incorporated: 92 (tl), 119 (b)
Silent Source: 114
Sound Technology plc: 50
Starr Labs: 59 (r)
Topham Picturepoint: 96 (bl), 177, 316 (tr); Chris
   Clark: 332 (r); James McCormick/Arena
   Images: 323 (l); Richard Mildenhall/Arena
   Images: 317 (l); Odile Noel/Arena Images: 95
   (m); PA: 267 (r); David Tully/Arena Images: 95
   (b); UPPA Ltd: 112, 176; Colin
   Willoughby/Arena Images: 95 (t); 98, 129;
   James Wilson/ArenaPal: 135 (b)
William Worsley: 197
Yamaha Corporation of Japan: 28, 59 (l), 125, 264
   (b), 338, 352 (t)
All illustrations courtesy of Nils Davey
All screengrabs and photographs not listed
   above, courtesy of the authors and
   manufacturers

AUTHORS

Ronan Macdonald (General Editor, original edition) has worked as a technical music journalist since 1989. He has written features and reviews as a freelance contributor to a plethora of magazines, including *Future Music*, *The Mix*, *Hip-Hop Connection* and *Guitarist*. He has also occupied the editor's chair on *Rhythm*, the UK's leading drummer's magazine, and currently edits *Computer Music*, the world's first dedicated music software magazine. A rusty drummer and fanatical home studio rat, Ronan firmly believes that everyone has an inner musician waiting to be freed by a book like this one.

Rusty Cutchin (General Editor, this edition) has been a musician, recording engineer, producer and journalist for over 25 years, and his articles have appeared in *Cashbox* (of which he was East Coast Pop and R&B editor), *Billboard*, *Hits*, *Musician*, *Country Fever*, *International Musician* and *Recording World*. Songwriting and production work for Atlantic Records and Motown led him to a studio career during which he worked on recordings by artists such as Mariah Carey and Yoko Ono, as well as on countless jazz, dance and hip-hop records. At the same time he built a pro-quality home studio, before returning full circle to journalism as senior editor (later editor-in-chief) of *Home Recording* magazine and technical editor of *Guitar One* magazine. In January of 2004 he was named an associate editor of *Electronic Musician*, the leading US magazine for the home-studio musician.

Sonic Boom (Foreword) was founder member of cult band Spacemen 3 and released several critically acclaimed LPs in the early 1980s . He has continued to stretch the boundaries of his trade with Spectrum and Experimental Audio Research. Lauded by many as a founder of the 'Lo-fi' music trend, his projects have always used many unusual and experimental aspects of music technology in order to capture the essence of his work.

Roger Cawkwell studied at the Royal Academy of Music in London before working as a freelance musician, composer/arranger and teacher. He became interested in making music with synthesizers in the 1970s and computers in the 1980s. After training as a psychotherapist in the 1990s, he now divides his time between working for a health centre, teaching music at a university, writing for *Computer Music* and creating his own genre of laid-back compositions with his computer-based studio.

Adam Crute has been recording and producing music for over 15 years. During this time Adam has worked with countless bands and artists and specified and installed dozens of recording studios (both 'real' and computer-based). He also has a close working association with Future Publishing, producers of *Computer Music*, *Guitarist* and many other popular music-making magazines, allowing his work to be seen by thousands of magazine readers every month.

Stephen Evans has always been interested in the technical side of the music business, and in 1988 started to run his own 16-track studio. In 1992 he signed his first record deal with MCA, learning all the tricks of the trade. He is now working as a producer at studios including Real World and Abbey Road, with artists such as Robert Plant, Goldfrapp, Joe Strummer, The Lockdown Project and The Girls.

Douglas Kraul has been involved in music technology as a developer, entrepreneur, writer and musician for over 30 years. Today his articles and columns are featured in prominent music technology publications, and his licensed synthesizer designs are found in commercially available products. Douglas has also contributed to the development of PC products since their inception nearly three decades ago. His company licensed a number of award-winning commercial products and also developed and manufactured some of the first MIDI products.

Orren Merton has been a musician since his days in U.C. Berkeley in 1988. He has been writing in the professional audio field for over five years, writing *Logic 6 Power!* and *GarageBand Ignite* (Course Technology) and writing for numerous pro audio magazines. He also helps moderate the Logic User Group, an online community of over 13,000 Logic users.

Tim Oliver recorded his first session with an early incarnation of James back in 1982. Since then he's teamed up with artists including Stone Roses, Happy Mondays (amongst many other Factory bands), Simply Red, New Order, M-People and Sinead O'Connor. He's just been working with Robert Plant and his band Strange Sensation and is currently writing a new album with David Blazye, formerly The High and Lonesome.

Michael Ross is a guitarist/composer/producer and music journalist in New York City. He contributes to *Guitar Player*, *Guitar One* and *Future Music* magazines, as well as puremusic.com, and No Depression (nodepression.net). The facets of his musical personality are on display at www.myspace/prehab and www.myspace/voodootrainmusic.

Dave Simons is a musician and journalist, and has covered the recording arts, past and present, for a variety of publications including *Home Recording*, *Guitar One* and *Musician*. His recent books include *Studio Stories: How the Great New York Records Were Made* (Backbeat) and *Read the Beatles: Classic and New Writings on the Beatles, Their Legacy, and Why They Still Matter* (Penguin).

Scot Solida has been playing and recording electronic music for a 25 years. As a professional sound designer, his samples and patches have appeared in some of the most popular software synthesizers and samplers available today, including those from Arturia, Bitshift, Linplug, Muon and many others. His work in sound design makes regular appearances in *Computer Music*'s monthly cover disc. He writes for a number of publications, including *Computer Music*, *Future Music* and *Grooves* magazine. As a musician, his work can be found alongside such underground luminaries as The Legendary Pink Dots and Ol' Scratch Recordings (www.olscratchrecordings.com).

INDEX